"Dedicated to *all* who have suffered great loss,
with a love that was greater than the misery."

i

"Don't Leave Weak"

(MY STORY - HIS GLORY)

H. Alisa Fowler

iii

Chapter One
Triumphing Over Tragedy

With God, all things are possible! There is not one thing He cannot do, absolutely nothing. As you read this book, I pray it will encourage you to push past what your mind can comprehend and cause you to believe with great expectancy that you will achieve the inconceivable with God working on the inside and allowing Him to flow through you. Do not permit your circumstances to dictate how you will react, but instead, may your greatest trials and tragedies empower you to do the things you once thought impossible.

Pushing through the pain of unbearable weakness forces you to be stronger than you ever dreamed you could be. What fulfillment and accomplishment this will bring on your weakest days when you can set aside all the torment, grief, and pain and choose not to let it control you but instead resist *its* tormenting taunts! That is what will stimulate the strength it takes to keep from quitting in the middle of your journey to overwhelming, overflowing, unexplainable, unending peace and joy; and finally, be able to triumph over your tragedy!

Pain doesn't exclude you because of your refusal to confront the hurt, and has the unique ability to take you under its power and hold you prisoner. Despondent, helpless, and feeble, you are forced into submitting to its authority. Many times, we are left feeling paralyzed, unable to function under its control, but we can *choose* to let it be the catalyst that propels us toward the strength needed to overcome our biggest obstacles in life and promote us to our greatest victories. *"Yet amid all these things we are more than conquerors and gain surpassing victory through Him Who loved us."* (*Romans 8:37 AMP*)

For as long as I can remember, every time my Papaw got a chance, he reminded me of the time I came to his house angry and upset because of something that had happened. I went for a drive to clear my head and ended up at my grandparents. As I was

1

explaining to my Mamaw the incident that had gotten me into such a state of anger, my Papaw listened in and mentioned how he wished he had someone to help with some much-needed leaf raking. I jumped up and said, "I'll take care of it." With no help at all, I raked a two-acre yard full of crispy fall leaves in a short amount of time. I didn't allow my rage to control me and cause me to become a victim, but used the pain-induced energy to motivate me to do something worthwhile instead. That kind of fire and fervency is what I would like to encourage you to desire. When something excruciating happens in our lives, we can sit around and feel sorry for ourselves, or we can figure out how we can use the same energy it takes to stay mad and use it for something positive. Trust in and know you can decide to be pitiful or powerful but you cannot be both! That is how this book became a reality in my life. When I lost my son, Justin, I felt I had to make sense of all the hurt, anger, grief, and pain that was deep inside me. I knew if something good could come out of such a devastating loss, then maybe, just maybe, I could understand why our family had to suffer indescribable, intense sorrow in this manner.

For so long after losing our son, I avoided doing all the things that reminded me of him. It wasn't easy to make potato salad for the holidays because the memory of how he would always come in the kitchen and eat all the boiled eggs before I could add them to the mixture. He was no longer there to run in, steal them away and devour them as fast as he could peel the shells off. For a very long time, I didn't want to make this dish because it was too painful when the memory would rise to the surface. Our family often ate Sunday dinners at my parents' house; I couldn't bear the site and smell of beef tips and rice or sweet potato casserole which Mom often made, because Justin loved it best. I felt guilty that we could still enjoy his favorite meal and he was no longer with us to fill *his* plate. There were so many other things that I side-stepped for the same reason.

Whenever I would hear a car that sounded like Justin's two-door Honda Civic, with its loud exhaust and screeching gears going down the road, it caused my heart skip a beat. Every time I heard his most loved songs or passed by his favorite foods in the grocery store, sadness would fill my soul like a dark, ominous cloud unashamedly eclipsing the sun. The heaviness I felt in those moments debilitated my will for a desire to carry on.

When I was eventually able to stop permitting these encounters to affect my emotions, I regained control of my life. I finally concluded that I might not be able to dominate everything that happens but did have the ability to conquer my reactions to the moments that tried to rob me of my priceless peace and joy. The very sense of accomplishment and bravery I gained from doing something so difficult was the purest form of exhilaration. I felt as if I'd climbed the tallest mountain or stared down a lion without being eaten. Now, the times that once seemed impossible are no longer filled with overwhelming sadness, but with joyous memories of my unforgettable son. Although, there are still days when I feel and though I fell off the mountain, only to land right in the middle of an angry lion's den. As long as I don't surrender to my enemy, just as God protected Daniel from harm He will cautiously watch over me. I now see or hear gentle reminders of my son, and my heart leaps at the satisfaction he brought to our lives while he was here, rather than the unbearable heartache I felt when he left. I've learned to search out the positive at every opportunity and not focus on all the negativity this life often brings. Learning this valuable lesson coupled with God's mercy saved my life many times over.

When I first began to write this book, my desire was to share my story with family and loved ones who have been close by my side through every event, good or bad, happy and sad. It started out as a Christmas gift, a keepsake of my memories over the last few years. I wanted everyone to understand in vivid detail from my personal point of view and to show them how hard I'm trying to do my very best with God's help to bring myself to a consistent level in my thoughts and emotions. I can only imagine how difficult I've been to live with in my altered state of being. In composing my story, I

3

inadvertently created an opportunity to share my faith in God and give a detailed account of how through much fear and trembling I encountered a victorious life through Christ. God never ceases to amaze me how He can take our ideas and plans and mold them into His will and way when we give Him room to move in our lives. The dreams, ideas, and visions we have for ourselves will pale in comparison to the perfect plans God has in store for His children.

The events leading up to our devastation unfortunately can never be undone. Many of the choices made are irreversible; this is why we must put careful thought into every decision we make. It's crucial that we all think before we act! The thoughts and notions we decide upon can often be dangerous and life altering. I beg you to carefully consider every move you make especially when it involves taking risks that affect everyone around you. From the moment I became a mother everything I've done or ever will do has been, and will always be, in the very best interests of my children. The day we become parents whether you acknowledge it or not our life is no longer our own. When I held my firstborn son for the first time I knew my life would never be the same. As soon the other two boys arrived the responsibilities increased substantially. I began making choices differently than I had done in the past. I no longer took chances that I once gave no thought about. I knew I was responsible for the life of a rare, priceless, beautiful, living souls. For that reason, I never tried purposely to put myself in harm's way. Those sparkly eyed bundles of joy greatly affected my love for thrilling rides at the amusement parks and I learned to be conscious for my health and my own well-being. I remember times when Justin was a teenager, and he was trying to convince me he was grown up enough to do something that I didn't agree with, he would say "Mom I *can* do what I want, it's *my* life." My response would always be "Well, I'm a grown woman, and I *should* be able to do whatever I please, but I don't because my decisions affect you and you brother." I would give the example that I *could* move to Hawaii but then I would miss you and hopefully you would want me to stay with you instead. He would sweetly reply "Mom you don't have enough money to live in Hawaii." To that I commented "You are exactly right and besides, I would never choose to be far away from you even if I were a billionaire!" The real truth is, when we choose to live in God's kingdom our life forever belongs to Him. Living no longer becomes what we want but what He chooses is best for us. I have often wondered do we often struggle with completely selling out to God based on the falsity that we have better ideas and plans for ourselves than He does? The truth is no one will ever be able to imagine the grand and glorious life God has in store for those who commit their lives fully to the Lord and wholly trusting in Him. His Word declares, God's plans for us are good. *"For I know the thoughts and plans that I have for you, says the Lord, thoughts, and plans for peace and not evil, to give you an expected end. Then shall ye call upon me, and ye shall go and pray unto me, and I will hearken unto you." (Jeremiah 29:11-12 KJV)*

I want my sons to know that I have not always done things perfectly, and they will be first in agreeing with me on those facts, but I have loved them to the highest level of my natural ability from the day they were conceived. If I could ever spare them one moment of pain or anguish, by taking it myself, I would gladly take on their heartache instantly never considering the cost. If giving up my own life would spare them from losing theirs I would do it in an instant, without one moment's thought. My cherished Fowler boys *if* you ever read this book know that only God could love you more than I do!

As time passed this project took on many distinct characteristics. My desire and prayer now in scripting my heart on these pages, with God's assistance, is to bring hope and healing to those of you who are hurting, lost, or silently dying inside. My intention is to encourage you to find the desire and boldness within yourselves to be determined to live your life to the fullest, even after tragedy has tried to strip you of your willingness to forge ahead. I can never promise you that the piercing pain and gnawing grief you feel will ever completely go away. I *will* assure you that eventually, things will be more bearable and that you will experience moments of pure, unpolluted happiness. With your willingness to persevere with God's help, you *can* survive after an unexpected and unimaginable loss of any kind. There will be many days your struggle feels like a constant up-hill battle. If you feel as if you are always on the losing end of the fight, remember never wrestle under your own ability but rely solely on God's unyielding capability to conquer every conflict. Can I encourage you to keep your focus on God and not on the current condition you may be struggling with? Discipline yourself to be focused on the outcome and not the process. *"The Lord shall fight for you, and ye shall hold your peace." (Exodus 14:14 KJV)*

My degree of my sorrow will bleed through every chapter. I have reached extreme highs on this journey, and have plummeted to the lowest of lows, but have obtained a level of victory through it all. This manuscript mimics my life in that I can go from zero to hundred in mere seconds, from complete sadness to utter joy in a moment's time, but I promise that when *my* story ends, it will be on an encouraging, hopeful, high note. My prayer is just as this book ends on positive message, when my life concludes my God will also ordain my walk to end in a joyous crescendo. Knowing that one day my trials and tragedies will be a distant, faded memory gives me the confidence to continue my existence on earth. The promise of Heaven as my eternal home, *if* I don't give up motivates me along life's treacherous highway. I aspire for you to share each emotion and be able to experience the delight I have discovered by making it through the many roadblocks and even being able to find joy in my journey. As you read this, I hope you will witness how God has brought *me* through the inconceivable and taught me along the way that, with Him, all things are available to you *if* you will trust and believe in a God that has no limits and loves with a passion that is unable to measure.

What you must realize and understand is that my thoughts

throughout these pages come from the deepest depths of my heart. I know that every loss is different, and likewise, everyone's heartbreak is very personal and distinctive. Some grieving parents anticipate seeing a rainbow, which brings some comfort and extraordinary joy, while others are driven into a deep depression at the mention of rain. I've learned that it's essential to go through some storms to deeply appreciate the radiant, resplendent rainbows. I recognize what helps me may not be something you would ever consider, but I'm inclined to go out on a limb and give it a try. I will always be indebted to those who took the time to invest in my well-being even though, at the moment, in *my* eyes it seemed useless and unnecessary. I have since learned that possibly I owe my life to them for their concern and compassion.

I'm giving you fair warning because a few people have mentioned to me that this book is a little "preachy," and I *may* have to agree with them on that statement. The truth is, the only wisdom I can share that will hold any weight will be taken directly out of God's Word. I've tried to back up key statements in this book with Scripture, as I don't want you to take *my* word for God's. You will notice that through-out this entire book I will always refer to various names of God using a capitol letter. One of my biggest "pet-peeves" is receiving a text message, email, or note from someone not honoring God's name as a proper noun or pronoun; you will quickly notice also that I will not recognize the various names of the enemy such as satan with as a proper noun even when prompted numerous times in spell check. I refuse to give the accuser of the brethren credit, respect, or honor of any kind.

Reading the Bible has assisted me in gaining insight that has provided help, healing, and wisdom during my recovery after my heart had been crushed by catastrophe. Studying the Scriptures for yourself coupled with my shared knowledge and experience will hopefully aide you in better understanding God's Word. I hope to coax you into adopting at least some of the strategies used on my grief-stricken path to restoration. My intent is that you would develop a desire to study God's Word daily so that you will realize it's worth and begin to apply it to your life; in doing so, it will bring stability and strength to your soul. My references to the Scriptures used in this book may not align with your perception of or belief in them. What you must understand, however, is that God has revealed specifically to me, through His Scriptures, how to have confidence and expectancy during *my* time of grief. What I have endured has caused my faith in God to increase. I've no other foreseeable explanation. If you take faith completely out of the equation, how does anyone or anything have the ability to exist? I once met a man who said he was an agnostic, meaning he didn't believe in anything. How does that even make any sense at all? How does he explain that he's able to survive without God's help? More than once I've heard it said, "If you don't believe in anything you will fall for everything." Without my hope and faith in God, I would have nothing to believe in or hold onto or any reason to continue this life. I trust that, just as He did for me, God with His infinite wisdom can also reveal to you exactly what you need at the precise moment you need it. I have often been told, "Prayer is talking to God, and when we read His Scriptures, He is responding back to us." All we need to do is go to Him in prayer and listen for Him to speak to you and allow Him to move on your behalf.

Others may interpret the same Scriptures in diverse ways. That's what makes God so extraordinary and unique. He's a Father, who has countless children with various needs, so what brings peace and comfort to one may not have the same effect on another. That reminds me of my boys when they were babies; one enjoyed being bundled, cuddled and rocked to induce sleep, while another loved to be bounced on a big pillow, having his back patted gently. Then there was my strong-willed-wonder you had to put in his bed and let him *sing* himself to sleep. Just as I learned what brought comfort to my sons God knows exactly how to acquire the necessary provisions for His sons and daughters. No matter what you require to soothe your troubled souls, I pray you will allow God to speak to you through His Word and bring healing to your brokenness.

In reading this book, know that you're getting an intimate, unfiltered look into the depths of my heart that in no way has been easy to spill out into words. Many times, there's simply no way to explain adequately the emotions that are packed so tightly inside. The emotions were buried so deep they had taken root and increased until I finally submitted them all to God. He then dug up, cut away, and groomed the contents of my soul and continues to develop it into a beautiful garden for His glory to shine. *"Every branch in Me that bears no fruit, He takes away, and every branch that does not bear fruit He prunes to make it even more fruitful." (John 15:2 ESV)* Notice "Me" is capitalized in this Scripture meaning Jesus. When we are in Him and He is in us *we* become One. *"As He is so am I"* (paraphrased from *1 John 4:17 KJV*)

In no way am I looking for fame, favor, or acceptance on this project from anyone. The only validation I will ever require is from God Himself. If I hear only one "atta girl" in this life it will hold no weight when compared to the approval I strive to acquire from my heavenly Father. I have no doubt that almost anyone could write a book. However, who is fully committed and dedicated to sit down and take the time to do it? I'm sure the numbers would greatly decrease when it came down to conquering the "literary beast." I've had countless reservations about releasing this book. Remembering that God doesn't always call the qualified to do His work as it has been proven throughout the Scriptures, I have given myself over to His hands to use me as His willing vessel. I have said many times, "I may not have the choice to be taller, prettier, or popular but I can choose to be faithful and willing and obedient." I have trusted that God will provide me with what I need to do the work He has designed for me to do. Before I was able to see that God was more interested in my commitment than my comfort, my fear remained primarily that others may read my work and voice judgment and condemnation, possibly coming from those I love most. I have since

9

learned to place my worth not in what people think but in God's analysis of my value. I have worked on this manuscript for nearly five years and have rewritten it at least a hundred times. I have strived for perfection in hopes of giving God my very best efforts. I have recently relinquished my ideas for God's plan and have surrendered this book to God knowing that He can take my mess and speak forth His message. There have been numerous times since the beginning of this task that I've wanted to give up and quit because it seemed too difficult to relive the painful memories of my journey. Many times, it felt easier to just keep the annihilated wreckage buried deep inside, allowing no one to see my atrocious pain unmasked. With the hope that it would be worth it all in the end if even one person could be spared some hurt and given an ounce of hope, I knew I had to continue. Each time I stopped working, something deep inside pushed me to persevere through the pain and keep going, thereby making this a completely God inspired project. I believe with all sincerity that my inability to give up on this vision proves that it does not belong to me but to God. When He invokes a burning sensation deep inside our soul to do something, and aspires to use us to help others, He motivates and creates a desire inside, and nothing or no one can stop His intended plan or its purpose.

Although Justin never cared much for reading, I would like to think that he's been right here with me every step of the way. That is why at times it has been somewhat therapeutic to permit my heart to pour out its contents into this book. Every memory I've shared throughout put me right back in the moment, able to relive every tear and gain the same happiness or sadness as the day it happened. I've felt his presence in one way or the other nudging me to say specifically what he and God felt would be the most advantageous to others.

I would like to take a moment now to thank my wonderful, kind, caring, and compassionate husband, Barry. I'm certain I would not have had the confidence to be who God has called me to be and to do what He needs me to do without your showing me what unconditional love means. You have been with me to help with this project and have supported me in every way possible. Even with the pain you also have endured through this loss, you've been constant, strong and steady, motivating me through the valleys and celebrating with me on our mountain tops. I never doubted God's amazing love for me when He blessed me with you!

Thank you, family and friends, for supporting me in this adventure. To those of you whom I haven't been able to chase away, scare off, or wear out, I'll be eternally grateful for the love and compassion you have unselfishly given me.

Most importantly, I've been incredibly blessed by my heavenly Father, without Him this endeavor would never have been possible. One of the main reasons I'm sharing *my* story is to bring my inadequate, miniscule portion of glory to my God. If I had the ability to praise Him all the days and nights of my life it would never repay the debt I owe. Thankfully through His shed blood on the cross I'm relinquished of all my debts. Through everything I've experienced and overcome, He alone gets *all* the credit and honor, for truly, without Him, I wouldn't be capable to stand under the strain of the constant anguish that tries to choke the breath out of me daily. With His unrelenting grace and power, I can submit my afflictions under God's control. On the days, I relinquish my will for His way I have the power to defeat my "grief enemy." I don't always get to that place of victory, but it continues to be my goal. My prayer is that, I will always be obedient to God, and step aside to allow His Holy Spirit to move, work and breathe in my life. My intent is to exist on this earth with a purpose and to be a blessing to those in need that I encounter along my way.

I ask God to hold close, bless and heal all those who have suffered a shattered heart. Always remember, what the psalmist said: *"He healeth the broken in heart and bindeth up their wounds."* (*Psalm 147:3* KJV)

Chapter Two
We All Have Our Own Story

While in a waiting room one day, I met a lady who encouraged me to do something I've always wanted but never dared. She took a seat beside me; after a few moments of conversation, out of the blue she suggested, "I think *you* should write a book!" I quickly responded "Who? Me?" I looked at her a bit confused and labored to respond as I pondered her statement. How did she know *that* was one thing I've always said I would love to do but worried that no one would want to read my work? Whether she realized it or not, she was being obedient to God's design for my life. He was using her to prompt the fulfillment of a lifelong dream. Not fully realizing it then but, *that* very day I was receiving confirmation, it was finally time to do that which I had hesitated over for so long. Ironically, the story I thought was inside me all these years was not at all the one God allowed me to tell. Perhaps the reason I had not completed my vision was that the book I was called to write had not been revealed to me until that specific moment. I now know God led this woman to encourage and motivate me, she later became one of my dearest friends. I will always be grateful that God caused our paths to cross that day. My newly found companion helped me in so many ways in the beginning stages of this book to make it a reality. *Finally*, the time had come for me to tell *my* story.

We *all* have a story inside patiently waiting to be told; each having a different catalyst to help bring it forth. It's the real-life movie of our lives, and we are the lead characters. Ultimately, God is the Executive Director and Producer and He, no doubt, has a perfect role for each of us to portray. His divine order and timing are always precise when we are willing to wait upon Him to order our footsteps that direct our way. *"The steps of a righteous man are established by the Lord, and He delights in his way." (Psalm 37:23 KJV)* Life would flow so much easier and smoother if we would choose to walk with God and not always try and run ahead, thinking we know the right way to go. From my journey thus far, I have learned time and time again that the path chosen for me is, more often than not, one I would never have chosen for myself. I'm convinced that *if* I depend solely on God no matter what happens and follow where He leads, I know that He has the best course mapped out for me with only the brightest outcome. In the end God is the One that will welcome us home with a standing ovation for a job well done. *"His Lord said unto him, Well done, thou good and faithful servant." (Matthew 25:21 KJV)*

To say this road has been full of many ups and downs and twists and turns, resembling a boisterous ride on a runaway roller coaster, is an understatement! Many times, I've tried to leap off this ride I did not choose. Each time I was on the brink of losing all hope, God's infinite grace and mercy kept me sheltered in His secure, warm embrace. Once I realized that I had nothing to go back to, my faith in God began to increase. I concluded that if I lost everything and only God remained then He was all I needed. All that was left behind me was the bitterness, pain, and heartache of what used to be. While on this unplanned ride, I concluded that my highs were never so extreme that I attempted to walk alone. I learned I needed God's constant help to make the mountains climbable and the valleys bearable. In order to conquer the heights along the way, I had to commit to the work involved in scaling them. Throughout my healing I spent many hours in the valley of the shadows. As I held tightly to the Scriptures His promise to me was found in the Psalms: *"Yea though I walk through the valley of the shadow of death; I will fear no evil: for Thou art with me; Thy rod and Thy staff they comfort me." (Psalm 23:4 KJV)* A gentle reminder that God was with me during the dark and dismal times. With God beside me what did I have to be afraid of? The Bible teaches me that perfect love cast out all fear. With God being the example of untainted love, *He* destroys all my fears. I soon discovered that in my valleys of fear and frustration I could find rest for my weary soul, or I could eagerly battle to escape. With the mountain climb being tiresome and tedious, I learned to rest and relax in the valleys and know that God *is* my constant strength and hope in times of great trials. There were many other times of being there that my respite and stillness closely resembled depression and defeat as I grew weary from the struggles. I'm grateful that they were never so intense I couldn't rebound. I decided to search for the treasures deep in the valleys, knowing that is where the beautiful lilies grow. I've learned throughout my experiences that I may not conquer every battle along the way, but am determined to win the war. My husband often encourages me by saying, "You lose only if you quit." Knowing God is on my side through the trials and tribulations of this life gives me a confidence I've never known on my own. *"If God be for us who can be against us?" (Romans 8:31 KJV)*

There have been many times through this journey I pleaded with God, insisting that I could no longer walk this walk, my strength was all gone, and I had no will to continue. However, through His constant encouragement, I was reminded that *all* things are possible through Him to those who believe. He hasn't called me to embark on this journey alone or to carry the heavy burdens of life. He intends to walk with me every step and shoulder the responsibilities I surrender to Him. Yes, He has a work for me to do, but I had to learn to take each day as it comes, lean hard on Him, and leave the heavy lifting to His capable hands. I place no faith in myself, but trust in Him alone, knowing that although it may seem inconceivable, God has more faith in me than I have and sees me stronger than I do myself. I desire that you, too, will learn to see yourself through God's eyes and also know that, *"He hath said, I will never leave thee, nor forsake thee." (Hebrews 13:5 KJV)*

As parents, there is absolutely nothing in this world we would not do for our children, but God's love for us is even greater. Just as I could never love one of my sons more than the other, my heart in fact, tripled in size over the time spanning my sons' births, to make ample space for each one. The Bible promises that God, our Father, loves us all the same. *"For the Lord, your God is God of gods and Lord of lords, the great God, mighty and awesome, who shows no partiality and accepts no bribes." (Deuteronomy 10:17 NIV)* His love cannot be purchased or earned, but is a product of who He is and given freely for all to receive. When I think of the adoration and appreciation I have for my sons, I know it's only a tiny portion of the great love and compassion God has for *His* sons and daughters. There exists no conceivable way to explain, describe, or measure the depth of His affections for us. It reaches to the highest heavens and travels to the deepest, darkest valleys. Our job is to learn to rest with extreme confidence in knowing that He is working all things out to achieve the very best outcome in every circumstance; and yes, especially through the hard to bear, inconceivable, tragic trials, and tribulations He *will* create something incredible! Jesus loves taking our broken messes and making exquisite, priceless masterpieces.

I can remember as if it were only yesterday, the sweltering, humid day in mid-July when Justin's graveside service concluded. I don't ever recall being as exhausted as I was on that particular day, completely drained from the heat and the previous day's events. Our family had been invited to attend a dinner at our church in our son's memory. I had no momentum left inside me to make one more gathering in this funeral ritual. The blistering heat and emotional turmoil had stripped me of any motivation I may have had to continue, and I asked my husband if it would be possible for me just to go home and rest in air-conditioned comfort. He said, "Honey I think it would be better if you try and go to the dinner, even if it's only for a little while." Searching for courage, I then looked up to the skies, stared at the blazing sun, and cried out to God, pleading for endureance to press on, somehow to make it through all the hurt, pain, and grief. I thought back to the simple phrase our son Justin always used to declare daily, "Don't leave weak," and asked for the perseverance to press on and never to "leave weak." Within moments the clear blue sky filled with countless black clouds and the heavens opened up to yield the most refreshing, calm, lingering breeze. As we all stood silent, drinking in the coolness of the moment, I realized this was an instant answer to my prayer and it presuaded me from that moment on that when I call out to God in my time of great distress, He will always answer. He showed me that He would send sufficent help to make it through all things. For many reasons I've never forgotten that day when I experienced the undeniable power of prayer, but mainly I'm grateful I was able to have first-hand knowledge of God's amazing love for me. From then on if ever my heart has been unsteady, feeling lost and undone, I visit this reminder and am convinced God is in total control of the winds and the rain, whether they be physical or spiritual. We attended the dinner and had a memorable time with family and friends, proving that God's power in us is alive when we rely on Him. *"My soul melts away for sorrow; strengthen me according to your Word." (Psalm 119:28 ESV)*

Eventually making our way back to our home, I again received another powerful message from God. As I got out of the car, I noticed several flyers from Justin's memorial service scattered all over the driveway. They had been trampled on and torn. I don't know how they go there. Did someone accidentally drop them or place them there on purpose? I quickly began to gather the papers up feeling hurt and troubled by the occurrence, and my soul immediately again cried out to God once again. I felt His spirit speak to me; "That's how they did *My* Son. He was despised and violated while on the earth, and yet I loved those who persecuted Him with the love I have for my Own Son." *"He was hated and rejected by men, a man of sorrows and acquainted with grief; and as one from Whom men hide their faces He was despised, and we esteemed Him not."(Isaiah 53:3 ESV)* In that very moment, I could clearly see how we are guilty of disrespecting God's own Son with our actions and by our words. That day I could finally understand that as upset as I was over the disregard of *my* son, God must also suffer intense grief when we place no value on the life Jesus gave so we can live eternally. I ask Thee, my God, forgive us of our sins

16

against You!

Learning to live after loss brings so many new, and unexpected, emotions to the surface. We often feel guilty *if* we experience laughter or pleasure. We may even feel as though the love for our loved one is diminished if we don't cry every day or if our degree of grief seems easier to bear on "sunny" days. I often refer to my level of pain as "sunny" or "rainy." A "sunny" day is one on which I feel "not so sad" and have the capacity to face it with a hopeful attitude; whereas a "rainy" day is unbearable, filled with darkness and endless tears. These emotions, by the way, have absolutely nothing to do with the actual weather outside but is the weather inside me that dictates my daily forecast. Just as the weather is ever changing, my emotional barometer could go quickly from sunny and hopeful to dismal and cloudy at break-neck speed. I've now learned through trial and error to look to God to settle my turbulent times and realize He rejoices with me when victory is within reach. I've often said, "It's hard to earnestly enjoy the pure radiance of sun if you've never experienced the desperation of darkness." What we have to allow ourselves to trust in and lean on is that those who've gone on before us, as well as those that remain, want us to continue as best we can with God's help. Each of our departed loved ones would prefer us to live with some level of pain-free normality in our lives, without the cloud of undeserved guilt and blame hovering all around. On my loneliest, oppressive, days, I encourage myself by being thankful for the blessings of unconditional love and support my remaining family members bring daily. The good Lord has afforded me so many benefits often taken for granted and gone unnoticed while in my pit of sorrow. May I never forget to lift up a shout and a praise for the capability I have through Christ to be victorious over death, hell, and the grave. *"I am He that liveth, and was dead; and behold, I am alive for evermore, Amen; and have the keys of hell and of death." (Revelation 1:18 KJV)*

I've tried to write this book to the best of my God-given ability in hopes of offering help and encouragement to those who, like our

17

family, have suffered the harrowing, distressing, heartache of the death of a child or loved one. After losing my son, I looked desperately for anyone or anything that would help me deal with the excruciating pain which only worsened as the days progressed. I spent time with other people that had lost a child and read every book I could get my hands on to try to force my heart, mind, soul, and body to go from point A to point B. The truth was and still is, however, no one thing can take you through the process faster or make it easier except our heavenly Father. You must walk through every step, cry every tear, make it through every sleepless night, with God's help to lead and guide you. There are no shortcuts in this sorrowful journey, and many days you may feel as though you are going backward instead of gaining ground. Nonetheless, you must do your very best to keep one foot in front of the other and try to live one day at a time; and when even that much seems unbearable, I highly recommended that you learn to take it minute by minute. It takes a great amount of time to nurse a battered, bruised, and broken heart. There is no time limit on grief. Those that have never endured loss must not ever put undeserved pressure on you to conform to their unrealistic expectations. They should never require you to "be better" or to "move on" according to their standards and timeline of recovery. Your healing and road to restoration is between you and God.

My husband/pastor often reminds me not to let a dreadful day turn into a miserable week, lest it turns into a horrible month, and then the months into disastrous years. What I have discovered is that this grief encounter is not a race; it's an unplanned adventure filled with ups and downs, highs and lows. Everyone arrives at the checkpoints at various times. There will be days when it appears you're crawling and still others when you have moments of prosperous progress. While on this particular path we have unwillingly entered the race at our lowest possible level. We feel unqualified, untrained, and completely physically and spiritually depleted of any stamina to compete. What you have to realize is that God doesn't judge us on how we start this monumental marathon, but God's focus is on how we finish. If you ever explore some of the people in God's Word, you will notice very quickly He didn't always call the most qualified ones to represent His kingdom. What you will find is that everyone He called God invested the time and attention to equip them with everything needed to do the job He required of them. Each day I find the ability that can come only from God to encourage me along my way. I pray every morning for Him to replenish and restore my heart. I ask that He settle and establish my mind, so I will be able to accomplish things I that I need to do and continue in the work He has called me to complete. When my world is crashing down around me and I lose the will to go on, I pray, *"Surely God is my help; the Lord is the One Who sustains me." (Psalm 54:4 NIV)* There are days I may feel I've done well, only to be followed by another that is one of the hardest I've experienced to date. There are times when the six-and-a-half-year mark feels like the six-hour mark, which means that I've often felt worse years later than I remember feeling in the beginning. Grieving parents are placed in a dark cloud of denial in the early months. As the reality of the tragic truth sets in the horrendous hurt begins to surface and the pain is no longer numb; it throbs with a desire to destroy its victim. I now know that I'm never to trust in how I feel but focus on what I know through God's teaching me. Despite these discouraging moments, you *must* keep moving forward. If you stay stationary for too long, you will eventually find yourself having to take today's steps along with making up for the ground lost in days past. *"Watch yourselves, so that you do not lose what we have worked for, that you may be fully rewarded." (2 John 1:8* ESV)

Whatever path or adventure God has called you to, I encourage you to seek out the lessons along the way and search for what He desires you to learn from your experiences. Take each step at His leading, and know that it's okay to close your eyes, take a deep breath, and rest in Him. If you allow Him, He will guide you over the holes, bumps, and ditches in your way, but you must learn to trust in that which you cannot see. I've often thought that if I could just close my eyes, I would be able to see more clearly that I need not know what lies ahead, but solely focus on God to take me over, under, around, or through each danger, knowing He'll shelter me from harm. *"For He will hide me in His shelter in the day of trouble; He will conceal me under the cover of His tent; He will lift me high upon a rock." (Psalm 27:5 ESV)*

Do not expect or require your friends or family to be able to do for you what only God can. *"The Lord is my rock, and my Fortress, and my Deliverer; my God, my strength, in Whom I will trust; my buckler, and the horn of my salvation, and my high tower." (Psalm 18:2 KJV)* I had a friend warn me about something I hadn't expected or thought about. She said, "You will lose friends and exhaust family members, especially when you're going through a tragic loss." That's unfortunate, but I've found it to be irrefutably true. On the bright side, God will give you many other people along the way in unexpected places to lift you up and support you. I am grateful for God's gift of friends as I know He realized we would need and enjoy fellowship with one another. *"And I will come down and talk with you there. And I will take some of the Spirit that is on you and put it on them, and they shall bear the burden of the people with you, so that you may not bear it yourself alone." (Numbers 11:17 ESV)*

One good thing about gaining different friends is that they're unable to compare your former self with the newly grief-stricken person you have become. The new people that enter your life won't be able to judge you when you don't act the same as you used to, due to the fact they never knew you before loss ravaged your heart, leaving it unrecognizable. When you've been touched by tragedy it changes the way you act and react in every area of your life. Know that it is burdensome for your family and friends to offer continuous support when they feel incompetent in their endeavors to keep you from falling into the depths of dark depression. They may eventually feel as if they have failed to ease the pain when they can no longer find words to encourage, comfort, and console you. Thinking it is the best thing for you, they may react by making themselves invisible and disappearing from your life all together. Nothing could be further from the truth. In fact, the very act of being there to listen, even if they don't utter one word, is one of the best therapies I've encountered. Take advice from my own experiences--doing *something* is far better than doing *nothing* for a friend in need. As you sow seeds of kindness in others God will give you a harvest you cannot contain. *"I the Lord search the heart and test the mind, to give every man according to his ways, according to the fruit of his deeds." (Jeremiah 17:10 ESV)* Remember whatever you do to help others God will in return bless you abundantly.

In my first few months of grieving, I wasn't sure that my faith in God was strong enough to sustain me. In fact, I was convinced God was punishing me by taking my son. I remembered the prayer I spoke aloud every day from the moment I felt my son's tiny body begin move in my womb: "Lord, please never take this child from me. I couldn't live my life abundantly without him;" and now, having to live through this ultimate loss, I questioned God, "Why was this *my* story?" I would never have picked *this* to be my reality. No parent ever would, and that is, in fact, the answer to my question. *You* would never choose such an impossible, monumental task for yourself, but God knows that with *His* assistance you can make it through all things so that *your* story one day can be used for *His* glory.

I once had someone tell me that I should feel honored God selected me to walk this path because it shows the great faith He had in me. She went on to say that undoubtedly God knew I could do it or I would never have been chosen to walk that path. Instead I was convinced God was punishing me for everything that I had ever done wrong. I've often felt certain He most assuredly had me confused with someone else but realize now that God sees us differently than we see ourselves. He sees us as He anticipates us to be and not the jumbled mess we see when we look in the mirror. *If* I was going to be all God had created me to be, I had to begin to see myself through God's eyes and not go by my own perception. I simply had to learn to accept the things that could never be reversed and muddle through as best I knew how. There are times when I find myself complaining more than celebrating. I know through reading God's Word He warns us that our mummering, gripping ways halt the flow of blessings in our life. Not wanting to prevent God's best gifts from being poured out in my life, I do my best to refrain from negativity slipping out in my speech. So, on days when I feel forgotten by God and His Scriptures seem foreign, I think of what my granddaughter, Skylar, always reminds me: "Ya get what ya get and don't pitch a fit, Slick." Which is what she calls me instead of the traditional names like grandmother, granny or mamaw. I won't confirm or deny that adorable little phrase as being in the Bible in some form or fashion, but you must admit it does lighten the mood when the stress levels are over the top.

Now more than ever before I'm fully trusting God to keep the breath in my lungs and my pump to keep pumping because I could easily have quit breathing and begged my heart to stop beating had it not been for the undeserved love, grace, and mercy He has shown me every minute of every day. I often *remind* God that He created my body to function properly the way it was designed and if I'm meant to do that which He assigns me, may He continue do the work in me necessary to carry out His plan for my life.

I pray that as you read my story, it will encourage you to trust in God to see *you* through endless days, sleepless nights, and every painful step no matter what you may encounter. Whatever your journey may be and wherever you are on the course, be of good cheer to know God Himself is for you. Your path may include loss of a different kind. You may be dealing with the loss of a spouse through death or divorce. You may have lost your home or job. You may have lost all hope in God because you somehow believe He has forsaken you and left you to figure out your own way in life. No matter what calamity you may have suffered, know that God is with you and He is fighting *for* and not against you, and when you call out to Him, He will hear you. He's more than able to see you through the darkest night and bring you into His marvelous light. What may look like a prison of darkness right now will one day give way to a palace of beauty when you allow God to erase all your bitterness, pain, and, sorrow.

Romans 8:18 AMP says, *"For I consider that the sufferings of this present time are not worth being compared with the glory that is about to be revealed in us and conferred {granted, bestowed} on us!"* Knowing this Scripture and keeping it hidden deep inside my soul helps me realize that whatever I may face on this earth, it can in no way compare to how spectacular, exquisite, and breathtaking the glory my eyes will one day behold; that is *if* I'm patient and steadfast while walking in the fullness God has ordained me to travel. So, although there is no visible finish line, there is to all of those that believe, a triumphant resting place in that land beyond the skies.

One of the most crucial factors while on your course is never to get tired of doing what is right even when it goes unnoticed by others. *"As for you, brothers, do not grow weary in doing good."* *(2Thessalonians 3:13 ESV)* God sees each and every one of the things we do to honor Him. We must also make it a priority to do unto others as we would have them do unto us, as directed in *Matthew 7:12*. Even when we're treated unkindly, we should always respond with kindness. Never try to gain ground while pushing others to the side. Do all you can to help others along their course having compassion on all you meet along the way. When our time on this earth finally subsides, and we gather with our loved ones as they patiently await our arrival with great expectancy. I wish to reassure you, as I also do myself, to keep moving, keep going, never give up or quit; do your very best to stay focused, resolute, and committed. Don't leave weak; allow God's Holy Spirit to activate and motivate you. *"But you will receive power after the Holy Ghost is come upon you." (Acts 1:8 KJV)* It won't be easy, and God never guaranteed it would be, but He *has* promised to be with us always. *"So, do not fear, for I am with you; I will uphold you with my righteous right hand." (Isaiah 41:10 NIV)* Even though you may feel lonely, you are *not* alone. God sees you as a strong and mighty warrior, especially when you are at your weakest, for this is the point at which He is strongest in you. Concentrate deeply to see yourself as God sees you; that will empower you and encourage you along the way, especially when you are past the point of giving up. We are our own worst critic; we often see ourselves helpless and under-equipped for the task at hand, but God sees the final result of who we will become *if* we follow in *His* footsteps. *"You are the light of the world. A city set on a hill that cannot be hidden." (Matthew 5:14 ESV)*

As you will soon learn in reading this book, I rest in all assurance knowing our son is in Heaven, as he was able to confirm his salvation to me a few weeks before the accident. For that, I will be eternally grateful. That's not to say that I'm content with fully accepting he's gone, but since he *is*, I'm satisfied knowing he was a believer and that his eternal home is in Heaven! There's never been one day so far that I haven't selfishly wished Justin was still with us, so I could watch him fulfill his lifelong dreams. Rather than be continually disappointed that he's gone from my sight, I take solace knowing he remains forever in my heart. I've chosen to be at peace with God's decision to call him home even though I may never understand why. I'm so very fortunate that not only did God give me one son, He blessed me with three incredible young men who each bring an overwhelming amount of sunlight to my darkest days. Jacob and Caleb, never forget how much I unconditionally love and adore you with every part of my heart and soul.

If, however, you're reading this book and don't have the assurance of knowing where your loved one eternally resides, please understand that you must not let that fear and doubt consume or destroy you, but rather leave your apprehensions in God's mighty, capable hands. You may not have been able to hear an affirmation of faith expressed, but that doesn't mean that he, or she, is not in

Heaven. I know without one doubt that God hears each one who calls upon His name. *"Behold, the Lord's hand is not shortened at all, that it cannot save, nor is His ear dull with deafness that it cannot hear."* (*Isaiah 59:1 KJV*) When Jesus hung on the cross with thieves on either side of Him, did He not promise the one who believed in Him that he would be with Him in paradise? He most assuredly did. *Luke 23:42-43 KJV* says, *"And he said unto Jesus, 'Lord, remember me when thou come into thy kingdom.' And Jesus said unto him, 'Verily, I say unto thee, today shalt thou be with me in paradise.'"* That man who was convicted by the world but forgiven by God didn't have to climb down off his cross and run around trying to "earn" his salvation. *"For by grace you have been saved through faith and this is not your own doing; it is the gift of God, not a result of works, so that no one may boast."* (*Ephesians 2:9 ESV*) God did not save us based on what we can do for Him, but solely out of a love that defies all comprehension. God loves us no matter what we've done and forgives us as soon as we ask. There is *never* one thing we can do to make God not love us. So, don't be so overcome with the stress and anxiety of not knowing the condition of your loved one's walk with God, which is very personal and intimate. Some are more comfortable sharing their relationship with anybody and everybody, while others feel that a much more private one best describes their walk with the Lord.

Jesus is the lover of our souls. He is more than able to reach down and pick us up the instant we fall. He longs for us to call upon Him in our time of need and rejoice with Him when our victory is in sight. His heart's desire for each of us is to come to the saving grace and knowledge of Him. We all need to realize that He doesn't expect us to get through this life not ever having to need His help. I'm sure Jesus is much like we are with our own children, eager, willing, and waiting to help us out the instant we are in need. He looked ahead in time and knew we would require a Savior to save us from our sins. God does not consider us weak when we call on Him. He longs for us to need Him and takes great delight in helping each of us on every occasion.

God, Himself, is the only one that I have met so far Who loves me in spite of myself. He is more than able to do all things, yet He wants and desires me. God demands nothing from me, and yet offers me all things. He never limits our abilities but increases everything we surrender to Him. He loves me without limits or conditions and respects the intent of my heart. He doesn't esteem me higher when I do right, and never would He turn away when I mess up. His Word speaks of His great loyalty all throughout the Bible. He says that we are kept in the very center of His eye and tucked safely under His mighty arms. *"He found him in a desert land, and in the waste howling wilderness; He led him about, He instructed him, He kept him as the apple of His eye." (Deuteronomy 32:10 KJV)* Another Scripture goes on to say; *"Behold, I have graven thee upon the palms of my hands." (Isaiah 49:16 KJV)* How awesome is that to know that God has a constant reminder of each and every one of us imprinted on His nail-pierced hands!

Understand and know, as I said in the begining, this is *my* story told the best way my heart can speak. I've tried to describe as effectively as I can its contents even when I had no adequate words to explain accuraetly what I was feeling. My prayer is that you will be able to gain from it a hope and a desire to know that no matter what you are faced with in this life, you can and will make it through and be able to walk in victory. Rest assured that no matter what you may be dealing with, if it's important to you, it's important to God. There's nothing too big or small that He cannot or will not handle for you *if* you but ask and receive His assistance. He's standing on the right hand of the Father ever interceding on your behalf. *Romans 8:34-35 AMP* asks: *"Who is the one who condemns us? Christ Jesus, Who died, {to pay our penalty} and more than that, Who was raised {from the dead}, and Who is at the right hand of God interceding {with the Father} for us. Who shall ever separate us from the love of Christ? Will tribulation, or distress, or persecution, or famine, or nakedness, or danger or sword?"* We find the answer to that question in verses 38 and 39 of that same chapter: *"For I am convinced {and continue to be convinced—beyond any doubt} that neither death, nor life, nor angels, nor principalities, nor things present, and threatening, nor things to come, nor powers nor height nor depth, nor any other created thing, will be able to separate us from the {unlimited} love of God, which is in Christ Jesus our Lord."* I pray that you will let *this* truth be infused deep in your heart, mind, and soul and that you will allow it to transform your relationship with God to know Him as the Healer of the broken, your constant help in times of trouble. May you come to know Him in the fullness of Who He is, to seek His face rather than His hand. My request and plea is that I will not always be in need, but seek out what I can do for others. I never want to beg God constantly asking that *my* requests be granted but instead thank Him for all the many blessings He has graciously given.

I must add that I don't believe those particular Scriptures give us a free pass to live our lives any way we want to with no consequences. *"And Jesus answered him, "It is said, 'You shall not put the Lord your God to the test.'"* (Luke 4:12 ESV) I honestly believe we're all held accountable for the way we live and that we should do all we can to live Godly, with the promise that our obedience always leads to blessings. That goal can be achieved solely when we allow His life (the Holy Spirit) to live within us. I have often told my sons that I would rather each of them be obedient to us as parents because they love us and not out of terror that they would get in trouble if they didn't comply. Is God not the same way with us? Would He not desire us to serve Him out of our love and devotion rather than out of fear that our disobedience would cause us to go to hell?

I have met many people who consider *my* belief all about religion, to whom I politely reply, "My walk with God is not a religion but a relationship." Because I love Him, I want to follow His leading which is for *my* good and *His* glory. I choose to serve Him out of love, not duty or fear. My relationship isn't based on a huge list of do's and do not's. *"For we maintain that man is justified by faith* apart from works of the Law." (Romans 3:28 NASB) Many well-intentioned Christian organizations believe in the Law, while I choose to reside in God's unmerited favor and grace. I have many times thought how it would ever be possible to keep every letter of each law or rule. The Scripture plainly says, "Whosoever shall keep the whole law, and yet offend in one point, he is guilty of all." (James 2:10 KJV) I in no conscious way deliberately sin since receiving my salvation many years ago; but I recognize that I sometimes slip up or fall short in my daily walk. Freedom came when I realized there is only One created perfect and His name is Jesus. For many years I was afraid that if I did this or that, God would take away my blood bought redemption. I was concerned that if I messed up, He would withhold His love or turn His back on me, refusing to respond to my heart's cry. As my relationship with Him has grown through the years, I no longer worry that I will *lose* my salvation, but I also never take it for granted. "For through the Law I died to the Law, so that I might live to God." (Galatians 2:19 ESV) I always try to do my part to live a life that is pleasing to God, much like we do with our loved ones here on earth. We do what we can to please *them*, not because we *have* to, but out of love. Just as I enjoy doing things for my family and others, I delight in serving God. To this day I have no idea why God loves me; I cannot understand or explain it, but I no longer question that, I'm just thankful to have His love abiding in me.

"But God commendeth His love toward us, in that, while we were yet sinners, Christ died for us." (Romans 5:8 KJV)

Chapter Three
Good Morning, Son-Shine

When my boys were young and just starting school, each morning they would come into the kitchen where I was busy making breakfast and preparing lunches for the day. I would always greet them with, "Good morning, Son-Shine." Thinking back I know they probably thought I was speaking of the "sun" and not "son." Being so young, they could never fully comprehend that, truly, they were the ones who could light up my world as brightly as the sun, even on the gloomiest of days. I can still see their toothless grins and their tousled hair as they scurried around, gathering backpacks, lacing shoes, and scarfing down a bite of breakfast before running out the door. Thinking back on those days, life seemed so hectic and stressful, only when those days were gone did I realize how invaluable they truly were. What I wouldn't give to go back in time and do it all over again--the good, the bad, and the outrageous. I could savor each moment, never taking one minute for granted. I would spend less time stressing, griping, and complaining and enjoy more time smiling and soaking up the brief time of pure happiness they each brought to my life. I think I could relax more and not be under the tremendous amount of pressure to do things perfectly so my children would turn out with absolutely no flaws, as if that were even a posibility. The truth is I was never expected to rear my children as little soldiers. No one on earth can be a perfect parent; the only *One* Who *could* hold that job abides in Heaven, and I respectfualy honor Him as my heavenly Father. I know I missed the *mark* in many ways, but I'm convinced that where I fell short, God picked up the slack and worked things out accordingly. I've always tried to mirror God's way of parenting in rearing my own children; I desired to meet their physical needs with His assistance and asked Him to provide spiritual needs.

I've been a stay-at-home mom since the birth of our youngest son, Caleb, whom I will always refer to as my "spice of life." I re-member praying, "God, *if* you plan to give me any more children, would it be possible to give them to me before I'm thirty?" Caleb was born three days before my thirtieth birthday. God sure has a sense of timing, and in that case, it lined up exactly the way I'd hoped, to my complete surprise! (Oh, me of little faith.) *Matthew 8:26 KJV: "And He saith unto them, Why are ye fearful, Oh ye of little faith?"*

Many of you who know me well remember that I very much wanted to have a daughter. My second son, Jacob, was our first at-tempt for a girl, and Caleb was our second, which brings up the pro-verbial "third time's a charm." However, I am convinced that had I not had a tubal, after the birth of our third son, my husband would have left me at the hospital to find another ride home. He, of course, was done trying for a girl and I had only just begun. I now realize that God knew precisely what He was doing when He blessed me with my handsome, wise, and gifted sons. I have since concluded that boys are exactly what I needed to complete our family. I've al-ways secretly felt like a queen in house full of kings, as they each in their own way make me feel special; fortunate and fulfilled that they let me live in their palace and share their lives. I'm an absolute be-liever that God gives you what you *need* and a lot of the things you desire. As we rely on Him to make the necessary provisions, *our* wants become *His* desires for us. *"Delight thyself in the Lord, and He shall give thee the desires of thine heart." (Psalm 37:4 KJV)* Therefore, the key is not in asking for *our* will, but *His* will, to be done. As we grow in grace and the knowledge of God as our Lord and Savior, we begin to build a hope and trust in Him which allows us to see that He *knows* what's good for us. Thank you, Lord, for always knowing what is best even when we think we should have our way instead. I once heard a powerful message on God's perfect and permissive will. His perfect will is when we give up all rights to having our way and release total control to Him. His permissive will is when we beg and plead for Him to give us what we want, and thereby renounce any thought of letting Him have control in our situations. I believe that when we refuse to let Him direct our paths, there are times when He will allow us to have our way, along with all the trials and tribulations it entails. Sometimes God permits us to learn the hard lessons we refuse to receive any other way. I've learned that it's best to keep the attitude of "His will, His way, always." That was one of the most difficult lessons I've ever been taught. I'll go into more in detail about this in the upcoming chapters. The benefits of understanding God's sovereign purpose early on will afford you a happier, less stressful, more uncomplicated life. I have now adopted the phrase "If I only knew then what I know now." That of course means I have finally "crossed over" to the older generation. You never hear young people using that particular saying. God's Word promises us that we can ask for knowledge and then we will have it, proving it doesn't have to manifest when you're older, but is available now for the asking. *"If any of you lack wisdom, let him ask of God, that giveth to all men liberally, and upbraideth not; and it shall be given." (James 1:5 KJV)*

Moreover, I have to admit that, without a doubt, I've been rather blessed with the best by the Best. God has given me the great privilege of rearing three incredible young men, who each bring an overwhelming amount of happiness and excitement to my life! Being a parent has been one of the hardest jobs I've ever had, but the benefits have been endless. Did I do it all right? My boys would give you the loudest "NO WAY" possible, and they would be correct. However, I do everything out of the sincere love I have for them. I hated saying, the dreaded "No" but knew that for them to be all God intended, their dad and I had to learn to use *that* word at times. I can't say it's been all fun and games, but I will say, as I have many times, that I've thoroughly loved being the mother of these amazing young men.

I've done my best to cherish my sons as much as humanly possible and have always confided to each of them that there's not one single thing they could ever do to make me withhold my affections for them. I treasure the priceless time we have together and find that every day I'm given with them, my love grows stronger and deeper. I pray they each embrace it and allow it to saturate their hearts over the years, and as they grow older may they finally realize and appreciate the devotion I've tried to give. Sure, there have been times I was angry with them, but it *never* has and won't *ever* affect or diminish my admiration for them. How much better this world would be *if* we were not always expecting approval or adoration to be based on performance, and *if* we could all be appreciated for who we are, with all of our imperfections and inabilities! I know that God's acceptance of us is so much greater than we can ever earn or deserve. We may never reach this goal with people, but with God, we always have the certainty He adores us with a pure, unconditional, unconventional love in spite of ourselves. There are many days when I lose sight of Who He is inside of me and I find it impossible to achieve personal acceptance, but in Christ I am always loved and accepted. When I can abide in that place of favor I am content and lacking nothing.

Everyone always says babies don't come equipped with an instruction manual but, in fact, God's Word gives us powerful insight as to how to bring them up. *"And these words that I command you today shall be on your heart. You shall teach them diligently to your children, and shall talk of them when you sit in your house, and when you walk by the way, and when you lie down and when you rise." (Deuteronomy 6:6-7 ESV)* Throughout the Scriptures, we're told that blessings follow obedience. It's our job as parents to esteem our children enough to compel them to behave in the proper manner so that their lives will be blessed. *"For the Lord disciplines the one He loves and chastises every son Whom He receives." (Hebrews 12:6 ESV)* When discipline is needed may we cherish our sons and daughters by administering guidance with an abundance of mercy and grace just as Christ has always shown us. Above all, we're to honor them with an unconditional, undeserved endearment that cannot be described or measured.

Knowing that God cares for me in the same way I admire my children, I ask my heavenly Lord and Savior Jesus Christ to go through the streets of Heaven and find that 6' 1½", blonde-haired, blue-eyed son of mine and give him the biggest, tightest hug, the kind where you can't breathe until you're let you go and it feels as if your bones are being crushed. I ask God to tell him every morning and night how much his family loves and misses him and that we will see him again very soon. Knowing that God hears my heart's cry, I rest assured that Justin can still hear his mom saying to him as I did each day as long as I was given the opportunity, "Good morning, Son-Shine." Although Justin may not be able to hear me physically, I know that the God I serve not only listens intently to me but loves and cares enough to take the time out of His busy day to assure our son of our steadfast and undying love for him.

I fully presume that everything we consider significant in our lives gains full attention from God. He understands our pain as we continually miss Justin and grieve his loss, for He also endured the loss of a Son, His *only* One, when He gave Him up to die on a cruel, rugged cross for our sins so that as a Christian, we will never suffer death as a sinner and thus have the assurance of life eternal. God gave so that we never entirely lose our loved ones that belong to Him, but are separated only until the day we'll reunite in Heaven. What a day, what a day that will finally be when we see Jesus face to face. *"Verily, verily, I say unto you, He that heareth My word, and believeth on Him that sent Me, hath everlasting life, and shall not come into condemnation, but is passed from death unto life." (John 5: 24 KJV)*

Chapter Four
Glimpses of Heaven

It's ironic that memories of a tragedy impact your mind in a way that they can never be forgotten. It's incredible to think how in one split second everything could be irreversibly changed. The effort it takes to remember the events of last week is exhausting, but the memory of that night is something I've tirelessly expended all my energy trying to forget. There are many days it still plays over and over in my mind, and *if* allowed to continue, would occupy all my time all day every day.

The events leading up to that horrific, life-altering night debil-itate my mind and are a factor behind every thought I have or deci-sion I make. There are, however, some memories of things which happened that still make my heart smile, such as one occasion when my two younger sons and I were at the mall shopping for school clothes. It was an annual event, and practically the only time my boys enjoyed shopping with me, mostly due to the fact they were the ones profiting from the all the purchases. My phone rang, and it was my oldest son, Justin, calling to see what we were doing. As I began to explain our plans, he said, "Well, I *was* going to come and see you all at the house." I immediately said, "In that case, we'll hurry back home." I always jumped at the chance for him to come for a visit, especially since he and his wife had recently moved into their own home. After getting married they moved into a basement apartment in our home, which enabled them to save money for a place of their own. We all worked together painting and fixing it up nice. I didn't get a chance to see him as much as I used to when we all lived to-gether, of course. It always made my heart happy to have each of the boys with me as much as possible.

When he replied, "I'll just meet up with you at the store," I said, "Great we can get you some new clothes as well;" but he protested, "Mom, you don't have to spend your money on me." That very instant I realized he had experienced a "reality check" and was learning how to live outside the comforts of his parents' home. While living with us he never had to earn money for necessities such as clothing, food, and, of course, a roof over his head; he had finally learned how expensive things were. My oldest son was finally a man, able to work and provide a living for himself and his family. That was a proud moment for a mother, but also somewhat bittersweet. I had always taken immense joy in giving my sons the things they needed and most of what they wanted. Early on we didn't have an excess abundance of finances; I would gladly wear bargain store shoes, thrift store designer dresses, and clearance rack clothes just so my children could have the best of what their hearts desired. The bittersweet part was seeing my son becoming a man and losing the boyish ways he had worn so proudly for so long. The baggy jeans full of holes had now become less saggy and not so holey. The time he spent taking cars apart so he could see how quickly he could re-assemble them to become better and faster was now dedicated to family and friends for the enjoyment of just being together. Yes, my son was finally acting and thinking like a man, making wise decisions, living life all grown up, and just like that, in a blink of an eye, he was gone. Take my advice and savor the good times no matter how small or insignificant they may seem, because only once they're gone, will you realize that those little moments were possibly the greatest memories of your life.

As we continued on our mission of clothes shopping and waited for Justin to arrive, we made our way into one of the boys' favorite stores, where I spotted a beautiful bright yellow polo shirt and thought of Justin. When I saw it was his size, I grabbed it, and we made our final purchases. I couldn't wait to show it to his wife, Courtney. I knew she would be thrilled that I had found a collared shirt he could trade for the "worn out" one he loved so much and always picked to wear to church or special occasions. It was beginning to look a little tattered and torn which seemed to be the reason he liked it best. Courtney worked at the mall, so I hurried to show her the shirt I'd found. She took one look and said, "He won't ever wear that shirt; it's way too bright!" Trying not to show my disappointment, I carefully placed the shirt back into the bag, feeling a bit let down that she didn't share my excitement over the purchase. I decided to keep the shirt anyway. *I* liked it so maybe Justin would as well.

The boys and I sat down and visited awhile as we waited for Justin to arrive. I texted Barry and asked if he wanted to meet up with us after he got off work. He gave me his usual response, "Sure Honey, anything for you." How did I get so blessed with such an agreeable hubby and three wonderful sons? Life was so good! After some time had passed, I looked up from our conversation and saw Justin coming toward us. I remember thinking that I'd never seen him look so handsome. It was as if he were glowing with iridescent colors all around him. I ran over quickly and lovingly hugged him, as I said, "Son, you look so beautiful!" I'm not sure why I've always told my boys they were beautiful instead of handsome. All I know is, in my eyes, I've never seen a sight as captivating as my three sons, and they will forever take my breath away and melt my heart each and every time I see them. When I gaze into their eyes, it will be the closest to Heaven I've ever encountered on this earth.

Justin had ridden his motorcycle and always hated the way the helmet messed up his hair, so he said, "Mom, I look awful!" He gave his hair a quick toss with his hand and threw his head back to perform his traditional side hair flip, and it looked as good as ever. As long as I live I'll never forget the shiny, radiant look he had, a luster that the weariness of a windy motorcycle ride could not destroy. His countenance that night is what I see when I close my eyes if my heart ever whispers doubt as to God's perfect plan for my son. Could it be that I was able to see the transformation that was in the process of happening, that he was beginning the journey to Heaven to a glorified body, and I was able to catch a glimpse of it here on earth? My heart tells me, "yes" even when my mind tries to convince me otherwise. To this day the battle continues between my heart and mind.

Doctors have surmised the distance from the brain to the human heart is eighteen inches; seems more like a million miles when you're trying to get your heart to understand what you mind can't comprehend. The question always remains, *why* is it that only after he left this earth am I fully able to understand what I physically saw that night before the accident, when it was too late to try and alter the events that took his life? Sometimes my mind holds me prisoner with thoughts that I could have done something differently or could have recognized what was about to happen and the fact I missed an opportunity. All around there were signs that his time on earth was about to end, but somehow, I didn't see them until it was too late to change the outcome. My flesh trembles at the thought that if I'd known then what I know now, maybe I could have prevented his departure and he would still be here with us. My mind uses these thoughts to paralyze me and cause feelings of fear and failure as a mother. After all, moms are expected to know things about their children that no one else could ever know. If danger is lurking, shouldn't a mother be the first one to know if her children are in harm's way? Isn't it true that moms are supposed to have a sixth sense or eyes in the back of their heads? Nothing should get past their suspicions. A mother sees and knows all, right? Wrong! God is the only One Who truly has that ability.

So, I need not let my mind tell me I was negligent or incompetent as a mother for not recognizing the signs of Justin's impending departure. Was I the only *one* able to see the transformation taking place? The realization then that what I was seeing was my son transitioning from this earth to his final resting place in Heaven, would have no doubt made it impossible for me to accept. The inability to stop this event from happening would have catapulted me into the deepest, darkest depression of which I would never have climbed out. Whether my eyes are open or closed, the vision I have of him, the way I see him still to this day, is exactly the way I saw him that night, a shining, brilliant light through the darkest of nights. Justin had the brightest, shiniest blue eyes I have ever seen;

they were large and perfectly round. Seeing that smile of his which shone through his beautiful eyes and illuminated his face like fireworks on the Fourth of July, brings happiness to my heart on the days when it feels empty, heavy, and alone. Whether his lips spread into a grin or not, his eyes always seemed to flash a dazzling, contagious smile, which will always be one of his many qualities I love and miss the most.

God's plan for Justin and our family was already in motion. The power of life and death is in God's mighty hands, and though we all can make choices to lengthen our lives or hasten our deaths, God ultimately has the final decision.

Now on the happy days, I am thankful I was able to catch a glimpse of how great and glorious Heaven must be because I have faith to believe I saw that picturesque place in my son that night, which is what keeps me going forward. You see, God prepared me every step of the way to say and do all the things the necessary things to make sure that he was ready. I had the chance show him the bright yellow shirt which he loved and was able to wear to his final celebration on this earth.

Later, we all went for dinner, Barry joining us at the restaurant after work. We were seated quickly and began talking about our day. As usual, we were all talking at the same time, but Justin spoke up and his words silenced all other chatter. He said, "I'm just ready to go home." I immediately responded, "Son, you know you're always welcome to come back anytime you want to." I then added, "Just go to your house, and you and Courtney pack up, grab Sky and head back to ours." He dropped his head as if I didn't understand what he was saying. The waitress interrupted with our food, and for some reason, we never returned to the conversation about a homecoming. That discussion haunts me to this day. I remember vividly now that Justin did not say, "I want to 'come' home" but said, "I just want to 'go' home." I regret that I didn't question him further to understand accurately what he meant. What in fact was he trying to tell us? Did he have an idea he wouldn't be on this earth much longer? Was he saying goodbye? When I see my son again, I'm almost sure I will have this subject at the top of my list of much-needed conversations I plan to have with him! That is if I'm even able to speak, from the sheer excitement of finally seeing him once again.

After the meal, we gathered in the parking lot; I remember my husband going over to Justin as he climbed onto his motorcycle. He grabbed him in one of those special hugs he's shared with each of his sons on numerous occasions. Barry held him tight and prayed a very special prayer over him that only God and Justin could hear. Afterward, we all went over to Justin and said our goodbyes; I told him to be careful and that we loved him. We all stood in silence, watching as he drove out of sight into the night.

As I continue to relive each moment of our time together that evening, I blame myself for not being more attentive to what was happening. What *did* Justin mean? I ask myself that question almost every day since he left. Did he know that he was about to leave us for his heavenly home one night later? I believe that just as I saw the signs predicting his departure, he, too, had little hints along the way but didn't fully understand. Utter darkness was looming in the near distance, and we were all unaware of the devastation that was about to become our reality. As I said earlier, God has a perfect plan for our lives, even during complete destruction. Although at times our hearts will be broken from what we must endure, one day God will reveal to us how the tragedies in our lives led us to the greatest blessings. *If* He allows your heart to be broken into a million pieces, He and He alone will bless you with a brand-new heart, stronger than the one you had before. *"For Thou desirest not sacrifice; else I would give it; Thou delight not in burnt offering. The sacrifices of God are a broken spirit: and a contrite {crushed, crippled, broken} heart, O God, thou wilt not despise."* (*Psalm 51:16-17 KJV*)

Each day since that night I saw Justin beaming with glowing light all over him, I've been trying to capture glimpses of Heaven and have been privileged to see in many ways the signs and wonders of God's elaborate handiwork. There have been numerous occasions when I look to the heavens and see the sky vividly colored with such glory and magnificence that only God could paint. One night while my husband and I were driving home, I looked out the window and beheld one of the most awe-inspiring sunsets I'd ever seen. I grabbed my camera so I could somehow capture it. As I snapped picture after picture trying to obtain the perfect shot to depict its unexplainable beauty, I asked my husband to slow down so I could portray a glimpse of each stage of its going down. My eyes began to fill with tears, so I put down the camera and just stared out the window. Under my breath I uttered a prayer, "God you are *so* wonderful, and Your exquisite masterpiece on this earth is overwhelming my heart. You, my Lord and Savior, completely take my breath away. I adore you, Lord, and to me, you are the most kind, loving, compassionate Father, full of grace and mercy. You are the lover of my soul and the Healer of my hurting heart. There is nothing more glorious than You, my God." Within seconds the skies began to flicker; the clouds seemed to come to life with exquisite light, but their radiant rays yielded no thunder; not a sound could be heard. There was just the quiet sparkle of light as it brilliantly illuminated the sky. In my heart, I felt God was speaking to me about how He sees me as His daughter. He was flickering the Heavens right back at me with light just as I had flashed the skies while taking pictures of the sunset. As breathtaking as the Heavens were that night, my God sees me as His beautiful creation. *"How precious are Your thoughts about me, O God. They cannot be numbered! I can't even count them; they outnumber the grains of sand! And when I wake up, You are still with me!" (Psalm 139: 17-18 NLT)* Much like I saw the marvelous light surrounding my son that night, our heavenly Father sees us all as the most precious priceless treasures on this earth. He daily rejoices over us with singing. *"He will rejoice over thee with joy; He will rest in His love, He will joy over thee with singing." (Zephaniah 3:17 KJV)*

Chapter Five
Going Home

The Saturday morning which was to be our son's last, unknown to our family until later that evening, I received a phone call from Justin. I had grown accustomed to his calling on the weekends as he was interested in what we had planned. We talked a few minutes as I suggested several ideas and asked if he wanted to grill some burgers out by the pool, or would he rather pull our boat to the lake and go skiing. I waited for his response, knowing he never liked to make decisions without first talking it over with his wife. (Did I also mention he was an intelligent young man?) Justin then said he would call back when he got off work, and we could decide how to spend our time. I then got up and started my day. My mother called a brief time later and said she was fixing lunch if we wanted to come by and eat. Because she is such a great cook and we all enjoy being together, I told her that, of course, we'd be there. Next, I texted Justin to let him know we could eat lunch at Nana's and then we could all swim and hang out beside the pool. He responded with a message saying Courtney was having car trouble, so he probably wouldn't make it. I told him just to come when he could and if he didn't show up, that I would understand. I told him his dad would be happy to help if he needed him, and he said he would figure things out and let me know. He eventually arrived somewhat flustered by all the day's events. We had just gotten home from Nana's when Justin entered the side door and I met him the kitchen and we sat down at the table, I remember his asking for something for a headache. As we always did, we prayed for healing, for all the pain to be gone, in Jesus' name. He began to share with me some of his worries and concerns, I realized the pain he was having was caused from stress. Hoping that encouragement would bring him peace, and calm his anxiety I tried my best to provide counsel on leaving his concerns to God. I told him that in time everything would be okay because God has a way of working things out for the best outcome even when there seems to be no way. We discussed plans for the next day after church, including going to a concert at a local theme park to hear a band he liked. I also mentioned that we were planning a beach trip and that he and Courtney should try and come with us. It felt as if I were doing all the talking and seemed that Justin's mind was a million miles away. He was hesitant to agree to any of these suggestions, saying he wasn't sure he'd be able to get off work for vacation and made various other statements as to why the concert plan might not work out. Again, I assured him that everything would be okay and for him not to worry.

Now as I replay every detail of that day in my mind, I wonder if Justin knew the real reason he wouldn't be able to make plans past that day. I may even go so far as to say that in some way *maybe* Justin knew his time on earth was coming to an end, which brings to mind his other actions during the previous months. He, his dad, and brothers had played a huge role in building our pool from foundation to finish. One day Justin had come by the house as I was working on the flower beds. He suggested we get the four-wheeler and ride through the woods to look for big rocks to use in the landscape. I quickly agreed, "That's a great idea, Son!" We had intended, eventually, to add a poolside waterfall but had a tough time getting started. I remember Justin's asking me to make sure Dad got all the supplies to finish, saying he would help. He was adamant about getting that waterfall built, much more than we were, so he continued to ask in the following weeks and then worked feverishly to make sure everything was completed. At that time, my mind couldn't understand why things were so important to him that they get done as soon as possible. Was there some spiritual force pulling my son onward and upward? I realize now that he must have sensed it, even if he could not understand for himself, that his race was coming to a finish and all loose ends had to be tied up. Could it be in the distance he could see Jesus waving the flag signaling his final mile? I hope he was watching from Heaven and was proud to see we finally did finish the project. Every time I look out and see it or glance at the boulders in the landscape, it reminds me of what a hard-working young man he was and how willing and eager he was to help others, whatever the need. The passion he had for life couldn't be contained, and it infected everyone in his path.

When I was with Justin that day, it never crossed my mind that this could be the very last time I'd ever see my son, sit and talk with him, and look into those huge, beautiful blue eyes. I'm sure that had I realized then what I know now, the final time I hugged him that day I would have never, ever let him go. I would have tried with all my might to hold on to him and would have never let him walk out that door.

Justin and I moved our conversation into the living room. I plopped down on the couch expecting Willow, Justin's spunky blue-eyed Siberian husky, to join me as he always did, but instead, the dog worked desperately to get into a one-person chair with Justin. Willow tried tirelessly to climb onto his lap, which was something he'd never done before. However, on this day Justin could barely keep a flow of conversation going due to Willow's determination to have his undivided attention. Justin mentioned how surprised he was that Willow was so aggressive and persistent to climb on him. We both were rather puzzled at the dog's actions that day. Thinking back a million and one times, I wonder, did even his fluffy, furry, best friend know this was Justin's last time to spend precious moments with him? How was it so obvious to an animal and not to me, his mother? As mentioned before, I believe it was part of God's grace that He didn't allow me to recognize the signs of my son's soon-to-be eternal departure? I believe now that was the key to my being able to accept his leaving. Had I known it was coming, I would have tried desperately to stop it. How could I have ever survived until now, if I'd known but still not been able to affect the outcome positively? Would I ever have been able to rebound from such a horrendous failure? I must trust what I've learned thus far, that not

43

knowing ahead of time the day and time of my son's death was another one of those unmerited blessings.

I remember a conversation Justin and I had on the boat just a few weeks before. As his nose always sunburned easily, I had asked him to put on sunscreen. Ironically, he replied, "Mom, I'm not worried about skin cancer; God is coming back, and it may be *this* year!" He was so adamant in his belief; I can still hear the forcefulness and determination in his voice. That haunting conversation plays over and over in my head, reminding me that it could have been one of the many signs I again missed.

The first year after his passing seemed to be the most agonizing, although it was spent in a fog that blurred reality. The words I held tightly were the ones Justin spoke that day on the boat, saying that *this* could be the year God comes back. I was convinced that this specific conversation with him was by no accident. In fact, it was my motivation to keep going when God came for him and I was left to carry on. As each day passed, I told my heart that even though the Lord did not return, splitting the eastern sky, I had at least made it through another twenty-four hours with the ability to keep breathing. I woke up each day convinced that *if* God didn't come back today, He very well may come tomorrow. I continued the ritual every single day that year. As each year came and went without the Lord's return, I then had to explore other avenues to make it through my heartache. I now try never to waste valuable time worrying about what *day* God will come back, but instead I focus on being ready *when* He returns. *"But concerning that day or that hour, no one knows, not even the angels in Heaven, nor the Son, but only the Father." (Mark 13:32 ESV)* I focused on my other two sons and my husband, grateful for my love and appreciation for them and theirs for me. That kind of devotion empowered me to keep living, especially on the days in the beginning when I felt God's presence was absent.

Of all the time, we spent on the lake with our boys, that last day was one of the most memorable. Later, as we watched the sunset

44

and headed back to the dock, a certain song came on the radio. Not a word was spoken as we all listened while the lyrics spoke meaning to each of us, in different ways I'm convinced.

It's like a storm that cuts a path.
It breaks your will, it feels like that.
You think you're lost, but you're not lost.
On your own. You're not alone.
I will stand by you; I will help you through.
When you've done all, you can do if you
Can't cope, I will dry your eyes, I will fight your fight.
I will hold you tight, and I won't let go.
It hurts my heart to see you cry.
I know it's dark this part of life
Oh, it finds us all, and we're too small.
To stop the rain. Oh, but when it rains,
I will stand by you. I will help you through.
You're going to make it, yeah, you're going to make it.
Cause I will stand by you. I will help you through.
When you've done all you can, and you can't cope,
I will dry your eyes; I will fight your fight.
I will hold you tight, and I won't let go.
--Rascal Flatts, "I Won't Let Go."

To this day it's still gut wrenching to hear that song; the very mention of its lyrics creates an immediate lump in my throat making it impossible to swallow, and my eyes overflow with burning, blinding tears. Although the pain is still raw, the words reassure me that the bond we had with Justin was not severed in death but has been made only stronger in his absence.

The importance of those lyrics was confirmed in a video my sister, Amy, made one summer afternoon a few weeks before the accident. On that particular day, the boys were working on perfecting

45

their dives, and Amy was trying out her new phone's video capability. The radio always played in the background when we were out by the pool, and as the phone was recording, that very song, "I Won't Let Go," came on, followed by "If Heaven Was Not So Far Away," and ended with, "I Saw God Today." I can't help but think God orchestrated that playlist.

Undoubtedly, my sister couldn't have realized at the time the importance of that film, but, thankfully she saved it, because it's the last footage we have of Justin and is very dear to us all. Scrolling through her phone the night of the accident, she came across that video and immediately brought it to me. Bittersweet, to say the least, it was a blessing to know that God allowed us to share that song together as a family and to have the reassurance that Justin won't let go of us. We, for sure, will never let go of him.

I've had many people try to talk with me about or help walk me through the grief process by offering suggestions and advice. Each aspired to convince me that unless I let go and moved on, I would never heal. As soon as those words came out of their mouths, I stopped listening to what they had to say. How could a mother ever truly relinquish her child? I understood the *principle* of giving my sons back to God because they do belong to Him. They are on loan to us, and when at an appointed time He may call them back home as He wills, but in *actuality,* to cut the ties that bind a child to his parents was impossible for me to comprehend. I began to pray for God to help me understand *if* this was what I needed to do to be healed of all my brokenness and pain, and if so, for Him to please guide me through the process. This particular battle lasted almost a year.

The summer following the loss of our son we chaperoned a youth convention from our church. One of the performers ended his musical set with an old-time favorite in every church, "I Surrender All." At that moment, my heart flooded with emotions that escaped out of my eyes and ran like a river down my cheeks. That was God's reply to me! You see, He didn't require me to actually "let go" of my

46

son, but His desire for me was to surrender him *back* to his heavenly Father. We were able to hold Justin for twenty years, five months, and two days and now, God would hold him until our reunion in Heaven. We returned to our home church and I received confirmation again when the worship team's song of choice was the very same one, "I Surrender All." Since that time, I've done exactly that; I've wholeheartedly relinquished Justin to God. I may not ever understand all the reasons he had to go so soon, but one thing I do know is that God has a perfect plan for us all, and no doubt Justin's early home-going was part of His plan for him. My prayer now is that I will not doubt God, but trust that even though I may not understand all the plans, He has for me, He has my best interests at the very center of His heart.

Many questions bombard my mind from day to day. Was Justin taken to Heaven to be spared the evils of the end-time prophecies? Would there perhaps have come a time when his faith in God would have been lost? I couldn't even bear the thought that this world might have tried to deceive him into believing *it* had more to offer, that my son would no longer embrace a love of God or desire to live for Him. These are all inquiries for which I may never have answers. Knowing that he is at rest and safe in the arms of God, filled with total peace and joy, and that he will never have to suffer the trials of this earth or have to endure pain or loss, sickness, tears, and sadness brings great solace to my weary mind and heart. I came to this place of peace one day while studying God's Word. He promises us in *1 Thessalonians 4:13-17 AMP*: *"Now we do not want you to be uninformed, believers, about those who are asleep {in death}, so that you will not grieve {for them} as others do who have no hope {beyond this present life}. For if we believe that Jesus died and rose again {as in fact He did}, even so, God {in this same way--by raising them from the dead} will bring with Him those {believers} who have fallen asleep in Jesus. For we say this to you by the Lord's {own} Word, that we who are still alive and remain until the coming of the Lord, will in no way precede {into His presence} those {believers} who have fallen asleep {in death}. For the Lord, Himself will come down from Heaven with a shout of command, with the voice of the archangel and the trumpet of God, and the dead in Christ will rise first. Then we who are alive and remain {on the earth} will simultaneously be caught up {raptured} together with them {the resurrected ones} in the clouds to meet the Lord in the air, and so we will always be with the Lord!"* I'm sorry/not sorry for the long Scripture reading here but it has such power I felt it needed to be shared. Finding this treasured nugget in God's Word brought me great comfort by the knowledge that my son is *not* dead but only asleep until God comes back to take us all home, and although he will rise first to Heaven with Christ's return, we will all follow when our time on earth is expired, and we assemble together in the sky.

One thing I know to be true, it will never be easy to lose a child, whether young or old. I've often said that whether you have your sons and daughters for a few moments, or a lifetime, there's no real way to measure the level of grief or the amount of time it takes to complete the mourning process. Three years after Justin was born, Barry and I were expecting for the second time, only to find out a few months later the baby wouldn't survive. I still remember the day we lost our unborn infant. Not ever getting to hold this precious little one tenderly in my arms, I often wondered could *this* have been the daughter I had asked God to give me? Never having the opportunity to say, "Good morning, she-shine," how could I *ever* begin to say goodbye? I wasn't able to look upon its tiny face or hear its first cry. My heart hurt deeply but the pain of the grief process was very different from losing Justin, still intense, but in time I was finally able to bear the burden of that loss. However, the absence of this precious child's presence lingers still to this very day. I've met other mothers who have also lost children through miscarriage, never receiving the opportunity to watch their unborn babies take one single breath. There have been other times I've had the opportunity to minister to those who have lost older children. Each experience is

48

unique, and every circumstance is not the same, every loss to be dealt with accordingly. No matter the length of time we're appointed with our children no parent ever wants to live without them. I've felt the sting of jealousy when others had longer with their children than *I* experienced. I also never fail to count my blessings that I was able to have the time I *was* given with our son. Some never push the pain aside and find a will to go on, while others continue the best that they can, living life with the missing vital part. Then there are those who remain unshakable because they know their loved ones would never want them to renounce merited joy. Justin hated to see me cry, and whenever I did, he was quick to try his numerous antics to make me smile again. So, I strive to be one of the courageous ones never to "leave weak." I don't always get there, but it's my goal each day to try and live my life to the fullest, knowing that's how my son lived, and that he'd want me to experience all that I can even if he isn't here to enjoy it with me.

When I stop to think about it, would we be living victoriously in total freedom *if* we had to live with the fear of possibly having to go through losing our children? Could we legitimately enjoy our sons and daughters with that fear ever present in our hearts? We'd be living in a prison of our design. Would we forever be forced to love half-heartedly for fear of our hearts being destroyed? Would we be constantly in fear of losing them, making it impossible to enjoy the time we're awarded? We know that children are truly one of our greatest gifts from God; and should He choose to call them back, we should be accepting of the fact that He sees the whole picture and has a better plan. There's an old saying that comes to mind: "It's better to have loved and lost than never to have loved at all." Getting that point across from your mind to your heart can be a long, painful, tedious journey and maybe a statement understood only by parents who have lost a child. I've often said that even if I had my son for a hundred years, it would never be long enough. If given a chance I would have never been able to give him back, no matter the length of time I was allowed. So, for now, I must *choose* to be

49

thankful for the years I did have with him and not angry for those I won't be able to enjoy. When my mind tries to sway me the wrong way, I think back on all the extraordinary memories I keep tucked deeply inside my heart. The joy of his presence in my life far outweighs the grief of losing him. If I were given a choice for him to live to an old age and then die and go to hell because of unbelief, *that* would be a heartbreak from which I could never recover. Knowing I have the promise of seeing Justin again, I will linger with enthusiastic anticipation of our long-awaited reunion in Heaven.

I once met another mother who had lost a son. She shared with me her own story of grief and explained that her son had given his heart to God at an early age. She said he was involved in a life-threatening accident while serving as a missionary overseas. Everyone prayed for him to be saved from death, including the mother who told me how she had begged God to spare her only child. Later the young man recovered only to turn against God and begin a life of crime that ultimately resulted in the loss of his life. She explained to me her devastation and unbearable guilt, knowing that *if* she hadn't pleaded with God to save her son from the near-death experience, he would have been taken up to Heaven. Instead, she now feared he was in hell. I listened to this lady with compassion for the loss and hurt we both shared. I wanted so much to encourage her in some way, but I couldn't find the words. I have now come to know a renewed hope in God that I pray she has also found. *"The righteous man perishes, and no one lays heart; devout men are taken away, while no one understands. For the righteous man is taken away from calamity." (Isaiah 57:1 ESV)* Those who are made righteous by God's grace are spared the torment of hell.

I must believe and trust that by God's choosing to call Justin back at twenty years, five months, and two days, it was the exact moment He appointed him to leave. God knew us before we were born. *"Before I formed you in the womb I knew you, and before you were born I consecrated you; I have appointed you a prophet to the nations." (Jeremiah 1:5 ESV)* Hanging onto that knowledge deep within my heart gives me an uncontainable hope and joy unending that *this* world cannot afford, knowing that God alone chooses when we enter this life and then calls us back at the appropriate time. We must never take that choice upon ourselves but leave the decision solely up to God. In times of fear and doubt of our ability to remain on this earth, we must focus on Him and gather His strength and peace.

As quickly as this precious bundle entered our lives, in a moment he was gone. The last text message I received from Justin was the night he left this earth. He said, "Mom, I'll see you at church in the morning." Having the assurance of knowing without one doubt my son woke up that next morning in the arms of Jesus, brings my heart unexplainable peace. Even though he may be gone for a little while, one day soon we'll all be together in our heavenly home. Until then, I will do the best I can to carry on, knowing that with each passing day, I'm one step closer to seeing my son again. *"For You have delivered my life from death; and kept my feet from falling, so that I may walk before God in the light and life of the living." (Psalm 56:13 AMP)*

Chapter Six
I Won't Let Go

Memories of last month, last week, or even yesterday seem a blur, but the memory of July 17, 2011, will be forever etched in my mind--a sacred memory that will *never* be forgotten. Driving past the tree once marked with bright, florescent orange spray paint, now faded, we remember *this* as the place which caused my family so much torment and agony. It has been a constant reminder of the day our lives completely turned upside down, and inside out making the life we lived before a distant memory of what it used to be. Although Justin is now in Heaven, he is still a vital part of our family. Not present in bodily form, but still with us in so many other ways, he holds an irreplaceable space in our hearts. However, we do struggle with accepting the fact that our family tree was forever forceably reconstructed the night of the accident.

Even though this gut-wrenching memory replays in my mind over and over whether I'm awake or asleep, I do have satisfaction in knowing that God is making me new every day that I permit His Holy Spirit in me to bring the peace and comfort that only He can give. *"Be careful for nothing but in everything by prayer and supplication with thanksgiving let your requests be made known unto God. And the peace of God which passeth all understanding shall keep your hearts and minds through Christ Jesus."* (*Philippians 4:6-7 KJV*)

During the first few months, most days were spent trying to focus on the tasks at hand, knowing that the busier I could stay, the faster the day would turn into night. Then I'd bury my head in the darkness and try to sleep so that I could count the days off faster until the time my family could once again be complete. Looking back now I can see that the habit of hiding under the covers or trying to rush bravely through the day with meaningless chores, was a complete waste of time. I realize I've spent so many hours and even days of my life being sad and depressed concerning things and situations over which I had no control. I now make a conscious choice not to focus on all the things I would have or could have done differently to obtain what I deem to be a better result. I desire to make the most of the time I'm given and not let the roadblocks along the way slow me down or detour me from God's appointed plan and purpose.

Keeping my mind on track while preparing for the inevitable distractions can be very complicated. When dealing with the loss of a child, you suffer a tremendous amount of trauma to the brain, which is now forced to function at only part of its capacity. That fact is caused by the inability of the mind to forget the events of your crumbled past. Hard as I try, my mind still has days where I can't get beyond the thoughts, feelings, and emotions of *that* night. When I'm in a conversation with someone, it's so hard to stay focused because of my mind's wandering back to the night my life was irrefutably changed. There are times in the middle of my daily activities when I'm frozen in my tracks as a thought of that horrible night leaves me acutely unable to operate with any degree of normality. For this reason, it doesn't take me long to grow weary and exhausted from the daily grind of activities.

So many times, I've thought how great it would be to recall only the happiest memories of our lives. What if there was a way for all the tragedies, grief, and pain to be forever erased from our hearts and minds? How great it would be if we no longer had to come to grips with the things we desperately wanted to reverse or reject. Would that not make for a perfect life? If only it could be as simple as that sounds, then I would not have to be continuously reminded of the night our lives were drastically changed forever.

The unforgettable day had started out rather uneventful, with no significant issues that were life altering up to this point. I was concerned for Justin because his happy-go-lucky attitude was clouded by his unusual behavior and seemingly troubled mind. However, since I had told him everything would work out, I, too, had believe that statement. As Justin went out the door that afternoon, Jacob insisted on going with him. He always wanted to be with his big brother every chance he could. Caleb chimed in wanting to go my sister's house, so he could spend time being the oldest in the family with his younger cousins. Having no boys home to "entertain" us, my husband decided it was past time for a "date night." We got ready and went for a drive, ending up a few hours from home. We enjoyed "window shopping" at some of the local car dealerships, *trying* not to be noticed by sales personnel, as we were not serious shoppers but just curious onlookers. We later visited our favorite restaurant before returning home. It had been a busy day, leaving me completely exhausted and looking forward to a long, peaceful sleep.

To this very day, six and a half years later, as hard as I've tried to forget what happened that night, I remember it as if it were only yesterday. It was a few minutes before midnight and I had just gone to bed. As I lay down and tried to get comfortable, there was an overwhelming uneasiness to pray for our oldest son, Justin. I always prayed for each of my three boys before falling asleep. My request had always been that they would affectionately know God as their personal Lord and Savior and have a genuine relationship with Him that would bring peace, joy, and happiness beyond what they had dreamed or could ever imagine. I asked God that my sons not only *know* unconditional love but freely give unselfishly the same away to others. Of course, I always prayed for God to watch over our children and keep them safe from all harm, but tonight was different. I could hardly get the words out. My heart began to beat very hard inside my chest, and the prayers would not flow as naturally as they always had in the past. It was hard to speak as if there was an unstoppable force paralyzing me. I had never before experienced such a heaviness. All I could do was focus my heart and thoughts on Justin and whisper the name of Jesus over him. I was terrified, shaking on the inside but unable to move physically. I knew my *spirit* had to pray, as my natural ability was completely impaired. I felt an urgent need to pray for his safety, for God to watch over him. Eventually the pressure seemed to let up some, and I was able to ask God to help Justin no matter what he was facing, that He would protect him from all danger.

Minutes later the doorbell rang. Barry immediately jumped out of the bed and within seconds he was on his feet and hurriedly ran to the door. I remember burrowing deeper under the blanket in such fear I cannot even begin to try to explain, even if mere words could describe. No time ever has a doorbell or phone call in the middle of the night brought good news. I heard voices and screams. Not knowing what was going on or what to expect, I slowly slid out from under the covers, steadied my feet on the floor, took a deep breath, and made my way to the front door. There I saw people gathered around crying and trying to speak to me, but my ears felt muffled and unable to tune in to what they were saying. The activity taking place before my eyes was utter chaos. Everyone was speaking at the same time, no one listening but continuing to shout loudly at one another expressing different opinions. I stood there trying to make sense of what was happening, but it was as if I were in a catatonic state, unable to grasp the meaning of anything that was being said or done. Everyone had so many questions they wanted my husband or me to answer, but neither of us knew what to tell them as they all scurried around frantically. When I was finally able to comprehend some of the deranged chatter, I heard someone scream, "Do you know where Justin is?" They had heard of an accident and that maybe Justin was involved. Not knowing what or how to respond to their question, thinking to myself "if" his friends who had all been with him earlier that night didn't know where he was, how was I supposed to know? I assumed he was at home. The last conversation I had with my son was earlier that night when he said how tired he was and how he'd had a horrible headache earlier that day. I suggested he go home early and get some rest, and he responded, "Good idea, Mom. I'll see you at the church in the morning." It never entered my mind that anything could possibly be wrong. After all,

I'd just experienced one of the most intense prayer sessions for my son a few minutes before. I pondered their questions in my heart, wishing I knew the answers, hoping with every ounce of my being that my son was safe no matter where his location. One by one the people gathered closer to my husband and me and began to share vague details of what they knew or had heard.

My daughter-in-law's sister began to speak first, saying that Courtney had called screaming uncontrollably. She said that all she could discern from her crying was that something horrible had happened and that Justin had been terribly hurt. As far as I knew, they had been together on Justin's motorcycle because he had picked her up from work; so, if there had been an accident, it would have been while they were riding home together. It made perfect sense to me that if Courtney was okay, then so was our son.

Barry held me tightly and promised he would have to go find out what was going on and for me to start calling the local hospitals and the police department to see if an accident had been reported. To this day, I don't know how I was able to find the numbers and make the calls, but somehow, with God's help, I did as he had asked me to do. With each number I called, no one could give me any information, which, in my mind, gave me peace because people always say, "No news is good news."

After making the calls, I went upstairs to see that my middle son, Jacob, wasn't disturbed by the confusion going on in the house. I tip-toed to his door and peeked into his bedroom, he remained quiet, so I assumed he was asleep. I passed by my youngest son Caleb's room and quickly remembered he was away from home, he'd called earlier and asked since he was already there could he stayed the night at my sister's house.

Completely confused, not knowing *what* to do next, I ran down the hill to my parents' house. I beat as hard as I could on their front door, screaming and crying, completely devastated. My dad answered the door within seconds, which was totally out of character for him because he'd always been such a sound sleeper. Weak from emotional exhaustion, my legs buckled, and Dad reached out his arms to catch me from falling. Completely baffled by my abnormal behavior, in hopes of consoling me he assured me things would be okay. He knew that something was drastically wrong; as to what it was, he had no clue.

My mother entered the room and tried to make sense of what was going on, but all she could understand was that it involved Justin. I calmed down long enough to try to explain what I knew while not fully knowing myself. My dad is the chaplain at the justice center and had some contacts he could call to find out any details they might be willing to share with him. While he was on the phone, I watched out the door for my husband to return. When he finally did, I ran to meet him before he continued up the driveway to our house. He quickly stopped the car and got out to grab me. He told me things were bad, really bad. I felt my heart fall into the pit of my stomach; I felt all the blood drain out of my body as though I might faint. I knew I had to pull myself together somehow. Barry pleaded with me to stay calm, pray, not to give up, hold on to God, and everything would be alright. My husband's faith has constantly been much stronger than mine, and he has always prayed and trusted God through every trial. This time could not be any different. If we ever needed to pull together and rely on God, it was now. I've learned so much through Barry's actions and his reliance on God's Word and knew that he trusted God's steadfastness that things would work out for our good. Unfortunately, the sinking feeling I had strangled what faith *I* once possessed. Fighting back all emotions, hand in hand we agreed that everything would be okay. I trusted that believing together our faith and prayers were stronger. *"Again, I say to you, that if two of you shall agree on earth as touching anything that they shall ask, it shall be done for them of my Father which is in Heaven." (Matthew 18:19 KJV)*

Barry gave me very few details about what was going on. There was, indeed, an accident and our son *had* been involved. He did tell me Justin was in a car and not on his motorcycle and he wasn't the one driving. He said to trust God and pray, and that's precisely what I did. It was all I *knew* to do. After Barry was convinced that I was holding up as well as could be expected, he went back to the scene of the accident to get more information. I walked back up the driveway to be with Jacob I asked him to please forgive me for leaving him alone for the time it took me to run to my parents' house. It was as if my mind couldn't function to do what was necessary; both my heart and mind were running a hundred miles a minuet. What I should have done was ask Jacob to come with me, but all I could do was listen to my emotions which told me to run. It made sense at the time but now, remembering back, I feel awful for running off that night and leaving Jacob alone without his dad or me around to help him understand even though we really had no way of explaining.

Jacob was responding in much of the same way I had. He was in a state of disbelief at what was being related to him. Being very confused, he said, "I was just texting with Justin a few minutes earlier," and in his way of reasoning, he knew his brother had to be alright. He said, "Just give me a minute, and he'll text me right back. You'll see; he's fine, Mom. Don't worry; everything will be okay. I know so!" He grabbed his phone and quickly began texting Justin as he waited and watched for a response. Those feelings of hope soon turned to unbearable pain, sadness, and grief when he realized that what everyone was saying about Justin being gone was becoming an absolute reality. Jacob's hope that these events were only a bad dream he couldn't awaken from had now become a horrible nightmare that got worse as time passed. He began to feel a heavy load of guilt and regret, certain that if *he* had been with Justin, his big brother would have been okay, and this terrible night would never have come to be. Jacob was blaming himself, thinking that he could have somehow stopped the accident if he had just been there. He kept saying that *if* I had let him stay with Justin that night, *this* would not have happened. I tried to reason with him by saying that he always tailgated his older brother to the point that if Justin ever turned around, he'd run all over Jacob because he followed so tightly behind him. My boys were always so close that their age differences never seemed to hinder their relationships at all. I used to say that Justin bridged the gap with each of his brothers. He could get along with Jacob so easily because they both loved the same things and Jacob wanted to be just like him. Even though there were seven years between Justin and my youngest, Caleb, it never even mattered to Justin. He could always be as old or as young as he needed to be to relate to each of them individually.

When Jacob finally got past the point of blaming himself for the accident, I tried to console him that saying both of them might have been involved in the wreck had they stayed together that night. I reminded him that he'd never been able to persuade Justin *not* to do anything. Justin was always so determined; when he set his thoughts to do something, he was going do it, and nothing or no one could change his mind. In fact, there were times when he would somehow persuade his dad and me that a certain something was, indeed, a good idea even after we begged him to reconsider, feeling as if in fact it was *not* a clever idea. With his strong-willed nature, we had won some battles and lost a few. I loved his determination, which was both a blessing and a curse for his mom and dad. I won't dishonor his memory by calling him a bit stubborn, but I will say he was definitely a determined young man. Justin had so many enduring qualities, but this will always be *one* of my favorites.

With Jacob's focus redirected, I was able to coax him to do what his dad had just asked me to do, which was to pray. After all, the *only* hope we had was to believe God for a divine miracle. In that very moment, we had to persevere under the tremendous amount of pressure we were facing. I told him we should keep our eyes on God to cancel out all fear and doubt. I knew if we were relying on what was going on around us, what little faith we had to pray and believe would quickly dissipate.

Jacob and I left the crowd of people and went into my bedroom to pray. Anyone who dared to enter and didn't have the faith to be-lieve Justin would be ok wasn't allowed to stay in the same room with us. Many tried to come in and commanded we accept that it was time to give up, quit, and let go, we refused!! I remember saying out loud over and over, "I WON'T LET GO, I WON'T LET GO, and I WON'T LET GO!!!" I just kept repeating myself. I know people were tired of hearing those four small words, but I could *not* stop saying them. Even when I *tried*, I couldn't. I believed that if I would keep confessing it, Justin wouldn't ever leave. *"Call those things which are not as though they were." (Romans 4:17 KJV)*

Chapter Seven
Not My Will

As the minutes of that ill-fated night turned into hours, more and more people assembled at the house. My husband returned to help us pray God's will be done and said that no matter how dreadful things seemed, we knew God was still in control. We moved our prayer group outside to the car-filled front yard, and I asked for people to gather around and help me pray for my son. They all seemed cooperative, and whether or not they believed in the power of agreement through prayer, didn't hesitate to comply with my request. As I looked at each face in the crowd, I saw many I knew who had been sheltered from certain death at various times in their lives. There was a girl in her twenties who had been born with a hole in her heart and wasn't expected to live very long but had gone on to live a full life. Another person had been involved in a severe motorcycle wreck that nearly cost him his life. With intense injuries to his legs, he *could* have lacked the ability to walk, but somehow God spared him this traumatic disability. Another lived through a devastating crash where the car was an unrecognizable crumpled mass of metal. I pleaded especially with each of them to help me pray and believe. Because God had saved *their* lives, surely, He would protect *my* son. They looked at me with empty eyes, unable to speak. Everyone was confused because they had assumed they knew how I was supposed to behave and my actions didn't line up with what they would've done. I had no idea what they were thinking, and it didn't matter; I needed their help to agree with me in prayer. Whatever their thoughts were, I had to follow what I felt was God's leading. I couldn't miss the chance to do whatever possible if it might help my son. As I began to pray and plead for God to let him live, they all stood in silence.

After some time had passed, I moved beyond the crowd of family and friends and found myself alone. Looking up into the dark sky lit with a multitude of stars, I cried out for God to spare my son:

"*Please*, Lord, let him live and not die." Just as this prayer left my heart, I immediately knew the impact of my request. I was overwhelmed with the magnitude of the concept of asking Him to save my son. If it meant that he would be left to suffer an impairment which would in any way rob him of the ability to be whole and live life to the fullest, then I could not pray for God to spare his life. The possibility of having to live with limitations and a lifetime of pain wasn't fair to him, so I knew I had to gain a new perspective. If God's plan for Justin was to take him to a place with no pain and no boundaries, I knew I couldn't ask, "*my* will be done." I had to pray, "GOD, *YOUR* WILL BE DONE!!" I knew deep in my soul that I had to allow God complete control of this situation; no matter how my heart was breaking, I knew I had to put my wants and needs aside and ask God to intervene in my son's life to do as He desired. You must know that was not in any way an instant decision but came only after some hard-learned lessons. You see, God had been preparing me for this journey since the minute He made me a mom. Just like many parents, I had a natural fear of losing my child as stated earlier. That gnawing, ever-present dread was manifested as soon as I felt that first flutter of movement in my belly. I will never forget that inexplicable joy when I heard my baby's heart beating in perfect rhythm with mine. I knew from then on, that my life would never be the same and couldn't ever be complete without my little Fowl(s). My fervent prayer remained, "God, please don't ever take my children from me."

June 30, 2009 Barry and I celebrated our twentieth wedding anniversary. We had just finished dinner and were down by the river watching the sunset when my phone rang. I picked it up, and all that I could hear were screams of pain and terror. The person on the other end of the line was a friend of my son who informed me Justin's motorcycle was in pieces all over the road right by where we used to live. I immediately dropped the phone and fell to my knees sobbing. Barry picked it up and tried to make sense of the unfolding situation. We began trying to call Justin's best friend,

Robie, because we knew the boys were meeting that day to play ball at the ballpark where they grew up.

I feared the worst, only to have fear became a reality when Robie's little brother, Ross, answered Robie's phone and said there'd been an accident. He tried to explain the details as best he could but quickly said he had to help his mom because she was so upset. We told him to get to Justin and let him know we were on our way. Ross then replied that Justin was completely devastated, he didn't have any idea where he was. I immediately asked, "Was he not on the motorcycle when it wrecked?" It was then Ross realized we didn't understand that it was not *Justin* who was involved in the fatal motorcycle wreck, but Robie who had taken my son's bike down the road for a ride and never returned. When their friends heard the crash, they all went running in fear of what they would find. I couldn't even begin to imagine the thoughts that ran through every young person's mind who witnessed that awful accident firsthand. I continue to pray for each of them for comfort, healing, and peace.

Overwhelmed with so many emotions, we jumped into our car, hurried to be with our friends to try and console them, and find our son to help him any way we could. There's no formal training to help you know what to do or say in a situation that is so beyond your control. Most cannot even begin to grasp the vastness of emotions during a time such as this.

I will never be able to forget those sounds of horror mixed with grief, anger, and confusion; they will continue to be heard deep in my heart when my mind wanders back to that tragic night. The ravaged look on our son's face when we finally got to him was indescribable. His beautiful, shiny blue eyes were puffy, red, and swollen from the tears that wouldn't stop pouring down his face. Just as I would run to my parents wanting them to make a horrible tragedy disappear two short years later, Justin ran to his daddy and me, hopeful we'd be able to make all his devastation go away. The only thing we could do was hold him, cry with him, and pray for him.

How I wish I could have spared him this excruciating pain by telling him it was just a frightful nightmare.

We loaded ourselves into the car and drove to the hospital emergency room where everyone but me got out of the car. I could *not* make myself move from the seat. I remember praying, "Please, God, don't let Robie die. PLEASE, PLEASE, PLEASE." As I sat in the car begging God to spare Robie's life, there was a knock on my car window and someone, whose face I didn't recognize, shouted that Robie was gone. At that very minute, so many doubts flooded my mind that I questioned my faith in God and had misgivings as to whether or not He had really heard my prayers. I even doubted for a brief moment God's existence. Thankfully, those thoughts held my mind captive only a short while. Had they lasted any longer, I would never have been able to survive my journey of grief, sadness, and heartbreak two years and seventeen days later.

I continue to give God praise for the incredible peace that settled on me the very next day. While outside praying for strength and wisdom to be able to minister to my friends in the coming days, God allowed me to see an image of Robie as I looked up into the sky across the tree line. I saw him dressed in white, smiling that winning smile brighter than usual, and there was a golden hue all around him. It reminded me of the time I saw Robie soon after he received his salvation. He was excited to share with me that he was going to be baptized. That image of him was so real I can still remember it to this day. I honestly believe it was confirmation that he was in Heaven. I'm so blessed God chose to give me that vision. Over the years it has truly helped me know God has a plan; and every once in a while, if we are searching for a sign and patiently wait on Him, we'll catch a glance of Heaven's glorious sights, and all our doubts will be erased from memory.

His plan may not be what *we* had expected, but if we trust Him, He'll see us through even the darkest nights. If we *let* God, He will take the difficult times, grief, and heartbreak we've gone through and shape us into the people He's called us to be for His glory. When

I was finally able to learn that I am who I am because of what I've gone through, it was very empowering. I've been made stronger and braver than I could have ever been had I not survived some of the greatest hardships of my life. Never being faced with significant obstacles would have left me with the inability to know the joy of being an overcomer. *"And they overcame him by the blood of the Lamb and by the word of their testimony, and they loved not their lives unto the death." (Revelation 12:11 KJV)*

I share this part of my story to encourage you to see that life is like a puzzle with some of the pieces missing. We can't see the full picture yet because God hasn't shown us all the parts that will complete it; but when He does, it will all make perfect sense. I have no doubt that if God gave us the ability to see our entire lives at a glance from beginning to end, with all the hills and valleys we'd go through, most of us would give up before the journey began. I hope that *if* possible, my victories, joys, and celebrations far outnumber my tragedies!

In retrospect, I realize that going through the experience of losing Robie in some ways prepared me to withstand part of the difficulties I've dealt with since the loss of my son. It seems I stopped only a moment to catch my breath and rest for a brief second. Then two short years later, as I looked up at the star-filled night sky, fearing the worst for my son but praying for the best, I was able to say with all sincerity, "Not my will but Your will be done, my God."

After taking a while to come to terms with what was happening in my own family, I gathered my thoughts and began to do my best to console others who were losing faith that Justin was going to be alright. Barry had just returned from the accident scene and insisted that we keep praying and believing for our miracle. He had great faith believing that no matter how terrible things looked, God in one instant could restore our son and bring him back to us. All my hope dissipated like a moth succumbing to the flame, when I heard a knock at our front door. As I opened it carefully, trembling and afraid I looked up to see our longtime friend who worked for the police department. With him were my mom, dad, sister, and our youngest son, Caleb. He confirmed to me what another policeman at the accident minutes before had already told Barry. Indeed, our oldest son, Justin, was gone.

There is no conceivable way for me to describe the stabbing pain we all felt at that moment. My heart went back immediately to earlier that night when I was so overwhelmed with the need to pray for Justin. In my spirit, I had known something was wrong, but all I could do was pray, pleading with God to watch over him and give him peace and protection. As I think back, I wonder if at that very moment if I felt like things had gone so wrong, why didn't I try to call his cell phone? I appease myself by believing that he would've thought I was overprotective. I can hear him saying many times that he was twenty years old and lived on his own, so he didn't need to be monitored; he'd have insisted that I stop worrying about him because he was a grown man. It's hard not to have those "what if's" -- the "would haves," "could haves," and "should haves" from time to time. I try not to linger on them because the truth is, it won't change a thing and won't bring him back. In fact, revisiting the past for any length of time only shuts down the healing process. We must consistently go forward so as not to hinder our progress. Trying to move ahead while continuing to look behind can only cause us trip and fall on our faces or land flat on our backs. During these times of fear and doubt, we need never revisit the past very often, but bend our knees in prayer to the only One Who can mend our broken hearts and settle our tormented, bewildered minds. If we must look back, let it be only to the good times that bring us joy for what we once had, and not focus on the turmoil and agony of what used to be or on the things that seems insurmountable, impossible to overcome.

What brings me the most comfort in all this torment is the confirmation of the bond my son and I share far beyond the grave. On the night he was destined to leave this earth, how could I have not known the exact moment he departed? I believe with everything in my whole heart that my overwhelming compulsion to pray so intensely for him was the exact moment he left this world and arrived safely in the arms of God. Justin was facing impending danger, and through his mother's prayer, he was spared the pain of hitting that tree and was already gone in spirit moments before impact.

After some time had passed, I was able to speak with our officer friend, who was first to arrive on the accident scene. He told me my son's accident was one of many he had responded to during the lifetime of his career with law enforcement, and assured me that by the severity of the wreck he saw as he approached, he expected the worst of injuries. Instead, he said he'd never seen a body in such peace as my son's, virtually unharmed from the crash. He commented that, "It was as if he had laid his head over and placed his hands under his cheek and went to sleep." He told me he'd seen other accidents with less damage yield far more injuries than those Justin had sustained. Having this information assured me that God did, in fact, protect my son as I had prayed for safety and continued life, although it didn't happen on earth but in his heavenly home. His address forever changed, and he no longer lives in a house we can physically visit, but in one our eyes cannot see on this side of life. Some of you may argue that my prayer that night was of no value since the outcome was his death. To that way of thinking I will always respond, "Can you imagine the possible turn of events had I not exchanged the prayer for my *want* to God's *will*?" I'll always trust that prayer *does* work and will change the results of situations even though we may have a far different picture of the outcome. After all, is there any place safer for him than worshipping with the saints around the throne where the King of Kings and Lord of Lords abides?

A mother's heart is to keep her child safe from harm, and she will always have the reflex to protect her own even when they are well able to take care of themselves, because no matter how old they are, they'll remain children in her eyes. When my boys try to convince me there's no need for my constant protection, I let them know immediately that, "It's what moms do." Justin always seemed so reckless with cars and motorcycles, being a daredevil at times, and constantly kept me on edge, always afraid something was going to happen to him. Thankfully, however, he was not the cause of the accident that took his life. The young man who had been driving the car was also killed. My prayer for his family is they would share the solace that I have in knowing God. After some time passed, I'm able to appreciate the fact, my son had a lot of fun doing what he loved. The times I told him, "No," he'd make his own choice to go ahead and do most of those things anyway, hoping I wouldn't find out. All the while I was praying for him to use common sense as God instructs us in His Word: *"Lord make me to know mine end, and the measure of my days, what it is; that I may know how frail I am." (Psalm 39:4 KJV)* With his having only a brief time on this earth, I'm grateful he did go ahead and experience life to the fullest. He lived his short life fast and hard, confessing many times over, "God knows my number of *my* days on this earth." He loved having fun and enjoyed every minute. I can still hear him say about his friend who died earlier, "Robie wouldn't want *me* not to have fun just because he's not here to have it with me." Feeling God knows best, I have to believe that Justin was here with us as long as He intended him to be. *"Since his days are determined, and the number of his months is with you, and you have appointed his limits that he cannot pass, look away from him and leave him alone, that he may enjoy, like a hired hand, his day." (Job 5:5-6 ESV)*

Chapter Eight
A Shattered Heart

A few days after the accident, in hopes of consoling me, my husband said, "Honey, I know your heart is broken." I immediately replied, "My heart is not broken; it's completely shattered!!" After all, we had just lost our son, and I was in shock that my damaged, destroyed heart could continue to beat. At that time, I had no hope that it would ever be revived. My faith was at its lowest point thus far in my Christian walk, and I just didn't know how to believe anymore. When you expend all your hope and faith believing what you ask for will be granted and quickly it dissolves before your eyes, not turning out at all the way you expected, it's extremely hard to believe in anything or anyone again. I knew I would have to find renewed hope in Jesus but had no idea when or how long it was going to take.

Previously, I had always had faith in God to defeat every sickness and disease, and many times I had experienced healing in my own body and had been witness to numerous others throughout my life. Whenever there was a much-needed restoration with our sons, we always prayed hard and leaned on God harder to bring a healing touch. My mind wanders back sometimes to a day when our family was at the lake skiing, and our son Justin took a bad tumble. When we got him out of the water, he was screaming in pain over his leg. Apparently, when he fell it had gotten twisted and pulled in the wrong direction; I was concerned it might be broken. We were a long way from a doctor's office or hospital, so the only thing we knew to do was pray. Isn't it strange how we consider prayer as a last resort. When in fact it should be the first and most important thing we always do.

My husband and I, along with our other two sons, gathered around Justin and began to pray for God to touch him. When we finished praying and started gathering our stuff to head back to the dock, Justin said, "Where are ya'll going? I'm fine; let's stay a while longer." The pain he was in had completely subsided! We were then able to enjoy the rest of the evening on the water. The next day Justin came over to the house and I asked, "How's your leg, Son?" He replied, "Good as new!" How thankful I am to be in a family that not only reads God's Word but believes every part of it. Truly, I know that there is healing in Jesus no matter what we may face on this earth. He is more than able to deliver us from any situation whether it be physical, mental, spiritual, or financial.

After the loss of our son, I had to get back to the realization that with God I was going to be able to make it, shattered heart or no heart at all, and that everything would work out for good if I allowed Him to rule and reign in my life. God cannot fix what we do not surrender to Him. When we give Him our brokenness, we have to wait patiently and realize it takes time to make the necessary repairs. The healing of my devastated heart wasn't as instant as when God touched Justin's leg that day. It was only after an abundant amount of time had passed that I was finally able to seek after God to replace my brokenness with His fullness.

I prayed for Him to give me the ability to have real joy again, as well as peace and hope, the kind that existed as if I'd never been subjected to heartache. I knew I must still be alive because I was still breathing and my heart was beating, but I wanted to know I could sincerely enjoy living again. All I felt was death *in* me and all around me. I knew the hand of God must somehow still be on me even though I didn't feel Him close by in those times I was in the pits of despair and grief. I must admit that during the deepest waves of anguish I didn't care if I lived or died. I just wanted the pain to stop and didn't want to go on living if there was never any hope of experiencing joy ever again. *"There hath no temptation taken you but such as is common to man: but God is faithful, Who will not suffer you to be tempted above that ye are able: but will with temptation also make a way to escape, that ye may be able to bear it." (1 Corinthians 10:13 KJV).* I held tight to this promise from God. I trusted that He would not cause me to go through something so terrible that His grace could not carry me past darkness and despair back to a place of happiness and joy. I knew that although I was perhaps in the fight of my life, God was with me. Just as He protected the Hebrew children who went through the fire unharmed, He would do the same for me. His love is unconditional, and mercy is unbiased.

As I grew more and more dependent on my faith in God to take me through what seemed like an impossible task to manage, He began to show and teach me things through His Word that encouraged my faith and, yes, began to restore my shattered heart. Like most things of precious value, that time spent in His Scriptures became priceless. God in His unmatched greatness could speak comfort to my weary soul as I depended on the Bible and let the pages fall open as He led me to a fresh morsel of encouragement every day. Once while studying the Scriptures, I read of God calling dry, lifeless bones to come to life, and indeed, He breathed life back into what was once dead. *"Thus saith the Lord God unto these bones; Behold, I will cause breath to enter into you, and ye shall live." (Ezekiel 37:5 KJV)* I knew *if* God caused the dead to live again in times of old, He most assuredly could do the same now. It was only after applying God's instruction to my own life that I was finally able to *believe* He would heal my shattered, crushed, broken heart and make me whole again. Knowing the truth of God's Word and adopting it for your life are two different subjects. We must *apply* the truth in order to have the power of His promises in our lives. *Hosea 4:6 ESV* tells us that, *"My people are destroyed for lack of knowledge."* If we don't read the God's instructions and believe that it is real in our lives, then how will it ever be activated in our circumstances? We can't just *listen* to the truth of God's Word; we have to *know* and do it. *"He who has ears to hear, let him hear!" (Matthew 11:15 NKJV)* When God speaks to our hearts through His Word, and we vaguely listen, never *hearing* or heeding, how does that do us any good? To give you a visual of what I mean, suppose you have a fear of water, concerned you might drown. If you are out on a boat and someone hands you a life jacket, it won't help you in any way unless you put it on. We need swimming lessons before we get our feet wet. You would never jump into deep waters without first knowing how to swim, which is an example of how God's Word works in our own lives. We need to be prepared for all things, such as knowing how to fight before we ever get into a battle. We can't wait until we're in trouble to figure out what to do. Even though I trusted that God would bring me back to life again, it took some time before I was able to begin to *apply* this knowledge to my life. *"And ye shall know the truth, and the truth shall make you free." (John 8:32 KJV)* Once I realized that God desired to set me free of all pain and agony, that I didn't have to live in fear and the torment of never being able to recover, I began to apply His Scriptures to my life and guess what? His Word works! We can do what He says we can do and *all* His promises are available to you are true!

I remember well the day I *felt* that my heart began to beat again. When you go from feeling dead inside, feeling absolutely nothing, numb, and empty and then out of nowhere you can physically feel movement deep inside, it's unforgettable! When you've felt bad so long, you often forget what it feels like to feel good. When God breathed life back into my grief-stricken soul, it was a breathtaking experience that I've never had the occasion to encounter except for the births of my three irresistible sons. Feeling my heartbeat for the first time after it was crushed, was the most overwhelming excitement to which nothing could compare. When God brought restoration and healing, He didn't *repair* my shattered heart; He created in me a brand *new* one. It wasn't merely pieced back together like a china cup that had been broken, and the owner tried to glue it back the best way he knew. That's just not how God does things. *"I will give you a new heart and put a new spirit in you; I will remove from you your heart of stone and give you a heart of flesh." (Ezekiel 36:26 NIV)* That cup fixed and repaired by the owner would never be the same again and probably couldn't ever be used for the very thing it had been created, but in the hands of the Creator, my heart would indeed actually *live*! It would once again be able to beat with the expectancy of greater things to come. Exactly like my salvation when God took the old me and made a new creation, I was made stronger than before, and my heart would never be the same. When we give God all that is broken, crushed, and destroyed, He can create in us a newness and strength which can be used for His glory. *"Therefore, if any man be in Christ he is a new creature. Old things are passed away and behold all things become new." (2 Corinthians 5:17 KJV)*

Chapter Nine
Not Looking Back

I know beyond all doubt God unequivocally answers every prayer. Sometimes He reacts the way we expect and sometimes in a way we never imagine. There may have been times you've felt as though your prayers went unanswered when in all certainty God has answered them all. I have been told that He often has *three* responses to our prayers. There are instances He says, "Yes," or He may say, "No." Then sometimes He says, "Not right now." We have to find it in our hearts to rely on the fact He has the best viable solutions to meet all our needs. There's a Scripture I often read in *Matthew 6:25-26 KJV: "Therefore I say unto you, take no thought for your life, what ye shall eat, or what ye shall drink: nor yet for the body, what ye shall put on. Is not the life more than meat, and the body than raiment? Behold the fowls of the air; for they sow not neither do they reap nor gather into barns; yet your heavenly Father feedeth them. Are ye not much better than they?"* Those words should give us great assurance that if God provides for the birds of the air, He will definitely give His sons and daughters what *they* need. I especially like the part about the *fowls,* as that is what my sons are all called by their friends. Take note, Fowls/ Fowler boys...God promises in bold, red letters in His Word that when we belong to God, He will always provide what you need!

It is so imperative to make prayer a priority in our lives. We need to learn to be sensitive to God's leading through His Holy Spirit in us so that we never miss an opportunity to speak with our heavenly Father. Just as God prompted me to lift up my sons to Him many times, the final prayer for Justin being the very most significant, we have to be obedient at every moment, people in need are depending on us! I often feel an enduring ache to pray for others, and I hope the ones I intercede for receive the peace and comfort prayer can bring. Knowing its advantageous importance and power, I never want to resist God's precise prompting. We may not ever know this side of Heaven how vital our prayers were to our family members or to others that may have benefited from our obedience to respond to God's leading us to do so. I will forever be grateful for every prayer that was lifted up to God on my behalf, for without faithful people supporting me, I'm afraid to venture even a thought as to where I would be today. Prayer can move mountains and calm the raging seas of our lives if *only* we would believe, just as praying for my son his last days on earth gave me peace that I didn't even know until later I would need. I'm resting in the assurance that because of those prayers and the urgency I felt deep down in my soul, I can now relax with complete confidence that my son is waiting for me beyond the skies in a place called Heaven. I will continue to pray for my peace to grow and multiply knowing that the passing of each twenty-four-hour period means I am one day closer to seeing my son again. *"If we then be risen with Christ, seek those things which are above, where Christ sitteth on the right hand of God. Set your affection on things above, not on things on the earth." (Colossians 3:1-2 KJV)*

I rarely meet anyone who hasn't faced an unbearable amount of grief or pain. There are times I feel a common bond with people who have suffered an inexplicable loss such as what I have. It may just be that someone comes up to me in a store and says, "I think I know you. You look very familiar to me." After a few moments of trying to figure out the relationship, we come to the conclusion that this person, too, has suffered the unexpected loss of a child. I can't explain how we're drawn to one another; it resembles a gravitational pull as if we have grief radar embedded inside our hearts; or perhaps I've now gained a new perspective that comes from a shattered heart, one which has been renewed to feel others' grief and pain. Before our lives were interrupted by tragedy, my compassion level was minuscule at best. I often prayed for others with what I thought was genuine concern, but I know now it was merely gratitude for the fact *I* had escaped the situations that were happening in *their* lives. Through this devastating loss, I know I've gained insight that I don't think I would've ever experienced had I not gone through it myself. I believe God allows us to experience certain things that cause us to feel sincere compassion for others, so we can effectively minister hope and help to those in need. He promises us that He *"comforts and encourages us in every trouble so that we will be able to comfort and encourage those who are in any kind of trouble, with the comfort which we ourselves are comforted by God."* (2 *Corinthians 1:4 AMP)* I feel that is one of the many reasons Jesus came down from Heaven and walked on this earth as a man. He could feel the things we feel and experience the same obstacles we face. *"For we do not have a high priest Who is unable to sympathize and understand our weaknesses and temptations, but One Who has been tempted {knowing exactly how it feels to be human} in every respect as we are yet without {committing any} sin."* (He-*brews 4:15 AMP)*

There are times I'm greatly comforted by being around someone who shares similar sadness because I know that they're the only ones who can fully understand what I'm going through. It brings a moment of solace knowing they may be able to provide support or advice to help me along my path. It also gives me a sense of strength when I can help in *their* bereavement. Then there are those dreaded times it just hurts too much to open the door to the pain, as it forces me to relive the anguish that I've packed away, down deep, as if I could ever take complete control of it either way. I've learned that grief shares a close resemblance to an ocean. It's as far as you can see and as bottomless as the sea. The waves are constant and unending. Often the surges are forceful and violent and other times indirect and shifting. There are times the swells of grief are over my head and other times they are up to my knees only. Whether the tide is overpowering me to the point I fear I may surely drown, or just splashing around my ankles, it doesn't lessen my desire to pray for the strength to overcome and walk in complete victory no matter what obstructions may be preventing me from moving ahead. With time being a rare and priceless asset, trying to control something that can never be manipulated is the most time-consuming, exhausting thing I can think of to spend precious minutes on!

As stated in previous chapters, prayer has always been so very essential to our family. I remember our family attending church together a few weeks before the accident, Justin sat beside me as we listened intently to a young man giving his testimony of going down a long road of drugs and alcohol. He shared how God changed his life when he asked Him to come into his heart. At the end of the service, he asked us all to stand as he gave an altar call. I noticed Justin bowed his head to his chest in what seemed to be overwhelming despair. I immediately felt the Holy Spirit prompting me to put my hands on him and pray. I had no idea what to say; it was as if I could *feel* his heaviness and I knew I wanted to intercede for him, asking God to lift his heavy burdens. I trusted the Lord to give me specific insight and wisdom to bring my son peace and comfort. I laid my hands gently on his back and began to pray under my breath silently, as I didn't want to interrupt his own prayer to God.

I have no recollection of the exact words I prayed that day. I wish now more than ever I could remember. I often have times when doubt enters my mind as to whether or not *my* prayer was instrumental in providing the necessary help for my son at the time. My husband assures me it was the perfect prayer required at that precise moment because God speaks *through* us when we allow Him to use us. Whatever the words were, they seemed to bring Justin a sense of calmness and relief. Later, at lunch that Sunday, as all three of my boys sat across the table from me, I asked each of them the following question: "If God called you home today, do you know that you will go to Heaven?" They all smiled and nodded yes, and Justin said, "You KNOW, Mom!" I'm grateful he never hesitated to assure me of where he would spend eternity. It may seem strange to have had a conversation of this nature, but when we faced the death of Justin's best friend, Robie, just a brief time before, it was something we were all forced to recognize: if it happened to Robie, it very well could happen again, anytime, anyplace to anyone. We never once since that tragic night thought accidents always happen to someone else but couldn't ever happen to our family. In fact, no one is exempt from tragedy; it lurks around like a revolting scavenger trolling for its next victim. I must admit now what I didn't even consider then: I was experiencing a fear the enemy was trying to create that now I had to worry about losing one of *my* sons. To combat this anxiety, I would randomly ask them to reassure me of their salvation so that I could have a renewed sense of peace that *if* I were to lose one of them, I would *know* that I'd see them again in Heaven. On days when fear seemed to consume me and suffocate any joy I had come to find I had to take measures to overcome my worst nightmares. On those days, I would run to God, climb up in His lap, and allow His Holy Spirit to speak peace to my worried, wayward mind and aching heart. On my journey with Jesus, I've learned that I can choose to walk by faith or I can crawl around in fear, but I cannot do both. That was a valuable lesson, I was made fully aware of when unexpectedly my worst fears did, in fact, become a reality. *"For the thing which I greatly feared is come upon me, and that which I was afraid of is come unto me." (Job 3:25 KJV)*

I trust that He'll never leave us or forsake us. Jesus promises us in *Matthew 28:20 KJV: "I am with you always, even unto the end of the world."* God will walk every step of the way with us and, in the end, all the glory will be His for without Him, in *my* hopeless desperation, it would have been impossible to make it even one day. He is what causes us to have the ability to endure. The quicker we all come to that realization the sooner we'll be able to carry the load we've been given in this life. With Him, we can make it through to the other side. We have to follow Him, listen for His voice, and do as He says, and we'll be able to live a victorious through Christ. *"Now to Him Who is able to {carry out His purpose and} do supernaturally more than all that we dare ask or think {infinitely beyond our greatest prayers, hopes, or dreams}, according to His power that is at work within us." (Ephesians 3:20 AMP)* What a blessing it is to know we have a generous, compassionate, loving heavenly Father, Who will go above and beyond to meet every one of our needs.

People often say, "God will not put more on you than you can stand." I've also heard that God will not call you to do something you cannot do. For many years I encouraged myself in those two statements when I felt I couldn't hold on one more moment. To this day I've never found either statement in God's Word. What His Scriptures *do* say is that is we are to *"Cast thy burden upon the Lord, and He shall sustain thee: He shall never suffer the righteous to be moved." (Psalm 55:22 KJV)* I also learned the hard way that God will allow us to go through things that are unconceivable for us to effectively manage on our own. After all, if we never had a struggle, how would we ever know that we truly need Him as an active part of our lives? If our own strength or ability were never tested, would we ever know God's omnipotent, limitless power? I do also believe God will call us to do some incredible tasks, but it's only to show us that without Him we are helpless but with God we can do anything. What we must realize is that when God calls you to do something, He will *"equip you with everything good that you may do His will, working in us that which is pleasing in His sight, through Jesus Christ, to Whom be glory forever and ever. Amen." (Hebrews 13:21 ESV)* That valuable lesson is one I've learned largely through the process of teaching it to my sons. I remember many times, especially with Justin, I would always encourage him that he could do even the difficult things with God's help and that anything and everything are possible. There were many mornings before school when stress and sickness would just consume him, and we would pray and trust God to be his strength. When we are powerless, God is at His greatest because we are no longer able to resist and He can work freely in our lives. I believe God's power is mighty and can be weakened only by our inability to believe He can and will move on our behalf. In time, Justin would learn that there was absolutely nothing impossible with God on his side. It's a lesson that I had to re-teach myself when dealing with his death; when my faith had been tested beyond my natural ability to believe. You see, we have the capacity to trust in and rely on God when things are going smoothly, but do you still believe when you are being tested by fire? I'm blessed by God that when my confidence in Him was suppressed to the limit it remained steadfast and unyielding. What a great peace and joy I have in the times when I fully trust in His strength and not my own to carry me through my life from the first day until the last. *"Even to your old age I am He, And even to your advanced old age I will carry you! I have made you and I will carry you; Be assured I will carry you and I will save you." (Isaiah 46:4 AMP)* God promised *three* times in that one scripture that He will carry you and me!

It surely makes for a more pleasant journey, when I wholeheart-edly believe that God means for us to enjoy our lives while on this earth. If we spend all our days miserable, we'll have missed some of the greatest opportunities to minister to the lost. After all, we as Christians are supposed to carry the light of Jesus, and to be His hands and feet while on the earth. When we go through this life-weary, broken, defeated, mad, ill and hateful why would others look at us and believe that God is all He promises to be and invite Him into their lives? If the world formed their opinion of the true character of Jesus strictly by watching us, would they want to be a follower of Christ based on our example of Him? Before my dad received his salvation, he believed he was *better* than the people he met in church. Perhaps those people were representing a Christian life in name only and not by their actions.

Justin always had a saying about cars: "Don't leave weak." It means that when you exit from one place to another, you need to give it all you've got, holding nothing back. I've now learned to apply *that* term to everything in my life whether it concerns the physical or the spiritual. I believe God also has a "Don't leave weak" message for each of us in the Scriptures. *"Whatever you do, work at it with all your heart, working for the Lord, not for human matters." (Co-lossians 3:23 NIV)*

Unable to sleep one night, I began to walk around in our backyard, a new habit that had formed when I couldn't find rest for my weary mind. By the light of the moon, I stared up into the star filled sky, sometimes for hours hoping to find answers to my numerous questions. On this particular evening, I didn't realize where my restless wandering had led me until I looked down and saw something prevented my feet from continuing. Before I bent down to see what it was, I noticed I was midway down my driveway, the same route I had taken weeks earlier when I went for help from my parents the night of the accident, which I hadn't been able to walk since that fateful evening. The object hindering my steps was a t-shirt. I immediately picked it up and began to look it over to see if I could figure out who had left it there. I didn't recognize it as belonging to one of my sons. A Scripture on the back said, *"I have been crucified with Christ; it is no longer I that live but Christ Who lives in me; and the life I now live in the body I live by faith in the Son of God, Who loved me and gave Himself up for me." (Galatians 2:20 AMP)* As I continued to read and re-read those words, I pondered their meaning and believe God revealed it to me immediately. The night my lost his life, a huge part of me died right along with him. I was still breathing, existing but not living. I now had the confirmation that I would survive, but only through the Christ within me empowering me to have life uninhibited, fearless and free after tragedy ripped my life apart. The power in that message on a crumpled-up t-shirt was meant just for me, placed precisely at the right location and moment that I was intended to find it. How it got there is still a mystery, and yet I know without one doubt it was one of my gentle reminders God had sent to encourage me that He was with me, leading and guiding my every step. God knows what is ahead of us because He's already there. If we're careful to go where He leads, the journey will be amazing; and should we stray off course, His mighty hand is there to steer us back on track gently and lovingly.

So many ask me how I can carry on during total devastation and heartache. I tell everyone who will take the time to listen that God given Scripture is what I trust in and lean on. I can live because He is alive inside of me. I now spend more time looking ahead than looking behind. I focus on what is to come and not what is gone. *"The Spirit of God hath made me, and the breath of the Almighty hath given me life." (Job 33:4 KJV)* Even though I *am* breathing, it is God Who gives me His breath, and His power *in* me enables me to live abundantly and continue on this unexpected journey through life. I now have perfect peace, love, hope, and joy not based on *my* efforts, because these priceless treasures can be found only in Him. I would like to encourage those of you who are dealing with the loss of a child or other loved one, that *if* you allow God to live and move in you and breathe life back into you, what He's done for me, He'll do for you. All you have to do is ask, believe, and receive Him into your heart. He won't ever force Himself upon anyone, but will enter your heart *only* if allowed. I may go as far to say that He will never ask you to do anything that He hasn't already done. So many refuse to permit God to come into their lives for fear of what they will have to give up too much. Would you trust me to tell you, when you surrender you lives completely to Him those things you used to enjoy doing will never hold a flicker of excitement compared to the ultimate satisfaction you will encounter when you meet Jesus.

There have been plenty of times I questioned God. I've also been distant and upset with Him and screamed out in anger during my dejected times of desperation. In the worst of times, I still somehow knew that *if* I were ever going to make it to the other side of the pain, He would be the only One Who could lead me through the darkest days and nights. Even when I didn't understand how all this turmoil had happened or even why, the one thing I never forgot was that without God, I knew I could never survive. *"For the mountains shall depart, and the hills be removed; but my kindness shall not depart from thee, neither shall the covenant of my peace be removed, saith the Lord that hath mercy on thee." (Isaiah 54:10 KJV)*

There *are* still times I visit the past and remember what life used to be like before tragedy struck, but only for a moment to gain encouragement that the fond memories always give. So many times, I reminisce about the day Justin asked Jesus into his heart, and I look back at the pictures of when he was baptized. Those reminders bring me a selfless pride, knowing Justin received his salvation at an early age and is now reaping his reward of eternal life in Heaven. People often ask, "How are you so confident in where your son is spending eternity?" I respond that it's by the various conversations over the years, in which there were multiple times he adamantly confirmed it to me. There were instances while growing up that he would come into our bedroom feeling down and out and lie across the foot of our bed and say, "Dad, Mom, we need to pray." My husband and I would then begin to petition God with our son, in agreement that every concern he had would be addressed by the Lord. We pleaded for peace and assurance of his salvation and he always walked away feeling confident in his relationship with God. Also, I tell them God gives me miraculous reminders when my mind tries to make me think otherwise. Sometimes confirmation of that fact comes through looking up in the sky and seeing a big puffy cloud filled "cross," letting me know that although Justin isn't physically visible, his presence will never leave. That seems to happen always just at the precise moment my thoughts try to doubt that of which my heart is already convinced. Often God sends a brightly colored, orange butterfly, Justin's favorite color, to sit close beside me, fluttering passionately so there will be no way for me to miss its appearance. Other times I see his favorite number, "three" strategically placed in my path, so I would have no chance to deny its presence. Often I'm at a store, and the only available line open will be lane three, or I may find myself needing gas, and the only pump with no waiting will be number three. Many of you may think these things are only small *coincidences*, when, in fact, to a mother who's dealing with the pain of losing a child, they're nothing short of divine miracles that hold the unique ability to restore life to the dead, empty

83

places in our hearts.

There were nights long before the accident when I would suddenly be startled awake from a deep sleep and look at the clock; it would be exactly 3:33 in the morning. There were very few nights when this didn't occur, and for the longest time, I tried to figure out why I would always wake up at that specific time. I think now that it was God's way of getting my attention. I believe He was using the repetition of the threes to get me focused on Him, so that later when I saw them, I would see *Him* and gain comfort from His undeniable presence. Just as Justin's favorite number was three, I believe God has a fondness for that number as well. The Bible speaks of it numerous times, with the most significant one proclaiming that "on the third day He arose from the dead." *"Thus, it is written, and thus it behooved Christ to suffer, and to rise from the dead on the third day." (Luke 24:4 KJV)*

I often revisit in my heart the very last time I was able to see Justin. The funeral director had called us in to say our final goodbyes; I looked upon the face of my son for the very last time until we would reunite in Heaven. Being unable to say goodbye, I leaned down and kissed him softly on the forehead and said, "I'll see you soon." As I turned to go, I noticed a basket that had been placed on a small table for cards and mementos. There was a sash tied to the basket which said, "Don't Leave Weak." I felt at that precise moment Justin wanted me to remember I couldn't leave helpless and frail and survive. That message of encouragement was going to have to be lived out in my own life. Somehow, I had to find the hope, faith, and stamina to carry on, knowing that God truly *is* my greatest refuge of strength in troubled times. To make it through this most difficult journey, I had to find God's mighty power in the midst of my complete weakness and rely on *His* strength alone. *"Lord, be gracious to us; we long for You. Be our strength every morning, our salvation in the time of distress. (Isaiah 33:2 NIV)* I had to give all I had to God and hold nothing back. That particular lesson I had tried so hard to teach each of my sons would now be the one *I* would have to practice daily. Don't waste time reflecting on all your insufficiency but reside in God's divine capability to transform your life as you submit to Him.

It's so challenging not to look back and remember all the great times we had as a family when our son was with us. Even though I said it's ok to revisit the past we must not become too settled and get lost in the moment. Those days were a time when I felt things were almost perfect but didn't entirely recognize it due to the distractions of minor conflicts which seemed insurmountable. Now I'm *choosing* not to dwell on the past but to set my sights on the present and what lies ahead. There are still days of trials, pain, and grief but I now know it won't last forever. God gives us a fresh dose of mercy and grace daily, just enough so that we can make it through anything He calls us to do. *"His compassions fail not. They are new every morning; great is Thy faithfulness." (Lamentations 3:23 KJV)*

I believe we could all live happier, fuller, and more victoriously *if*, when we get out of bed every morning, we would trust God to be in total control of our lives, the lives of our loved ones, and every care of the entire world. Isn't it pivotal to believe He's big enough to take care of *us* and everything we deem important? That's not to say we're supposed to sit back and do nothing. After all, faith is an action word. I merely mean that we need to seek Him and do as He says to do, and He in return will do what we are unable to do. As the prophet declares in *Isaiah 49:5 KJV: "My God has become my strength."*

If I will steadfastly look ahead and not back, there's a bright side of darkness: I had faith in the promise of *knowing* that although Justin's life had ended on this earth, it had only just begun in Heaven. Although I would far rather have my son here to bury *me*, as should be the natural order of life, his being in Heaven brings me a comfort I can rely on. That hope calms and settles my disheartened soul, and gives peace to my wearisome mind. I often feel guilty when I miss him so much, because he has the best Heaven has to offer. That is why we should never look at death to a Christian as anything less than a celebration of a glorious home-going. Heaven is our reward and not a brutal punishment. Although we may get consumed with our selfish ways of wanting to keep our loved ones close, since Justin had to leave, I will rejoice that I have the promise of seeing him again. *"For the Lord, Himself shall descend from Heaven with a shout, with a voice of the archangel, and with the trump of God: and the dead in Christ shall rise first. Then we which are alive and remain shall be caught up together with them in the clouds, to meet the Lord in the air: and so, shall we ever be with the Lord." (1 Thessalonians 4:16-17 KJV)*

Chapter Ten
I Can Only Imagine

Three weeks had passed since the accident. Thankfully, the days seemed to go by rather quickly at times, but then other days appeared to drag at a leisurely, mundane pace. I learned to keep my mind busy with everyday activities, knowing that *if* I could distract my mind, my thoughts wouldn't be able to viciously sabotage my day. This particular day had been a little more trying as I had the dreadful job of doing something that no parent ever wants to do. I had to be at the police station early that morning to claim my son's shoes. The police had kept them for various reasons and called to let me know they had been released so I could stop by and pick them up at my earliest convenience.

When I arrived, the man at the front desk told me to wait and someone would be right with me. I took a seat, and as I waited my mind began racing over all the events of that awful night when my son perished, and I lost one of the greatest gifts God has ever given me. Justin was our firstborn son and had a smile that could light up the darkness. Few people can smile in such a way that it shines from within through their eyes, that sends a glow over their entire face, but this child of mine had that unique ability. As I describe it just now, I can still see his gorgeous, sparkling grin. I pray I never lose the capacity to close my eyes and see his smile and those big, round, shiny, blue eyes.

As I continued to wait, I tried to focus on happier times. I remembered the day I purchased those shoes for Justin. He had asked for a particular color and brand. They were white Nike Air Max with an orange swoosh, which to me looked more red than his favorite— Tennessee orange, but he was happy with them. That's what mattered most! Justin was always so conscious of keeping them clean and seemed to be extremely proud of them. How was I to know when I purchased them that this would be the last pair he would ever wear?

After some time had passed, I was able to regain control of my thoughts, when I was interrupted as I sensed someone was nearby. I looked up to see a familiar face waiting patiently as I tried to wipe the tears away and regain my composure to speak. The officer was a longtime friend of our family and had been called into work the night of the accident. He had shared with me how difficult it was to see Justin that night. He mentioned how upset he was realizing he would have to be the one to tell us our son was no longer with us. Our friend had spent a great deal of time with my husband while at the accident scene, and indeed did have to deliver the news to Barry as he waited along the roadway never losing hope that Justin would survive. As he continued to speak my mind raced back to happier days when he and Barry coached baseball together. Back then our hardest decision was figuring out where to go eat after the game. Those days of uninhibited fun now seemed a million miles away.

It was both comforting and painful to have him be the one to deliver my son's belongings to me. I remember thinking *this* isn't the way things were supposed to be. However, it seemed there was more compassion with it coming from someone who also knew us and had grown attached to our son over the years. I could see by his demeanor that day that he was still very sincere with his heartfelt condolences. I am most appreciative of his sympathy and compassion for our family.

After we spent some time talking he led me down a long hallway to his office and presented me with a brown paper bag. Inside was a large plastic bag that contained my son's shoes. I held the bag, afraid to look inside, not knowing what I would see and fearing the worst; as I opened the sack, it was not at all what I presumed. His shoes looked as new as the day I had presented them to him. In a way, their unblemished condition made it somewhat easier, *if* that is even possible. Not to have to look at any remnant of that tragic accident somehow calmed my worn out, exhausted soul. I thanked my friend for being so kind and caring during this time, as I knew his job was never easy, especially when there was such familiarity. He assured me that if there was anything he could do to help, he was always available anytime day or night. We said our goodbyes, and he walked me to the door.

Later that night, the police department called to say they also had my son's phone they had received along with the shoes, but somehow hadn't given it to me when I was there earlier. I hung up the phone and called my sister, who has always offered a strong word of support, so I wanted to unload the day's events and receive her loving consolation she constantly supplied. Amy continues, to this day, to be a great strength and encouragement. My little sister has always had the unique ability to take whatever bad I happen to spill over on her, look at it objectively, and offer in return a more bearable solution. As soon as she heard my trembling voice on the other end, she asked if she could be the one to go by and pick up the phone, as she knew how anxious we were to have it returned. We desperately wanted to see anything at all that might bring some comfort or joy to us, even if it were only for a moment. It would have been wonderful to see pictures of him with his friends or to hear his voice on a saved message, to watch a video of him living his life to the fullest, to hear his laugh, or to see his smile. I wanted just a glance back to a time that wasn't filled with grief and unbearable pain. Would that be too much to ask?

I think of how hard it must have been for my sister to handle this one last "Justin-task" for me, to save *me* the torture of doing it. My son was also the light in her eyes and the happiness of her heart, and she would gladly bear any grief she could, so I wouldn't have to endure needless anguish. She was away at school when Justin was born and would come home every chance she had to spend time with him, always with her arms loaded down with gifts. I cannot imagine the amount of ridicule her friends gave her when they begged her to go out with them, but instead, she chose to come home to spend all her excess free time with Justin. The first man to fully captivate and steal her heart came into this world weighing a whopping 7lbs. and 15oz and a tiny 20inches tall. I'm thankful he lived long enough to realize the unconditional love that she unselfishly gave to him. There was nothing in life that he could ever do that she would not be there to lift him up, cheer him on, pick him up, or bail him out. She wholeheartedly supported him in anything and everything he attempted.

When Amy had completed her mission that night, she hurried to our house with the phone. Before I could even look at it, I excitedly asked her if they were able to retrieve any of the pictures or videos. She dropped her head as if she felt it was somehow her fault that there was no information available. She explained they had tried extensive measures, but were unable to find *anything*.

As she placed the phone in my hand, the emotions filled up inside me to the degree I felt my heart fall inside my chest. As I cradled the last thing my son had held that night, I imagined I could feel his hand in mine. As I looked at this shattered box of glass and plastic, it was as if I were right back to the night of the accident, and those events rushed in and flooded my mind with debilitating misery all over again. Was I ever going to be able to breathe easily, to experience a much-desired worry-free life, and to have uninterrupted joy? Would I forever be faced with the constant reminders of that horrible night when everything completely turned upside down and inside out? The answers can be found in God and Him alone. *"My grace and peace be multiplied to you in the knowledge of God and of Jesus our Lord. His divine power has granted to us all things* that pertain to life and godliness, through the knowledge of Him Who *called us to His own glory and excellence, by which He has granted to us His precious and very great promises." (2 Peter 1:2-4 ESV)*

I remember impatiently waiting each day for the return of the phone, I was hoping it might somehow fill in part of the gaps from the night of the accident; perhaps he tried to text us a message just before the wreck. Maybe there would be details as to why he was where he was or why he even got into the car with an impaired driver that night. Did Justin try to call us, or did he try and text saying he needed help and wanted for us to come? We would never know what his final moments were. The phone revealed no answers to my endless questions. The events and moments leading up to the accident would remain a mystery. That may in fact be a blessing instead of a curse. I'm powerless to change the outcome of that horrific night; maybe the absence of specific information helps to decrease the intensity of the torment.

I placed the phone back in the plastic bag I had received it in, put it inside the kitchen cabinet, and began to get ready for bed, always my place of retreat to hide from things I didn't want to face and accept as my reality. I would slide deep under the covers, squeeze my eyes tightly shut and try my best to make all the unbearable pain disappear as it attempted to strangle and suffocate me. My continuous efforts to find relief were in vain and only made things harder each time I refused to relinquish my pain, discontentment, and discomfort to the One Who could heal every hurt. After much time and fellowship with God, I was able to give up, let go, and let Him have all that was messed up, broken, and destroyed. If I were careful not to try and take the pieces back before He had the chance to make the necessary repairs, He would create in me a newness only the Master Carpenter can construct. *"And He that sat upon the throne said, Behold, I make all things new. And He said unto me, 'Write: for these words are true.'" (Revelation 21:5 KJV)*

My youngest son, Caleb, was having trouble going to sleep. In fact, we all were deprived of the ability to relax, due to the fact our minds were repetitively racing through the events of the previous weeks. We mostly rested in shifts, and in the rare case we did drift off, it was only enough to make us feel even worse than before we had lain down. So, on most nights, it was easier just to stay awake. At least that was what *I* did. Many nights I found myself outside sitting in a lawn chair in the backyard staring up at the black sky lit with tiny diamond-like stars. Somehow the quietness of the evening

91

brought a peace that the days did not allow.

On that particular night, I ended up lying down with Caleb until I felt like he had finally drifted into a restful sleep. I slid out of his bed and crept down the stairs to climb into my own, looking out the bedroom window to see that it was nearly daylight. As I lay my head down on my pillow, I could hear a racket coming from the other room. I couldn't make out what it *was*, except for being something I couldn't ignore. I tried to close my eyes, but my ears would not tune out the noise. Then I got up and walked to the door, and it got louder as I made my way through the house. I looked outside to the back porch to see if it might be the radio left on from the previous day. I made my way to the kitchen and saw my husband's phone beside mine, but neither was making a chirp. My eyes were drawn to the cabinet where I had placed my son's phone earlier. My mind was convinced that surely I must be dreaming, or imagining I heard anything at all even to entertain a hope it could be Justin's phone; but as I walked nearer to the closed cabinet, the sound got louder. I opened the door and inside that plastic bag was a light as bright as the break of dawn. I grabbed it and ran back through the house to find my husband. I hurried as fast as I could go, fearing the sound would cease before Barry was able to validate the treasure I'd found. I needed someone to hear what I was hearing, or to tell me I didn't hear what I thought I did, or that maybe indeed I was correct. I forcefully pushed open the door to see Barry standing at the bathroom sink shaving. I couldn't *speak*. All I could do was wave the phone back and forth near his face, hoping he'd understand what I was trying to say, while I remained speechless. He was running late trying to get ready for work and didn't seem to have much time to fiddle with what he *thought* was foolishness on my part. I will never forget the bewildered look on his face. With my inability to speak because of the tears and excitement, he was baffled as to what was causing my behavior. He, too, was perplexed by what he was hearing. When he was finally able to tune in to what was going on, we both dropped to our knees and listened to one of our most favorite songs, "I Can Only Imagine," which talks about what it will be like when we all get to Heaven and are surrounded by God's glory, what we will see and do. Will we sing, or dance, or even be able to speak? Our eyes filled with tears as we felt as close to Justin as we had since he left. After some time had passed and the song continued to play over and over, for some reason I felt a need to check the time. When I went back into the bedroom and looked at the bedside table, the clock showed a few minutes after 6:00 a.m. That song was the sound that woke my son up for work each day. His thoughts were on Heaven at the beginning of every morning! As I began to think over the events of the last few minutes, I realized that had it been an alert for a text or email, it would have quit long before I had ever heard it or had a chance to find the phone; but because it was an alarm, it continued to play long enough for me to locate it. The song played over and over with not even a pause. Eventually, we had to take the battery out in order to make it stop; it was ironic that the phone wasn't going to quit until we knew all too well the significant meaning it was meant to accomplish. This phenomenon was intended to encourage us that if we doubted our son's whereabouts, then all we had to do was remember this moment when something that seemed impossible became a reality. As that phone somehow miraculously began to work through its shattered brokenness, our hearts would also begin to heal.

What a joy and a comfort it brought to my heart that my son no longer had to wonder what Heaven would be like; he was now able to experience it to the fullest. No longer would I be forced to listen to the doubts in my head of the certainty my son was *really* in Heaven. God showed this fact to me by causing a shattered box of glass and plastic to work flawlessly. He proved that things a man thinks are impossible, are ALL made possible by Him. Just as He worked through the brokenness of that phone, He would also be able to work through the nothingness of my shattered life.

Even though we made many attempts in the following days and

weeks to get that phone to play again, it had been rendered completely useless and never made another sound, but that is fine with me. I know without a doubt God caused it to operate just at the right moment and right on time. The memory of that event has been forever etched upon my soul and continues to play in my heart and mind every day and will never be erased. Knowing that my flesh may feel all sorts of ways, I can rest in the assurance that my soul can be at rest even through complete devastation. *"My flesh and my heart may fail, but God is the rock and strength of my heart and my portion forever." (Psalm 73:26 AMP) If* I'm patient and wait upon Him to renew my might by trusting His power entirely and not my own, then and only then will I be able to stand in the times of trouble and know that He holds me in the very palm of His mighty outstretched hand. My load of grief and care will never be too much for God to handle; with His Holy Spirit power living inside, I'm enabled to endure all things. *Isaiah 40:28-29 AMP* declares: *"The everlasting God, the Lord, the Creator of the ends of the earth, does not faint or grow weary. He gives power to the faint and weary, and to him who has no might He increases strength."* That Scripture means that no matter how tired or exhausted we may feel, His strength will see us through until the end. God never grows tired or becomes weary; His power never fails. To further encourage us, His Word professes that the very same power that raised Jesus from the dead lives in us. *"And if the Spirit of Him Who raised up Jesus from the dead dwells in you, He Who raised up Christ Jesus from the dead will also restore to life your mortal bodies through His Spirit Who dwells in you." (Romans 8:11 KJV)* I don't know about you, but when I think that God himself lives in me and empowers me to do the impossible, what do I have to fear?

Through the paralyzing devastation of tragedy, God demanded my attention if I was ever going to be healed. I believe that's why He placed signs and wonders all around me during the time of complete weakness so that I would not be able to deny His power at work in me, to carry me through every step of the way. I know that if you, also, have things that you're going through which seem impossible, He'll show you the same grace and mercy He has shown me. I pray each day for God to quicken my mortal body back to abundant life. I pray that He will give me clear understanding and a heart and mind focused on Him and not on my problems. I ask God to strengthen and establish me to do all things that He has called me to do with His help. I ask Him to heal every hurt and replace and multiply everything that the enemy has tried to steal from our family. I know if I'll believe in Him and never doubt, He will most assuredly answer every prayer. *"If any man asks in faith, nothing wavering. For he that wavereth is like a wave of the sea driven with the wind and tossed." (James 1:6 KJV)*

Chapter Eleven
Finding Joy in the Journey

I am confident that God desires for everyone always, in all things to have the ability to find complete joy in our lives. *"And these things write we unto you, that your joy may be full."* *(1 John 1:4 KJV)* I won't ever believe that He gave us this time on earth so that we would be happy only when we all get to Heaven. He doesn't intend for us to live in this world weak, weary, angry, bitter, and disgusted, but with a shout of praise, knowing that if God brought us to it, He most definitely would bring us through all situations. That doesn't mean it will always be easy. I'm not saying that we'll have only joyous times and that if you follow God, everything will always go the way you planned. We gain our strength through the tough times and the adversities of life, much like bodybuilders gain strength through resistance. We should seek to find happiness no matter what we may have to walk through, realizing that this world is not our home but merely a brief stop on our journey to Heaven. What we face in our lifetime will not last forever. *"As we look not to the things that are seen but to the things that are unseen. For the things that are seen are transient" {temporary}, but the things which are unseen are eternal."* *(2 Corinthians 4:18 ESV)* Knowing that the hard times will eventually come to an end encourages me to keep my eyes on Jesus and keep moving ahead. The trials we will have to walk through can be overcome with God's help! *"And He said unto me, My grace is sufficient for thee: for My strength is made perfect in weakness. Most gladly, therefore, will I rather glory in my infirmities, that the power of Christ may rest upon me."* *(2 Corinthians 12:9 KJV)* That verse speaks volumes to my heart and soul. It not only says that when we are depleted of all natural ability, He will, in fact, *be* our supernatural strength, but goes on to say that we can have joy even in our weakness. That means that in Him I can find joy even through all adversities. We need to make diligent decision not to let our circumstances rob us of joy.

We must determine in our minds and hearts that whatever comes our way we can and will make it. When you trust and believe in God's Scriptures, they will become rooted deep in your soul and you'll be able to live in perfect peace. There's not one storm you will ever face that God's power can't deliver you from. The key to having this kind of freedom is speaking it, believing in it, and receiving it. Never speak doubt and negativity over your current conditions. Don't ever use phrases like "I'll never be able to do that" or "Things will never get any better." The truth is that by repeating those nullifying comments you are inadvertently giving your enemy power over you. We never need to make it easy for our avenger to destroy us. Don't ever let the word "can't" be in your thought process or enter your vocabulary. Pray and speak life over your every situation and need. There is power in the phrases we proclaim. Let your words be life and not death as you speak into the atmosphere. *"Death and life are in the power of the tongue." (Proverbs 18:21 KJV)*

Our joy is our strength, and without it, we are powerless against the wiles of the devil. The Word of God tells us that we have an enemy in this life and he tries with all his might to get us off the path that God has planned. *"Be sober; and vigilant: because your adversary the devil, as a roaring lion, walketh about, seeking whom he may devour." (1 Peter 5:8 KJV)* Even though we have someone working against us to steal our joy, we, in turn, have a God that's giving us a life of abundance to the point it is an overflowing supply that will never run dry. We have a dear preacher friend who reminded us that "the devil is in contempt of court!" We are no longer under the adversary's judgment but have been justified by God's grace. Jesus settled things once and for all on the cross!

If we seek to find joy in all things, knowing that God is for us, we'll be able to endure to the end and do so with a gladness that comes from within. *"May the God of your hope so fill you with all joy and peace in believing that by the power of the Holy Spirit you may abound and be overflowing with hope." (Romans 15:13 KJV)*

I'm committed and determined not to let anyone or anything come between myself and my gladness. The main thing that motivates me to continue is I believe beyond all doubt that one day my walk will become easier and eventually my life will get better. I have *decided* to become addicted to finding happiness each day in all things, to search out something worthwhile in even through the bad that may come my way. *Psalm 39:13 KJV* gives us great hope in knowing that God does not intend for us to be in this world merely surviving, but that in Him we can live a life full of joy and, yes, happiness even after a significant loss and unbearable grief. *"O look away from me and spare me, that I may recover cheerfulness and encouraging strength and know gladness before I go and am no more!"*

There's a prayer I've often prayed, even before the death of my son. It is simply, "Lord if you choose *not* to change the situation, and if it is Your divine will for me to encounter this opposition, please change me that I may be able to endure it to the finish with great enthusiasm." The despair we must walk through on this earth is not by choice. I have often thought *if* we were able to select only the blessings or the easy things in this life, when would we ever be able to learn the hope and faith that comes only from knowing God? Of all the things I've experienced, I've learned that the hardest changes we'll go through are the forced ones, those we would never seek out of our own free will. We can choose to move to a new city, or we may be pressured to go there because of circumstances. We can decide to buy a new car, or we may *have* to do so because the one we own has broken down. Almost everyone, myself included, takes pride at being in control of the choices we make. Nevertheless, we all must face things as they come and do the best we can with God beside us. Pride says, "Look what I have done;" God responds, "Look what I have done so you didn't have to." *"Have I not commanded thee? Be strong and of a good courage; be not afraid, neither be thou dismayed: for the Lord, thy God is with thee whithersoever thou goest." (Joshua 1:9 KJV)*

There are times when hardships come on slowly like a loved

one's long-term illness, or some things suddenly come upon us with no warning at all, such as the fatal wreck that consumed our son. It's sometimes through facing these hardships that we come to realize we need a Savior. By going through destructive situations, we gain the ability to trust Him, to make it through this life, not just surviving but being able to thrive victoriously and also having joy while going through devastation.

Never be lazy and sit silently expecting God to do all the work to get us thorough all life's detours. We have a role to play, which is to pray continually, keeping an open line of communication with our heavenly Father, and He will move on our behalf in every situation. I always say, "Jesus is *alive,* and He is active inside me, and for that reason God keeps me going." I could never be happy sitting around doing nothing when God is living His life in me. *"You make known to me the path of life; in Your presence, there if fullness of joy; at Your right hand are pleasures forevermore." (Psalm 16:11 ESV)*

You may wonder how it's possible to have joy when things turn tragically wrong and don't line up with the way you intended when the life you expected has been irrevocably interrupted by an unexpected, grievous tragedy. I know all too well the difficulties of trusting in something that seems inconceivable; God's Word is exact and will bring you healing if you believe what it says and do as it instructs. You see, I in no way planned my life to live without the privilege of having each of my sons live a long happy, prosperous life, never having to ever lay my oldest to rest. I've decided to walk in peace knowing that God had another plan and trusting that He loves us so much, He freely gave His Only Son so that my son now has eternal life. Even though I didn't pick this journey, God chose it for my family. I wasn't given the option whether or not to give my son up, I do have the choice to continue with joy and hope that's ultimately found in God. Even though it isn't easy, I know that somehow with God's help and my faith in Him, I will survive. *"The Lord is my strength and my shield; in Him my heart trusts, and I am helped; my heart exults, and with my song, I give thanks to*

Him." (Psalm 28:7 ESV)

Even though God has a perfect will for our lives, it's never without difficult or trying times, but the knowledge that He is with us through it all causes me to hope in Him alone. There's not one step that I'll ever take that He will not be with me. He has called me to this journey, and I will finish the race with joy. God knows that I can do it, or I would not have been chosen for this path. There will be times your own healing from heartache will come quickly and others that it may take longer, but I know that through Him you'll have the stamina and endurance to walk through your life victoriously.

There's never been a day, at least up to this point, that I can honestly say my heavy load of grief has been totally absent. It's an unpleasant, unwanted, unkind guest that shows up without warning or invitation; it's with me from the moment I wake up until I lie down to sleep. I wrestle with it both day and night, trying my best with God's assistance to keep it as far away as possible. My heart is steadfast and determined not to let my desolation overpower me. I know without God's help to win the battle, I will be quickly devoured. I'm in a monstrous monsoon of perpetual, raging emotions, torturous and unending. As the tumultuous sea pulls me under, I fight to stay afloat, holding onto God's promises and trusting in His mighty hand to pull me to higher ground when I'm consumed with fear and doubt. The Bible speaks of a great thunderstorm in the book of *Mark 4:35-41*. The disciples were in a large ship, Jesus was asleep, resting peacefully. The winds blew violently while relentless rain pounded the vessel, filling it up quickly with water. The men cried out in fear; concerned they all would surely drown, they immediately woke Jesus. He then arose and rebuked the tempest, and a calmness covered the sea. He then asked His disciples, *"Why are you so fearful? How is it that ye have no faith?" (Mark 4:40 KJV)* You see, even though these men were supposedly well-*trained* fishermen they were utterly panicked, unable to function during the storm. They had to rely on Jesus to rescue them from the squall, proving what my husband always says, "You can know how to do something flawlessly, but can you still preform effortlessly in the middle of chaotic turbulence?" Just as the fishermen cried out for help, we too can call upon God during troubled seas and He will extinguish any danger. Make it a habit to walk in faith not fear; either you will trust that God can handle it or you won't. One thing is certain, He can't help us if we don't ask and believe He can and will.

In all that has happened I've finally learned not to trust what I feel or where my emotions try to lead me. Walking in fear is terrifying and dangerous and annihilates all quality of life. Walking in faith can also be scary, but never dangerous because of God, our Shield goes before preparing the way. Faith allows us to enjoy life and the blessings along the way, whereas fear paralyzes us from having that ability. Fear is unbelief while faith believes beyond the natural ability to comprehend. Both fear and faith are unseen. Fear is what the enemy holds over our minds to prevent us from stepping out and doing great and mighty things. Faith is what God gives us to walk a victorious path. Should you *choose* faith, it will yield endless, glorious results in your life.

Just as I cannot maneuver the winds that blow or stop the damage from a hurricane, I know I cannot control the degree of grief that I'm forced to deal with daily. My adversary would like nothing better than to keep me bound by intimidation and unbelief, but I know God desires me to walk in the fullness His life in me affords. God is the one voice that can tell the ocean it can come only to a certain point upon the earth. He is also more than able to control the turbulence of this life, and I know that He and He alone can calm the raging sea inside of me. *Isaiah 43:2 AMP* says, "*When you pass through the waters, I will be with you; And through the rivers, they will not overwhelm you. When you walk through the fire, you will not be scorched, Nor, will the flame burn you.*" The realization of this truth was not an instant fact in my heart, for, in the beginning, it was so easy to get caught up in the waves of emotions and own the right to give up and quit. After all, many before me have renounced the battle to continue living life after loss. Would I, too, choose to abandon the fight to survive?

Time marched on despite my relentless efforts of refusal to proceed along willingly. I found that I had built walls all around me which indeed resembled a prison. I was convinced that if I remained behind those bars, nothing or no one could get to me, nor me to them. It was a way I could protect myself from others and in return safeguard others from myself. I didn't have to worry about acting as others felt I should, and no longer did they have the burden of trying to pacify me with kind words or gestures. Then one day I realized that I held my very own set of keys to the dungeon in which I had chosen to live. If I was ever going to escape and be free from the grief in which I was living, I had to make a conscious decision to break loose from my self-induced bondage. If I were going to make it, I had to choose to do my part and use the resources within me to escape the barricade I had built around myself. I knew I had to focus not on my constant pain, but instead on God's promise that no matter where I go, He is there. I had to follow the instructions from the Scriptures: *"Draw near to God, and He will draw near to you."* *(James 4:8 KJV)* I have now learned not to rely on my own strength to survive, but to lean on God in order to make it through the tempestuous storms this life brings.

I have *determined* to hold strong to my trust in God, refusing to dread what is ahead and knowing that *"God has dealt to every man a measure of faith." (Romans 12:3 KJV)* I believe our willingness to *use* our faith determines our level of confidence in Him. Some may trust in God with their *whole* hearts while others may allow Him only a small portion. I have committed to giving Him *all* of me. God puts His faith in *us* when He calls us to walk through tumultuous times. I realized if I could just keep my eyes, heart, and mind focused on Jesus, I would have the strength to walk through the hardships of life and be more than able to make it to the other side.

Are we going to continue to live our lives, never determined to find joy in the journey and believing the lie that we can never make it past the darkest night? Or will we choose to allow whatever we've gone through--the loss of a child, spouse, loved one, home, job, or health--rob us of our remaining time and force us to sit on the sidelines and watch our lives go by? *"For we are His workmanship, created in Christ Jesus unto good works, which God hath before ordained that we should walk in them. (Ephesians 2:10 KJV)*

I urge you to allow God to walk your path with you, beside you to guide you through all the twists and turns this life may hold. Know, trust, and believe that without a doubt, you can do all things with Him. You can and will be able to rejoice in time on this road you did not choose, *if* you allow God to carry you when you have no power to continue. In Him, there is perfect joy, peace, and hope. *Psalm 35:9 KJV* declares this victory: *"And my soul shall be joyful in the Lord; it shall rejoice in His salvation."*

Through loss I've discovered a hope and gladness this world cannot teach. I've heard it said that being joyful is a state of mind, a place of *being* and not a destination. That is far different from being happy. Joy is a free gift from God while happiness is a reaction to a particular event or encounter. To explain it more clearly, overflowing joy comes from Jesus and happiness sometimes happens. Joy is constant, and happiness is conditional. *"So also, you have sorrow now, but I will see you again, and your hearts will rejoice, and no one will take your joy from you." (3 John 16:22 ESV)* I strive to get to that place of peace and fulfillment in my own life, where I can find solace along the way, even when the trip includes unexpected unplanned stops. Whether I'm faced with loss or blessed with much. I strive for the same amount of happiness no matter what condition I may go through on this earth. I know it's a goal I will never achieve on my own. It's an unexplainable joy we receive when we accept Christ and can allow Him to uncover a satisfaction that goes far beyond our natural understanding. When we give Him our complete sadness, He will in return give us joy unspeakable and full of glory. That life is found only in knowing God and allowing Him to be our complete source of peace, love, and contentment, a deal I couldn't refuse since all I had to offer Him was my pain, grief, and despair. God's divine Word promises us: *"These things I have spoken to you, that My joy may be in you, and that your joy may be full." (John 15:11 ESV)* How great is that! His perfect joy overflows mine. To this day, it has been the best deal I could ever ask for, greater than I could have ever imagined. If we choose to walk in it, it's irrevocable--a priceless gift, one we could never earn or deserve.

Who on this earth could ever love us as Jesus does? His adoration for us doesn't diminish when we are unlovable, unkind, and unacceptable. He even loved us enough, while we were shameful, deceitful, immoral sinners, to give His life as a ransom for ours. Jesus took our sin debt and paid the price with His precious blood that we could be spared death and given eternal life in Heaven. *"Surely, He has borne our griefs and sorrows; yet we esteemed Him stricken, smitten by God, and afflicted. But He was pierced for our transgressions; He was crushed for our iniquities; upon Him was the chastisement that brought us peace and by His wounds, we are healed." (Isaiah 53:4-5 ESV)* God has only good intentions in store for us *if* we will but trust and rely on Him for every need, believing in Him and knowing that He has the very best plans for us. Not even the ones we have for ourselves will ever come close to those great and wonderful things He has in store for His children, as we are sons and daughters of the one and only *true* King. That knowledge brings the only constant satisfaction and tranquility I've known since the day I made Jesus Lord of my life. I will never forget the moment I surrendered to Him my afflictions and He gave me pleasures beyond my greatest expectations; in fact, I revisit that memorable time often when my emotions become unstable and undone. God never once promised us that in this life we would never have difficult days, but knowing that He is with us to help no matter what it may bring, permits me to experience genuine happiness. That has been one of the most difficult adventures I've ever encountered. By no means have I come to these conclusions overnight. I won't lie and say that I've always been able to find a joyous destination, but I've never stopped searching for it, and it's now often found in the simplest of things and not the big things that I once sought after. It's a sincere happiness that far outlasts what our eyes can see. It's an excitement that comes from the inside, and, if I allow it to shine, is noticed now on the outside. *"Let your light so shine before men, that they may see your good works, and glorify your Father which is in Heaven." (Matthew 5:16 KJV)*

Chapter Twelve
Just One More Day

I've often thought to ask God for just one more day with my son, to let him have a "day-pass" from Heaven to visit with us one more time here on earth. Would it be a punishment for him to leave all the comforts of Heaven and return to the world that could never even compare with the pleasures to which he has grown accustomed? When my heart is drifting far from reality, I reel in my emotions and desired expectations realizing, "How could just one more day ever be enough?" If given a chance to be with him for a short amount of time, would I ever truly be able to say goodbye with the understanding that the last minute of that day would mean going through the agony and pain of losing him all over again? Could I bear the torment and survive the trauma his departure caused again--the hurt, the loss, the pain and total devastation?

Anguish continues to attack my heart as it tries to strangle and suffocate my willingness to persevere under pressure. However, God is helping me day by day to lean upon Him for everything that's lacking in my life. I have renewed strength from focusing on Heaven and Him and not on the conflicts that are ever present. As hard as I try, there *are* still days, even now after six years and nearly six months have passed, I ask myself, "Is this real? Is he for a fact gone? Is this all a nightmare from which I cannot awake?" Many evenings while doing dishes I stare out the kitchen window, fully expecting to see my 6' 1 ½" tall, blonde-haired, blue-eyed young man walking down the sidewalk to the back door to tell me all about his many adventures. When reality sets in and I realize he isn't ever coming back to the life he once had, I tried to encourage myself in the Lord. He is God when things are great *and* when things are miserable. My hope and belief in Him will sustain and motivate me at all times and through all things. My job is to trust in Him to complete the plans He has for me and not hinder their progress.

There are times when it seems as if Justin has been gone an eternity, and then there are others when it seems he's just left. Some days the memories of that night hurt just as much as the actual night itself. It seems I must fight the battle each day not to lose sight of the victory I know God has already provided for me if I continue to walk with Him, never losing faith that one day things won't be so hard.

The first few months, I was in a state of total disbelief, a phase my mind went through to help me deal with what I could not accept. The best description I have is that it's like a dark, dense fog through which you cannot see or even attempt to move out of, for its thickness holds you like quicksand, and the more you struggle to get loose, the tighter the grip it has on you. Gasping for air you eventually relinquish the fight and surrender to its mercy as the breath is slowly sucked from your lungs.

Long before I realized there were actually people who shared their grief strategies online, I'd already discovered my own steps through disaster. I learned these symptoms by suffering each and every ailment with their intense side effects. The internet lists five main levels of grief: denial, anger, guilt, depression, and acceptance. I'm assuming this is based on factual occurrences and not some calculated theory. I've discovered my most valuable information on the subject from others who closely identified with the same devastation. Some people may have suffered fewer or more categories than these five, and others may have endured different degrees altogether.

Through *my* journey, there are three stages that I've come to know, each of which has brought me to my knees eventually, begging for mercy. The first one is wanting nothing. When you're at the beginning of pain and grief, there isn't anything you want, because nothing can take the place of that profound emptiness in the *very* pit of your soul. It's as if your body shuts down, and the only desire you have is to have your loved one back. The activities you used to love or do no longer bring you pleasure. You go without food for proper nourishment. There were days I would *forget* to eat. My mind consumed with the desire to have Justin back in our lives took precedence over every other thing. I denied myself to others and resisted their attempts to engage me. My unrealistic ideas to bring healing were inadvertently destroying my will to live, and isolating me from the ones who could help stop the emptiness.

Stage two begins when, after some time, the desire to have your loved one back becomes even greater, and you go from wanting nothing to wanting everything. That need causes you to want anything that will fill the huge hole your loved one once occupied in your life and in your heart. You try to replinish it with other things such as spending time on the computer or smartphone, watching TV, working endless hours at work or home. Often times we try to compensate by overeating, perhaps drinking or drugs, purchasing items you don't really need--you indulge in anything and everything to excess in an effort to smother the desperate deprivation you have deep within you, but it's to no avail. If anything, the "stuff" makes you feel even emptier because your loved one isn't there to enjoy or share it with you. The "debt" you acquire from trying to fill a bottomless pit is astounding and causes anxiety and stress to move to a deeper level. The thrill you achieve is minuscule and unsatisfying, so you then continue with the next activity, then another, and another, but total fulfillment is never within reach. These techniques mask the real issue & you are left emptier than before, void of any happiness from your selfish acts and stuck in a vicious cycle you created all on your own. Your self-prescribed remedy for healing becomes your demise. These survival techniques become addictions in one way or another. Some of the awful habits may seem to be more socially acceptable than others, but none replace God's antidote for healing the hurt, the hole, and the hunger. Although this took me some time to realize, I knew that nothing apart from God could meet my desire to be made whole. If you are empty, broken and incomplete, God came to bring hope and healing. People may not judge you as harshly if you are a shopaholic as they do if you are an alcoholic or a routine drug user. We often judge what is wrong based on our own perception and degree of severity; we think if it's only a *little* offense it's okay. God looks at each transgression the same in that they *all* separate us from Him. First, we must recognize the problem before we can receive a solution. When we attempt to find complacency or satisfaction from a substance other than God, we offend His ability to satisfy. I've often said, "Trying to heal your broken heart with anything other than God is like trying to put a bandage on cancer; it won't work!" I have come to know that God is jealous in that He desires to be the One to meet each of our needs; seeking for us to let Him fill all our lonely, vacant places. *"For thou shalt worship no other god: for the Lord, whose name is Jealous, is a jealous God." (Exodus 34:14 KJV)*

At times, we've all relied on others to plug up the huge void in our lives, but I've learned through the experience of losing Justin that I can no longer depend on others to meet the needs only God can fulfill. When we expect others to complete us or make us happy, it's a very unfair, selfish tactic to get our needs met. For so many years if everything was going well, my kids were happy, and my husband was performing as I thought he should, I reveled in a place that I thought was paradise on earth, when in fact that kind of luxury was only a counterfeit substitute. If we're looking to others to soothe our yearning desire to be made whole, lacking nothing, we'll always be dissatisfied, left with a hunger only God can sustain. To put it simply, if we experience contentment *only* when everything and everyone around us are preforming perfectly to our standards, we'll have very few moments of uninhibited happiness. What we must realize is something my dad used to say, "We all have a huge 'Jesus hole' inside of us and the only thing that can fill it is *Him.*" I've come to find that statement undeniably true. The only real prescription that will quench the thirst of your longing is to deepen your relationship with Jesus and trust His love to insulate all the gaps in your life.

The third stage on your road to recovery and restoration is

learning to be satisfied and to remember that it's not what you do *not* have but what you *do* have that will bring you back to a place of serenity. *"The Lord is my shepherd; I shall not want." (Psalm 23:1 KJV)* I have a dear friend who has no children and once asked me if I would have had children if I'd known that one day I would lose one of them. Would I be willing to go through all the grief and torture of losing my son for that chance to be his mom? It was with the loudest voice that I exclaimed, "YES!" Had I known the moment the doctor laid this tiny, blue-eyed, precious bundle of love in my arms, there would come a day, twenty years, five months and two days later when I would have to give him back, my answer to be his mother, still to this day six and one half years later, would be a resounding "YES," although with tear-filled eyes from a shattered heart. The day each of my sons was born I could not comprehend how such a small living, breathing creation could take up the biggest space in my heart. Having the courage to love is great, but greater still would be the boldness to do it knowing you would one day have that passion ripped from your soul, leaving the most extreme pain and emptiness that only God could rehabilitate.

Having one more day would only cause me to want one *more* day, then another, and another. *One* more day would at the same time be too much and never enough. The pain is far too intense for me to think I could ever endure it again. So today I choose to be satisfied for the priceless memories that can never be taken away. When tomorrow comes I will again have to commit to that statement and the next day, and day after that, until the ache inside subsides. All my life I've heard people say things like "when I get this," or "when I get that, then I'll be happy;" "if this happens," or "if that happens, then I'll be satisfied." The problem is that there's always going to be something else waiting around the corner to throw us off course. The best thing we can do is find a way to live each day with as much enthusiasm we can muster, because tomorrow may never come. We wouldn't want to look back over our time on earth and see how blessed we were and, yet never took the time to enjoy it to the fullest. We also don't want to be plagued by worries of things that may perhaps happen so that we have regrets because we let the "what if's" and the "maybe's" rob us. Several years ago, I heard a pastor say there are only two "for-sure" days and they'll be forever remembered because they're set in stone. One is the day we're born, and the other is the day we die. What matters most is what we do with space in between. Life is often not what we expected or planned it to be, as I've explained throughout this entire book. For that reason, it's necessary to make a decision to add more life to your living rather than just numbers to your years. A butterfly in all its beauty is given only days, *not* years, to live. With all the struggles of its transformation process, through all the changes it must endure, the life it has is spent fluttering about aimlessly enjoying all the moments it can partake of to the very end. We must make the most of the time we're given, we need to live life on purpose with lots of life in our living; because in a split second, one late night knock at your door can change everything. My dad used to remind his congregation every week that we are only one heartbeat away from leaving this world and waking up in another.

So, for now, I'll do my very best to live each day to its fullest potential, enjoying my family here and striving to make beneficial use of my time. Trying my hardest to encourage those God places in my path, I will wait patiently for that day I'll see my son again, and there will be no more tears, no more pain, no more sorrow. The best part will never be having to say goodbye. What a day that will be and such a glorious sight to finally see my Savior face to face, the One Who died that I could live, and finally to understand all the answers to my many questions; or--will any of that even matter because of the joy that lies ahead when all my concerns fade from memory? As I've said many times, I know God has a perfect plan for each of us, and if we rely wholly on Him we will witness the change as stated in *Isaiah 43:19 KJV: "Behold I will do a new thing; now it shall spring forth; shall ye not know it? I will even make a way in the wilderness, and rivers in the desert."* We all know that any-thing worth having is worth the struggle. I want to encourage you to focus *not* on the pain, but on God's promises for you. Don't let grief keep you bound behind prison bars, separated from your friends and family. Entrust God to lead and guide you to a place of peace and joy that only He can. *"Now the Lord is the Spirit, and where the Spirit of the Lord is, there is freedom." (2 Corinthians 3:17 ESV)*

Chapter Thirteen
No Greater Love

It seems only fitting that since this book has a chapter on peace and joy, there should also be one on love. The Bible tells us that *"Greater love hath no man than this, to lay down his life for his friends." (John 15:13 KJV) God* showed us just how much He cherishes us when He unselfishly gave His only begotten Son to die a cruel death on a blood- stained cross for our sins. Jesus died so that through Him we will live eternally in Heaven. How could there be such love for a world that is often filled with hatred, without hope, lost, and dying except for the ultimate sacrifice of God's own Son? I've often said I would never be able to give up one of *my* sons to die even for my best friend, much less someone who made it impossible for me even to like them, so in my finite mind I've wondered how God could do that; but He *did*, for the purpose that even just one single person would come to know Him and be saved. *"For God so loved the world, that He gave His only-begotten Son, that whosoever believeth in Him should not perish but have everlasting life." (John 3:16 KJV)* By believing in God, we have a covenant of eternal life. Although we can never fully comprehend that God loves us unconditionally, we can choose to abide in His great love. Knowing that encourages me to accept the fact He's fighting for us when our hearts are shattered and we lose the will to go on. *"He will be with thee; He will not fail thee, neither forsake thee: fear not, neither be dismayed." (Deuteronomy 31:8 KJV)* God never forces love upon His children; He gives us a free will. If we weren't given the option whether or not to serve God, we would be as robots able to do only as the master commands. Also, no one and nothing can ever separate us from His love: *"No height, nor depth, nor any creature, shall be able to separate us from the love of God, which is in Christ our Lord." (Romans 8:39 KJV)* I'm reminded of how God feels about us as I ponder the Scriptures that tell how Jesus chose to give up His crown and all the comforts of Heaven to come and walk this earth

113

not as a King but as a man, a servant leader willing to die as the ultimate sacrifice for our sins. Wow! His *choice! "But emptied Himself, by taking the form of a servant being born in the likeness of men, And being found in human form, He humbled Himself by becoming obedient to the point of death, even death on a cross." (Philippians 2:7-8 ESV)*

Christ's love for His children far exceeds that which even we as parents could ever comprehend. Also, while many of us would be willing to give up our own lives for our children, Jesus will forever be the ultimate example of the greatest display of affection when He hung on a cross and died for *His* children. The feelings that God has for us continues to this day to defy all my natural understanding, that someone could think so highly of me that He would be willing to sacrifice His own life so that I could be forgiven every sin I've committed or will ever commit in the future. His redeeming love paid our sin debt so that we could live in full-scale freedom. As a Christian, my goal is to love others with the same kind of love my Savior has for me. I'll continue striving to push my natural limits, to love the unlovable, and go above and beyond the call of duty for those I love. Of course, there are times when I do get upset or angry with my family and friends, but I will always, always love them. There are so many times I find myself asking God for the wisdom to make the right choices in every area of my life. I often wonder what Jesus would say and do in "this" or "that" moment, which always helps me to put the situation in perspective and set the mark for my children where God has set it for me, the goal we should all establish as the parenting standard of love. As I've said before, the love I have for my children is far beyond what I could've ever imagined, and I'm sure most parents would agree. There was no book to read or class to take to show me how to love my children. It was an instant reflex as natural as breathing. The very moment the Lord placed each of my sons in my womb, there was an immediate connection, a bond that no one or nothing, no amount of time or distance, not even death could sever.

My boys have always had the unique ability to turn my bad days to good by merely asking for help with something or by taking the time to come in and share their day. It requires only minimal effort on their part to put a smile on my face and positively melt my heart. I'm also always grateful to be included in their many activities. As our heavenly Father desires for us to come to Him in our time of need, I've always wanted to have that same relationship with my sons. I remember one day Justin was working on one of his many car projects and came in to ask for help as he had done many times in the past. He was using spray adhesive and fabric to give the hood of his car a new look. I remember it well because it was a smiley-face fabric which reminded him of the song he loved by Uncle Kracker, "You Make Me Smile." To this day, whenever I hear that song it immediately brings a mix of tears, smiles, sadness, and gladness as I recall the special memories I will forever hold in my heart. Justin was having issues with spraying the glue and smoothing out the material at the same time. Of course, I would never say, "No," even if I questioned why he would want to do such a thing, because, knowing him as I did, I was sure he'd have done it with or without help; and there was no way I was going to miss out on that valuable quality time! I will have to agree the car did look rather good when we were all finished, and I felt so blessed for the brief moments I was able to share with him. As this was one of the last times I would get to help him with a project, I do so cherish that memory in the depths of my being.

On one of my birthday mornings, when my husband told me, "Happy birthday," I replied, "Thanks, Honey!" *Although,* when Caleb, our youngest, remembered it was my birthday, I was elated! He was so excited to give me a gift and a card he had picked out all by himself. As my husband stood there questioning my excitement as to why that same joy had not been expressed when *he* wished me a happy birthday, I explained, "It's because Caleb seldom remembers, and you never forget." As I went on and on about the card and the gift, Barry jokingly replied "It was *my* money he used to buy the stuff." I told him it didn't matter to me who paid; I was just thankful he and Caleb cared. Jacob also has gift giving moments; one year for Mother's Day he had a card with money inside waiting for me laying on the kitchen table. I told him how much I appreciated it but wished he would keep it to get himself something; he said "Mom, you deserve something nice; spend it *all* on yourself." On the holidays Justin always insisted I go help him shop to pick out gifts for the ones on his shopping list. It only took one time to know the real reason he needed my help was to make sure he picked something that I really liked. He paid careful attention to what I looked at and then returned later to purchase whatever it was and give it to me as a gift. I love and appreciate Barry immensely, and thankfully he understands the relationship I have with the boys. He knows it's the little things that can bring my heart the greatest joy, mostly, because the moments are so few and far between with them. My boys are older now, becoming young men, and I've discovered they need me less and less, which is the proper order of life but still hard to accept.

As a Christian parent, I desire to make God's example of unconditional love a reality in my life. We don't deserve, neither can we earn this free gift from God. So many times, *our* love is based on the actions of others, and often those who do the most for us are more loved. We base our value so highly on what someone else thinks of us without even realizing that God loves us no matter what--when we *do* right, when we *believe* we do right, and when we completely mess up everything. That's not to say we should go about purposefully doing wrong because of the infinite grace and mercy He freely gives. It plainly means that our sins won't ever affect the degree of His love for us. Never has there been a time when I've done wrong that God has not forgiven me or that He has held my sins against me. By far His greatest display of love for us came when He gave His Son to die for our sins. *"But God clearly shows and proves His own love for us, by the fact that while we were still sinners, Christ died for us." (Romans 5:8 AMP)* Other than for my three sons, I know without a doubt that I would never want to pay the price for the crimes someone else committed. How many of you would agree with me on that one? When I think of and experience such great love, I believe it causes me to come to a more in-depth understanding of its real meaning and makes me want to be better, to love more, and yes, and to forgive always. How can we ever say someone doesn't deserve our forgiveness when we could never repay the bill Jesus settled for all the wrongs *we* have ever done? *"For if you forgive men their trespasses, your heavenly Father will forgive you."* *(Matthew 6:14 KJV)*

I will never ever forget the day I was forced to live that particular Scripture out in real life. We live far out in a rural community, there are very few people who live close by. We rarely have extra time on our hands to visit with others and take the opportunity only if we had a reason for doing so. One unusual day we had the chance to meet several of our neighbors when our adventurous Siberian-Husky, Willow, went on an unsupervised hiatus. I loaded the boys up in the car after spending hours searching the woods around our house. We went knocking on every door having no luck at all locating our beloved furry friend. The last person we asked suggested we go to the house at the end of the road. They were certain that if he didn't have him he would more than likely know where he might be, because he'd been known to shoot dogs if they were anywhere near his property. He added, that we had better pray our animal hadn't met a similar fate. We arrived at the man's house, and when he came to the door, my oldest son began to tell him about his dog disappearing, what he looked like, and asked if he had seen him. The man said he had not, but would be happy to help us in our search.

We quickly accepted his offer and looked everywhere until darkness fell upon us and we immediately called it a day. We were so heartbroken over the loss of our dog that we didn't get much sleep that night. Morning came, and we received a call from the neighbor who had helped us look for Willow. He said he was in a barn beside his house. Had I known then what I know now, I would have been more inquisitive about *how* Willow ended up in this man's barn. We quickly jumped into the truck and went to retrieve our dog. As Justin and I went down the driveway, he told me he sure was glad that his dog was finally found. I agreed with him and explained that was exactly how *I* felt every time *he* came home safe after a night of being gone without telling me the night before that he would *not* be home. He looked at me and said, "Mom I was scared we wouldn't find him," and I replied, "I know. It's no fun having to worry about someone you love, is it?" He answered, "No, it sure isn't." All ended well that day, and the man and his family seemed to make instant friends with our family and even spent some time at our house over the Christmas holidays that year. Soon Justin began to help him with odd jobs around his house.

All seemed to be going fine until Justin came home one day and said he was going to move into the man's house. He'd promised to give him a job if he would come to live there. Since we'd been going through everyday struggles with the dilemmas of kids growing up and Justin's wanting to do as he pleased and have no rules, regulations, or consequences, the offer to live with this man's family seemed appealing to him. Of course, even though Justin was determined to move out, Barry and I didn't think it was such a good idea. My mind gained encouragment from the Scripture: *"Train up a child in the way he should go; even when he is old, he will not depart from it." (Proverbs 22:6 ESV)* I took comfort in knowing that all of Justin's life we always tried to raise him as best we could to do what was right. Now I was unwilling having to put the that teaching to the test. I didn't trust this man or his motives but I knew for a fact my son was a reliable young man, I believed he was responsible and would do what was honorable. Every parent desires for their children to follow the staight and narrow path in life. We should never try to force them or beat them over the head with our beloved Bible, but encourage them to go in the right direction. The word "train" means to manipulate as to bring into desired form, position, or direction. For example, farmers use a distinct method of feeding young calves when they are weaning them from nursing.

They often use a bottle with the tip coated with syrup or honey to entice the young calf to drink the substitute milk. We need to motivate our children lovingly, so they'll not be adverse to following the proper path. If we make doing good *appealing*, it will be attractive and cause them to want to do good.

When the neighbor arrived at the house to get our son, I met him at the door and informed him in a not-so-friendly tone that he needed to mind his own affairs and not make our son his business. He seemed shocked by my actions as to be honest so was I, needless to say the man left and Justin stayed. As I began to replay the confrontation over in my mind, I felt terrible, embarrassed that I'd let my rotten attitude get the best of me. *"If I speak with the tongues of men and of angels but have not love then I have become only a noisy gong or a clanging cymbal. {just an annoying distraction}"* (1 Corinthians 13-1 AMP) Things were never the same after we had that naughty "neighborly" run-in. Justin soon learned that room and board was all he'd receive as payment for the work done, and that wouldn't put gas in his Honda Civic, so thankfully it didn't take him long to decide that was not the most profitable plan for his life. It was during times like this my son was becoming a mature adult, striving to make wise choices. I had confused his disobedience with the fact he was developing his wings and beginning to fly. I was trying to take control of things he was meant to learn through natural consequences, which is a mistake we often make as parents. We try so hard to shelter our children from harm, having no regard for the fact that sometimes it's more effective if they learn things by circumstance rather than our telling them, and *yes*, sometimes they have to learn the hard way. I can still hear my father telling me that it was his job to keep me from going through the "mud-holes" in life, to which I always responded, "I'll learn things my own way." Justin, too, was learning his personal life lessons. I now understand what my father already knew. It hurts deeply for parents to see their children go through challenging times that could have easily been avoided had they heeded loving parental warnings.

Justin settled down and things seemed to be going well, but relations with the neighbor appeared to take an evil twist. One morning sometime after the negative run-in, I let our dog go outside, after being gone a short time he returned and was limping and yelping the most extreme pain-filled sounds I'd ever heard. I screamed for Justin, who nearly broke his neck scrambling up the stairs from his basement apartment. He yelled, "What's wrong?" I told him about Willow, and we looked him over as best he would permit us to, finding only a few drops of blood near his chest area. He couldn't walk without a tremendous amount of discomfort, so I asked Justin and Courtney to load him up in the truck and hurry with him to the vet. As they got ready, I told them I'd stay to keep watch over Skylar, Courtney's daughter.

Time seemed to drag on as "Sky" and I tried to keep busy. We played around in the backyard, and when she found my rain boots sitting at the back door, she climbed right into them. Her antics made me laugh because she was so little that the boots came up high enough on her legs that she had to walk stiffley legged like a mummy, unable to bend at the knee. That didn't matter to her; she was determined to wear them anyway. She clomped around as best she could with me following close to catch her if she was about to fall. This adorable little girl with sparkling blue eyes has the unique ability to make me smile when all I want to do is cry. To this day, she and her mother hold a special place in my heart and always will.

Eventually, the phone rang, and it was Justin saying that Willow had been shot, the vet was going to remove the bullet, and he'd let me know more as he learned the details. I picked Sky up, and held her tightly; we began to pray that Willow would be okay, as I know God is concerned with every care we have. Moments later Justin called again to say the bullet missed Willow's heart by only a few inches but that he would be okay. I immediately hung up the phone, called the neighbor, and asked if, in fact, he'd tried to kill our dog? He responded, "No I didn't shoot your dog, but if I did, I would say I did." The question came to mind as to *how* did he know that our

120

dog had been shot if he didn't play a role?

Later another neighbor called, asking if our dog was alright. I asked her, "How did you know that something might be wrong with Willow?" She then began to explain that the suspected neighbor had recently told her he'd seen the dog near her house and asked if she wanted him to kill it. She said not to hurt the dog, that he never *bothered* anything. Apparently, the man took matters into his own hands and shot our dog anyway. How can a person be so bitter and brutal? Knowing Willow meant no harm and was causing no problems for *him*, why would he want to injure him? When Justin made it home, I told him what had happened, and he sat beside me while we called the man back to let him know that we knew he'd tried to kill our dog. Again, he denied it, but I felt compelled to tell him anyway that I forgave him, to which he made a rude comment and quickly hung up the phone. Being a Christian, I knew I had to forgive this man even if he didn't "deserve" it or ask for it. I know *I* will never be deserving of God's unmerited favor and grace, which He freely gives me every time whether I ask for it or not. *"And be ye kind one to another, tenderhearted, forgiving one another, even as God for Christ's sake hath forgiven you." (Ephesians 4:32 KJV)* Even though I harbor no anger or bitterness towards this man, from that day on I've always tried to avoid him and looked straight ahead trying not to notice him when we had to pass his house daily going to and from home. Although I *do* forgive him for his wrongdoing, it's still a difficult memory to escape.

Months went by, and we all assumed our problems were over and done with; we thought that if we left the man alone, he would return the favor. However, one day while I was shopping, Justin called to say the man had shot at him from his front porch as Justin drove past on his way into town. I asked him if he was serious, and he said, "Mom, I saw him and heard the shots as I hurried past his house." In shock from what I'd been told, I hung up and called my husband and recounted what had happened. He and my dad went down to the man's house, but he wouldn't come to the door. How could a man with the guts to shoot a gun at a car not have the courage to answer for his actions? Eventually, they decided they weren't getting anywhere and went on their way. I called Justin back and recommended he come home a different route and avoid any contact with our not-so-friendly neighbor, to put it *mildly*.

The Bible commands us to love our enemies and to pray for those who use, abuse, and curse us: *"But I say unto you which hear, love your enemies, and do good to them which hate you." (Luke 6:27 ESV)* It's spoken even more vividly in *Matthew 5:44 KJV: "But I say unto you, love your enemies, bless them that curse you, do good to them that hate you, and pray for them which despitefully use you, and persecute you."* What difficulty or reward is there in loving only the ones who care about *us*? *"For if you love those who love you, what reward you have? Do not the tax collectors do the same?" (Matthew 5:46 ESV)* It's far greater to show love to people who may never return it. After all, isn't that how Jesus behaved? He went along pursuing the very ones who set out to destroy His life by hanging Him on a cross to die a harsh, undeserving death.

While pondering that Scripture, trying to grasp what it truly means to love your enemies, I remember a time when I found myself on a narrow, steep, spiraling road of getting yet another assignment from the Master. A few weeks after the accident, this same mean-spirited neighbor phoned to let me know he had my son's hat and asked if I'd like to have it back. Justin must have forgotten it when he left after helping the man with some work around his house. I quickly responded, "YES!" I could hardly contain my eagerness as I waited for his response. He told me that he would let me know when I could come by and retrieve it. I waited several days for him to call back, but he never did. I grew impatient, so I picked up the phone and called him. He answered and informed me in a very harsh tone of voice that he would let me know when and where I could get the hat. I pleaded with him, explaining that I was eager to get it back, as I no longer had my son and it was ever so important to have as mementos the things which had once been special to him.

They were the only things I had left and were rare, priceless keepsakes. His voice angrily responded to my plea, "You will get the damn hat when I say you can!" My heart began to beat very fast and hard inside my chest as I felt the bitterness trying to grow; my mouth was dry, and my throat began to swell shut; I was having trouble breathing. My stress-filled anxiety fueled my fury and was getting the better of me. I couldn't understand all the anger and hatred in this man's voice. After all, *he* was the one who had reached out to me with the suggestion of giving it back. Why had he become so angry, especially after all our family had just endured with the loss of our son? My mind and my heart couldn't understand the man's actions as none of it made any sense.

I continued to call him several more times, but he became increasingly angry. Since he'd previously offered to give my son's hat back, I felt that maybe with all of the things that had gone wrong this was his way of making peace. So, if that were true, why was he so annoyed when I attempted to get the hat? Determined not to give up, I called and asked as kindly as I knew how for him just to place the hat somewhere I could find it please, and that I wouldn't bother him again. I suggested he put it on the porch, hang it on a fence post, or put it on the grass beside the road near his house. I was so desperate to have that hat and was trying to make it as uncomplicated as possible for him. To my fervent plea, he responded, "I don't have your damn hat; I burned it!" I was speechless and don't have any memory of what happened next. I can only venture a guess that I just hung up the phone. Afterward, I remember my sister calling me, and from my broken voice and scattered words, she knew something was wrong. I was eventually able to explain what had happened, and moments after she hung up there was a knock at my door, immediately followed by another call from her informing me the police would be coming so I could file a complaint against the neighbor for harassment. A brief time later there was a knock at my door. I opened it to see my officer friend from the night of the accident. I tried to explain to him that it wasn't necessary to seek to do anything. My feelings were hurt and I didn't understand, but I'd already been through the greatest loss any mother could ever sustain, so this man's actions were nothing compared to what I'd already encountered. How could what he was doing hurt me any more than that? He assured me that he would handle the situation and insisted I tell him what was going on. As I began to share the events leading up to that day, he listened intently and assured me that he *would* return with my son's hat. He stayed gone for some time, but came back with a smile and placed the hat in my hands. It had not been harmed in any way; the cruel-hearted man had not burned it but was only being mean and vengeful, for what reasons I still do not know. I will always be thankful for my officer friend, who was so kind and took such care in making sure to soothe this mother's grieving heart.

So, I know you must wonder, "You're able to forgive *that* merciless man for trying to cause you unnecessary grief, and if so, *how* did you do it?" My answer is "YES!" By the grace of God, I do pardon him for every one of the awful things he sought to do to me. *"Love never fails." (1 Corinthians 13:8)* That's how it's possible for us always, no matter what, to love the unlovable. No man or woman will never steal my joy because I will not permit it to happen. If someone is seeking to destroy you why allow them to get the utter hand and cause you to lose your composure? I choose not to be influenced by others' opinions or actions. My confidence is found in God not in man. That torturous trial will not cause me to miss heaven by creating bitterness and letting unforgiveness ravage my heart. We must all make a conscious decision never to let anyone deprive us of our contentment. Along these lines, I've made a choice not to be easily offended. *"Forbearing one another, and forgiving one another, if any man have a quarrel against any; even as Christ forgave you, so also do ye." (Colossians 3:13 KJV)* If I don't permit it, I won't be swayed in the wrong direction and lose my zest for living in harmony with all kinds of people. I encourage you to be emphatically motivated by love in all you say and do, expecting nothing in return, and you can most assuredly know that everything done with a pure heart will work out for your good and God's glory. I learned a long time ago that there will always be people who will come along and try to aggravate and discourage us, but it's *our* choice not to give permission for them to affect us by infecting our happiness with their needless, unwanted, undeserved malice. It has often been said that our trials are necessary and that they come to reveal our *true* character. God teaches us through His word that He's making us into His image. *"We all, with unveiled faces, are looking as in a mirror at the glory of the Lord and are being transformed into the same image from glory to glory; this is from the Lord Who is the Spirit." (2 Corinthians 3:18 HCSB)* What does your countenance look like when you're placed in the middle of difficulty or strife? Does your attitude resemble the God you serve? Would anyone recognize you as a representative for Christ? I've often heard it said, "What is in you will often come out when you're pressed up against a wall with no way of escape." Trust me, I know it's not an easy path we're called to walk. My husband always says that if we resemble or mimic the world, how will we become unique, as God has called us to be? *"But ye are a chosen generation, a royal priesthood, a holy nation, a peculiar people; that ye should shew forth the praises of Him Who hath called you out of darkness into His marvelous light." (1Peter 2:9 KJV)* In this life, we sometimes walk through unprovoked trials--those that are due to nothing we did or didn't do, but we serve a God Who will refine us as pure gold, and we'll never even have to smell like smoke from the fire we've experienced. *"That the trial of your faith, being much more precious than of gold that perisheth, though it be tried with fire, might be found unto praise and honor and glory at the appearing of Jesus Christ." (1 Peter 1:7 KJV)*

In the Bible we're reminded of pure, unyielding, unselfish love time and time again. One of my favorite stories speaks of two ladies, each with a newly delivered son. During the night, one of the mothers found her little one had died when she unknowingly rolled over during the night onto the newborn. She immediately took the life-less infant into her arms, placed it in the bed of the other mother, and took that woman's sleeping child as her own. You can imagine the anguish and confusion experienced the next morning when the healthy baby's mother tried to wake up the deceased angel lying there in place of the child that belonged to her! She had no idea how or why the other woman's son lay dead in place of hers. The two ladies began arguing, each insisting that the precious bundle full of life was hers. The rightful mother had an idea of how to settle the dispute. She demanded they take before the king the infant she knew without a doubt belonged to her and have him decide which woman was the biological mother. I'm certain the deceitful mother began to come up with a million reasons why this was not a prom-ising idea, knowing that she had tried to trick her naive roommate and would surely be found out if the king got involved. I can only imagine that with much coaxing and pressure, she had no choice but to take a chance, in the hope of winning the baby as her own. When the two approached the king's throne, each pleaded her case, and the king came up with a solution as to how to determine the actual birth mother of this infant. As he took the little boy, he drew out a sword and said he would settle this argument once and for all. He then proclaimed that he would cut the baby in half so that way each of them could have him. When the real mother of the boy heard his idea, she screamed out of the depths of her heart, "NO! Let her have my son." The other woman then replied, "Let him not be mine or yours, but divide him!!" WHAT? How could she be so cruel as to suggest the tiny newborn be severed in half? She had just tasted the punishing stab of the death of her own child; how could she in re-turn want to also heap unrelenting grief upon another? The sinister woman was prepared to let her unselfish, compassionate friend suf-fer the greatest pain, so she could reap from a love she didn't de-serve. That kind of evil is incomprehensible to me. There was no longer any doubt in the king's mind as to which mother the child legitimately belonged--the one willing to give the child up so that he could live. A pure heart is always willing to let go for the good of someone else, even when it means walking through unbearable grief on their part. Just as Jesus died a cruel death on the cross due to no sin of His own, we should spare others pain even if indeed it causes undeserved strife upon ourselves. (This Scripture reference is paraphrased from the book of *1Kings 3:16-28 KJV*)

Chapter Fourteen
My Father's Heart

While working in the yard one day, I received a call from my dad. He said in a rather calm voice, "Alisa, I need you to come quickly and take me to the emergency room." I dropped what I was doing and immediately rushed to pick him up from his house, which is within sight down the driveway from our own. Some time ago my dad had purchased the property and split it evenly among himself, my sister, and me. The plan was for each of us to build there so we would always be close, which was an excellent idea, especially on this day when my dad needed immediate help. I was thankful I could be there in a matter of minutes. When I arrived, and jumped out of my car to help him, he said, "Are you taking me dressed like that?" Typically, this type of banter would have hurt my feelings, as I thought a hat, sweatshirt and pants qualified for the adequate attire for an unplanned hospital visit! After all, how many trips to the emergency room are anticipated so that you can be sure to be properly dressed? His humor brought relief to my heart; I knew that if he still had his creative sarcasm intact, he was going to be just fine. All kidding aside, I knew he must have felt gravely ill for him to ask me to take him to the hospital since he avoided going to doctors in general. He always said, "They never find out anything wrong with me, so *why* should I go?"

As I drove hurriedly down the road, I began to ask him details of what was going on that prompted him to call me. He described the symptoms that to me sounded like a heart attack. I grew more concerned about my dad as he shared the details of what he was feeling. He'd had a lot of issues with his heart before, and cardiac disease related problems had been present on his side of the family.

He remained calm, and we finally arrived at the emergency room entrance. They immediately took him back and began running tests. I sat in the waiting room making phone calls to family members, asking for prayer for my dad. A brief time later, my mom and sister arrived, and I filled them in on the details. When we were finally invited in to see him, he was resting calmly but said he was in a great amount of pain. The doctors assured us they were doing all the appropriate tests to find out if, in fact, he was experiencing a heart attack.

After the results had come in, the doctor entered the room and assured us that my dad had not had a heart attack or a stroke. They said the blood work showed no signs there was anything causing the issues he was having, once again proving that dad, in fact, was right in his beliefs that they never find anything wrong with him. That made no sense at all to us. We knew that if he had decided to go to the emergency room for help in the first place, there had to be something significantly wrong. The doctors decided it best to keep him overnight for observation. We agreed because we all knew there had to be something going on that initiated the tremendous pain episode. Looking back, it seemed that for a while he'd been having issues one way or another with shortness of breath and chest pain. All we could do was hope and pray the overnight stay would give them time to search deeper and be able to find the cause of his debilitating distress.

There were several doctors involved, and as they began to leave the room, I was able to intercept one of them and have a private conversation with her in the hallway. I felt I had to make a plea to encourage her to dig deeper and try harder to find the source of this incident. I began to explain to her about the loss of my son, Justin, and told her that having him was a special blessing for my dad, as he had always wanted a boy himself and had been very close to his firstborn grandson. I remember my mom showing me how she wrote in my baby book the first words my father spoke after I was born: "Are you sure it's a girl?" As I recall he had the very same reaction when my little sister was born. I used to joke with him that when Amy and I were younger, he kept our hair cut short and raised us as "tom-boys" because, I assume, he wanted us to look and act like boys instead of girls. Since I was bald until the age of three, he nicknamed me "Slick," and my sister was called "Buffy," because she did in fact have enough golden locks for two side ponytails, begging the question "Why not call her "Goldie-locks?" The short hair came into play when I eventually had some to trim. Knowing my dad's desire, I was very thankful that God blessed me with sons so that my dad was finally able to experience the joy of boys.

Justin had an unusual name for his grandfather; he always called him "Buck-A." No one in our family has ever been able to figure out why, but that didn't matter to my dad who seemed to enjoy the title Justin had chosen for him and wore it with extraordinary pride. I always believed it was because he was trying to pronounce "Buddy." Dad always called Justin his "little buddy" so I assumed Justin concluded my dad was his "big buddy." He often said he liked the nickname because he was the only one he knew ever to be called by this title. He said if Justin hollered out in a crowd of a thousand grandfathers, he would always be the only "Buck-A" to answer. It was distinct and unique, as was their special bond, which I tried to explain to the doctor, and that I was convinced his health problems intensified with the loss of his firstborn grandson. I told her that everyone in our family hurt and their healing was at different degrees and levels, but that Dad seemed to have had a great deal more difficulty rebounding from the loss, which was evident to each of us as we noticed his health continuing in a dreadful, downward spiral.

I felt as if the doctor cared about what I had to say and listened with compassion as I told her about my father. Although she had a doctor's degree and knew far more than I ever would, she treated me with respect, and paid close attention, showing a vast amount of interest in what I had to say. With tears filling my eyes and spilling onto my face, I explained to her that there was no way possible that something wasn't physically wrong with my dad. He'd been to numerous doctors since Justin's death, and they'd all done many tests and hadn't been able to come up with an explanation as to why he felt so poorly. I explained how he despised those trips and that because he'd instigated coming this time, it was evidence of a plea for

130

help due to a considerable amount of pain. I told her I felt my dad's heart had been extensively broken since I knew all too well the symptoms of that condition. I, too, was trying my best to recover from the immense, constant, and at times unbearable pain of losing Justin.

She responded with words I can still hear to this day. She told me there was, in fact, a "real" medical condition caused by a broken heart. The doctor said it was called "broken heart syndrome," "stress-induced cardiomyopathy," or "Takotsubo cardiomyopathy," and is brought on by a surge of stress hormones which happens after an emotionally stressful event such as the loss of a loved one. It's often diagnosed as a heart attack because it has some of the same symptoms. In the case of "broken heart syndrome," a part of the heart temporarily enlarges and does not pump the blood properly while the rest of the heart functions normally or with even more forceful contractions.

Finally, an answer! I was overcome with relief and had sincere gratitude for the doctor who took the time to listen to my heart and give me insight into what was going on with my dad's health. We now finally had a possible, specific answer for his continual discomfort. The words she spoke finally confirmed that what we had experienced with the shortness of breath and heaviness in our hearts as if a thousand-pound boulder lay on our chests, was indeed a real "doctor's term" used to describe a legitimate condition, complete with official medical terminology and list of painful symptoms. His heart, in fact, was possibly physically shattered and broken, just as I had felt mine was the night I learned of my son's death.

With the knowledge she imparted, I posed the question, "What can be done about it?" She assured me she would speak with some of her colleagues and together they would find the definite source of my dad's health issues, so he could receive the help he had so earnestly been seeking. At that moment, I had increased hope that he was finally going to get some relief from the pain he'd been carrying so long. I stepped back into the room and shared with my father what I'd learned. I told him they were determined to search for and find plausible answers to help him feel better.

The next day after running more tests, the doctor met with us and said they were going to do some exploratory surgery to see what it would reveal. For what seemed like hours, we waited quietly, and prayed God would protect, hold, and keep my dad. I rested in the assurance that God was in complete control of everything and that He had a perfect plan for each of us. I knew my dad had no fear of death and often said he knew where he was going and that it's a far better place than this earth. He even went as far as to say, "I'm okay if I go and I'm okay if I stay, but *if* I stay, I would like to feel better." I always responded by saying, "I can understand that, Dad, but if possible, we would love it if you stayed as long as you can here with us." The assurance of my dad's salvation proved to us that whatever God had planned for him, we were in complete agreement with *his* Father.

There are times I've thought that in dying we could all be spared from dealing with the pain and grief of losing Justin *if* we could just join him in Heaven. Dad certainly would be willing to win the race, beating us all there so he could be the first one able to see Justin again. I felt my faith begin to rise, I was not concerned as much as maybe I should have been about the outcome of the surgery. I was placing all my confidence in my Father to restore dad, refusing to walk in fear. I rested completely assured that if God were not going to call him home, then He would heal him and work His plan through all this. He led us to the right doctor who was willing to listen and sympathize with our family enough to push through obstacles to appropriate care.

God had prepared and settled my father's heart to be at peace whatever the outcome might have been and had also increased my faith to trust *Him* no matter what. God truly worked out every detail ahead of time. He always knows precisely what we need and when we need it, even before we are aware there *is* a need. He strategically has each step we will ever take carefully planned out and numbered, and then goes before us to prepare the way. He even leads and guides us walking each mile close beside us. The key to making it through tough times is to have faith that is unshakeable, immovable, and unstoppable.

So much of the time, God's ways are opposite to those of which the world would try to *convince* us. Men say to believe only in what you can visualize or touch, whereas God says to believe in what you *cannot*. *"Now faith is the substance of things hoped for the evidence of things not seen." (Hebrews 11:1 KJV)* It's easy to believe in what your natural senses can observe, but God wants us to have hope and believe in that which isn't discerned physically.

Man's way says to keep all you have; the more you have, the better, right? God's way says, *"It is more blessed to give than to receive." (Acts 20:35 ESV)* God's Word also says the more you give, the more He blesses you. That doesn't pertain only to money, but to everything, whether the need is physical or spiritual. *"Give, and it shall be given unto you. They will pour into your lap a good measure--pressed down, shaken together, and running over {with no space left for more}. For with the standard of measurement you use, {when you do good to others} it will be measured to you in return." (Luke 6:38 AMP)* What you make happen for others God in return will do for you.

As I sat with my family and waited for the doctors to come from my dad's surgery, I didn't worry and fret but rested in the assurance that God held my heart and the heart of my father in His capable, mighty, nail-pierced hands. Whatever the outcome, we would rest in the peace of God that surpasses all-natural understanding. As we walk in the truth of God's Word and when it is fully activated in our lives we can have *all* the fruits of the Spirit working in us. Love, joy, patience, kindness, goodness, faithfulness, gentleness, self-control, all free gifts available for the taking.

There are times I feel great faith and other times I feel as though I barely have any. I'm constantly puzzled by the fact that I feel as if

133

my faith increases when things go according to my prayers and disintegrates when the outcome seems contrary to my expectations. My husband assures me that it is *not* our great faith or the lack thereof that moves or changes things. It's that the faith moves us into a position to receive what God has in store for us. God desires us to believe that He *will* move on our behalf! I am so thankful He requires that we have only a tiny bit of faith. He's not as concerned with the amount, as He is with the fact that we walk in His gift. *"I assure you and most solemnly say to you, if you have {living faith the size of a mustard seed, you will say to this mountain, 'Move from here to there' and {if it is God's will} it will move; and nothing will be impossible for you." (Matthew 17:20 AMP)* Wow! The measure of one, miniscule mustard seed is equivalent to the size of the lead at the end of a pencil. You can barely see it, but when it begins to move over the paper, there is undeniable proof it exists. Surely each of us, even on our hardest, darkest days, can conjure up a mustard-seed size faith. If we but venture out, God will meet us and walk right beside us every step of the way. When the days are hard and seem impossible, that's when I pull from my God His given measure of faith to find the ability to continue my journey. *"God has dealt to every man a measure of faith." (Romans 12:3 KJV)* I've learned through experience to trust Him when times are hard and when times are easy, to call upon Him in times of great need and to praise Him for the battles won.

The doctors came to the waiting room and explained to us that my dad was resting and doing fine. They did discover that he had three major blockages in the arteries leading to his heart. It was entirely possible that had they not gone in and repaired the damage, my dad may not have survived for very much longer. We were all thrilled and thankful that he was going to make it and would finally have some relief from the pain. I give thanks and praise to God for the doctors' knowledge and expertise and for guiding them through the surgery. I know without our being led to the right doctor and her listening to my concerns, he may have quite easily been sent home without further investigation into the source of his painful issues.

I am both blessed and fortunate to have known the love and care of an earthly father, but even greater than that, I have a heavenly Father Who loves without limits. I can honestly say I never completely understood the love my parents had for me until I had children of my own. Many times, we judge God's love for us based on what we know of our earthly father's example. If we have absent fathers, we assume God is too busy to care about our needs. If our earthly fathers are hard to please no matter how hard we try, we often believe God is the same way and thus avoid a relationship with Him, feeling we're never going to be good enough. The truth is that we can never do one thing to earn God's love. He wholeheartedly loves us because God *is* love. Who else could love us no matter what we've done or haven't done? Who else but our heavenly Father would exchange His Own Son's life to redeem us from our sinful nature? I often meditate on the many facets of God's love for us. Why would a God that not only created *all* things and is in complete and total control of *everything*, need me? Absolutely nothing is impossible for Him and yet he loves and wants me, knowing there is nothing I could do for Him other than give Him continual praise for what He has already done, as well as what He will do in the future. *"I will bless the Lord at all times; His praise shall continually be in my mouth." (Psalm 34:1 ESV)* Knowing the Father's heart toward us and being able to walk in His goodness and mercy, makes this journey bearable. It's only when we unequivocally understand that He absolutely, limitlessly, unconditionally loves us we can begin to walk by faith. He's working out a perfect plan for our lives in the valleys as well as on the the highest pinnacle. My heart's desire is to praise Him when I'm going through the dismal, dark, and destitute places as energetically as I celebrate on the magnificiant mountianto.

I pray that if you do not know the heavenly Father's grace, mercy, and unconditional love, you will give Him the opportunity to show you His heart, which is my favorite part of all. I'm very honored, humbled, and privileged that God has given me the priceless blessing of beautiful, loving, kind, and caring natural parents, a gift for which I am eternally thankful. It bears repeating that you may not have been blessed with the perfect father here on this earth, but you *can*, however, find one in a heavenly Father Who longs to be near you, to love you, to hold you, and to keep you from harm. *Psalm 46:1 KJV* promises: *"God is our refuge and strength, a very present help in time of need."*

God knows when we are heartbroken and when our hearts are utterly destroyed--fragmented into a billion pieces. He draws near to those who are crushed, torn apart inside: *"The Lord is near to the heartbroken and He saves those who are crushed in spirit {contrite in heart, truly sorry for their sin.}" (Psalm 34:18 AMP)* The realization that God is especially close to those with a broken heart is a bountiful blessing beyond what mere words could ever describe. God was right there when the doctors operated on my dad's broken heart, and He worked through their hands to heal it. *"Bless the Lord, O my soul, and forget not all His benefits, Who forgives all your iniquity, Who heals all your disease." (Psalm 103:2-3 ESV)*

God continues each day to bind up the wounds of our broken hearts and lives. I'm in awe of His work thus far in my own life. With every day I serve Him, I adore and cherish Him more. He's been my hope when I am hopeless, my strength when I am at my weakest, my faith when I am faithless, and my joy when all I have is sorrow. He's my song in the night, my mercy every morning, and has been my faithful best Friend, closer than any other. He's been my loving, heavenly Father, continuing to love me in *spite* of myself, and even when I don't like *myself*. He stands beside me and is my shelter in every storm. He goes before me preparing my path and is behind me to catch me when I fall. He is the One I live for, the One from Whom I can never live apart, my all in all. Some call Him "Jesus," some call Him "Master," some call Him "Lord," some call Him "Savior;" some call Him "soon-coming King." *I* call Him "Abba Father."

My heart, my life, and my breath I owe to Him. I serve Him because I *want* to, not because I *have* to or because He blesses me. Rather, I am blessed to be able to serve Him because I love Him.

Serving God has been one of the greatest decisions I've ever made in my life. I don't know how I ever was able to survive without Him living inside my heart. I realize now that it was His protection and mercy that I was able to exist. For years I felt so empty and lonely, however, I wasn't ever truly alone; even when I didn't acknowledge Him as our Savior, He stayed faithful. It wasn't until I found Him that I realized how much I needed Him. It hasn't always been easy, but I have no doubt it would have been impossible without Him. I have never regretted or turned back on my choice, even when things haven't gone according to my desires, but have trusted Him through it all. I console myself with the fact that when the things of this earth don't make sense to me, I know *Who* God is and accept by faith that His thoughts and ways are beyond my natural comprehension and that His plans for me are far greater than I could ask, think, or imagine. *"For My thoughts are not your thoughts, neither are your ways My ways, saith the Lord. For as the heavens are higher than the earth, so are My ways higher than your ways, and My thoughts higher than your thoughts." (Isaiah 55:9 KJV)*

Just as my earthly father always provided physical needs for me when I was younger, my heavenly Father provides for me and helps in the areas of my heart where my earthly father can no longer assist. *"Blessed {gratefully praised and adored} be the God and Father of our Lord Jesus Christ, the Father of sympathy and the God of every comfort." (2 Corinthians 1:3 AMP)* I know, just as my earthly father hurts when I do, God also is moved when I come to Him broken, helpless, and needing a hope only He can provide. *"The Lord is gracious and righteous; our God is full of compassion." (Psalm 116:5 NIV)* He knows every tear I cry, and one day I will weep no more. *"For the Lamb which is in the midst of the throne shall feed them, and shall lead them unto living fountains*

of waters, and God will wipe away ALL tears from their eyes."
(Revelation 7:17 KJV) Ironically *that* Scripture and verse is the day and month of my son's death, undeniably another sign from up above that God is speaking to me through His Word, proving once again that He is with me and always will be.

Chapter Fifteen
I'll Try Not to Cry

There comes a time in the healing process when you are very conscious of your tears. In the beginning, you have no control over your emotions, so the tears flow, and you are completely paralyzed even to *try* to stop them. Later, when a bit of time has passed, you feel as though others expect you to restrain yourself. They are resolute in their belief that by now you should be through grieving, so you try to hide your pain and cry only in complete privacy. God knows the tears we shed, whether seen or unseen and desires to turn them into laughter so we can rejoice in the victorious life He's given us. *"Greatly desiring to see thee, being mindful of thy tears, that I may be filled with joy." (2 Timothy 1:4 KJV)*

The tears never go away completely, and some days I must make a conscious decision to refrain from letting them escape. In so many ways, they're a release of the indescribable pain. At other times, they are disguised and masquerade as weakness. I had a beloved family member who tried to ease my mind by reminding me that as I have mentioned before, grief is not a marathon; it's a quest, a search for a better time and place. I've often assumed the amount of time it took to heal depended largely on the depth of your devotion for your dearly loved one. I try not to linger too long on that theory, as it may sentence me to a lifetime of weeping. People who think there's a timeline have never felt the loss of a loved one. Remember, as I said earlier, there is no particular time constraint or way a person *should* act, so I've learned that I must choose not to listen to what others think about where I should or shouldn't be in this process, or what I should or shouldn't do during. Instead, I decided to listen to the voice of the almighty God, to which I've dedicated my life. *"They that sow in tears shall reap in joy." (Psalm 126:5 KJV)* With the number of tears, I've cried thus far, I'm waiting with great expectancy an endless amount of overwhelming joy in my future.

As I've said before, we *must* choose to stay motivated to keep putting one foot in front of the other and refuse to give up. It's imperative to choose happiness, over sadness. That doesn't mean discouragement might not try to come against us, or that, at times, the desire to die doesn't seem to outweigh the will to live. The enemy would love nothing more than to consume us with the desire to quit, so, to oppose *his* plans, we must choose to keep going. Our thoughts and feelings will quickly lead us astray, which is why we cannot rely on them. We must proceed in faith and what we *know*, not by feelings and emotions, or we will forever fight a losing battle. We must believe in what God tells us in His Word: *"And be renewed in the spirit of your mind. And that ye put on the new man, which after God is created in righteousness and true holiness"* (Ephesians 4:23-24 KJV) If we confess that daily, we'll encourage ourselves to keep trying until we make it over, under, or through the mountain, or else it will be leveled to ground level, in Jesus' mighty name. Remember to celebrate the mountain peaks while you can, because, more likely than not, there will be other monumental hills to conquer shortly. The strength you gain with each climb will uphold you on the next perplexing obstacle. The victories we desire may be hard to come by, so we must take the time to celebrate even the smallest ones. When I shed tears all day, I can look back on the days I cried only a little and am encouraged because I know *all* my moments won't be filled with sadness. I can have hope that maybe one day will come when I won't cry at all.

My husband has always said he's grateful God never made the terrain in our lives completely smooth because then we wouldn't have a foothold to get to the next level. God never meant for us to carry the heavy load all alone. He wants us to yoke up with Him so we can make it through our difficulties. *"Take My yoke upon you and lean on me, for I am meek and lowly in heart and ye shall find rest unto your souls. For My yoke is easy and my burden is light."* (Matthew 11:29-30 KJV) He never forces His abilities upon us but gives us the choice of submitting to His assistance to carry the weight of our responsibilities and trials and tragedies. We can rest assured that our stresses and troubles and tribulations are not meant to pull us away from Him, but to draw us closer. He wants us to run *to* Him, knowing without a doubt that He is for you and with us, working everything out for the best beneficial outcome possible. Tests are not intended to destroy us, but to make us stronger. Would we ever manifest productive faith in God or trust Him if we're never faced with situations beyond our control? I believe it is through difficult and sometimes seemingly insurmountable situations that we can grow in our belief in God. He desires that I choose not to cry sad or bitter tears, but be full of joy and gratitude, realizing the choice is up to me. *"May the God of hope fill you with all joy and peace in believing, so that by the power of the Holy Spirit you may abound in hope." (Romans 15:13 ESV)*

I recall several times a day the phrase my son used it is one I have also adopted as my own: "Don't leave weak." I'm reminded of those words when I'm tempted to crawl into a deep, dark hole and refuse to come out until I can wake up from all the grief and disappointment to live in a world where there is no desolation. Then I realize that a pain-free world is available only to those who have gone on before us and that we, as believers, will receive as our reward one day. I ponder that one little three-word sentence, and it encourages me, with God's help, to climb out of the putrid pit I dug for myself and push forward to God's promised, designated finish line. I've often heard that in a race, the most challenging time, when most are ready to give up, is when the end is in sight. I've never run an "official" race or spent much time running at all, but rather enjoy walking to have some form of exercise. However, there *are* times I grow tired after only a little while, so I've learned that if I set small goals for myself that I know I can achieve, I feel a deep sense of accomplishment that inspires me to continue. I'll say to myself, "If I can *just* make it one hundred steps." Then when I've conquered that target, I set for myself another attainable goal of two hundred steps. With *that* one accomplished, I set another, and pretty soon I've reached the destination I thought, in the beginning, was way beyond my reach. I believe this method applies to many areas of our lives. *If* we can just remain determined not to give up, we'll soon be amazed at how far we've come. If something has any substantial worthy value, it's worth the fight to conquer it's worth, this was the example Jesus displayed on the cruel cross which cost Him His life. He loved us to unto death, knowing that we are worth the price His precious blood paid. God Himself looked ahead in time and knew the torture His only begotten Son endured would yield Him a bountiful harvest of sons and daughters that outnumbers the stars in the heavens. I personally believe that the greater the battle, the sweeter the victory. I've personally experienced both, in the natural and in the spiritual realm, that often it's after the darkest night, dawns the most beautiful light.

Many times, I go back in my heart and mind, to the moment I gazed my eyes on my son for the last time on this earth. He was sleeping the most peaceful rest, lying in a intricately detailed, black, wooden box that would be lowered into the ground, and forever shut until the Lord's return when the dead in Christ shall rise. I caressed his cheek trying to memorize every aspect of his face; I bent down to kiss his forehead gently. My heart seemed to fall hard inside my chest. Biting my lip to harness the tears and taking a long, deep breath, I said, "I'll see you again soon, Son."

The funeral director then came and released the hinge to open the bottom part of the casket, so I could see that he'd honored my request to put my pink and green polka dot sock on Justin's right foot and a bright fluorescent floral one from his wife on his left. Justin was always in the habit of "borrowing" my socks and kept the tradition alive when he married Courtney. It seemed natural to continue this custom. I've often wondered what Jesus thought when Justin entered Heaven sporting his colorful fashion.

The director then invited my husband to shut the lid of the casket; I reminded him not to close it tight for both of us were in full agreement that *if* it were God's will, He was more than able to raise him up at that very moment. What a time of rejoicing that would be! To be able to witness a modern-day miracle, seeing the dead come back to life. I must admit I hadn't given up hope that Justin *could* be brought back to life. After all, I had to hold on to my faith because it was all I had left. I lingered for long as I was allowed and then had to relinquish my plan to God's hand. My soul continues to anticipate the day when the dead in Christ will indeed rise! *"In a moment, in the twinkling of an eye, at the last trump: for the trumpet shall sound, and the dead will be raised incorruptible, and we will be changed." (1 Corinthians 15:52 KJV)*

My husband held me tight, as we shared a tear-filled smile and turned to go. We climbed into the limousine waiting outside the funeral home, I experienced a renewed sense of peace in knowing that my strength, power, and hope comes from the Lord and that when I trust in Him, there is absolutely nothing I can't do with His divine help. *"I can do all things through Him Who strengthens me." (Philippians 4:13 ESV)* The truth of this particular verse is power and life if we can apply it to our everyday lives. Realizing that the Greater One lives inside of us equips us to live a happy hopeful life filled with expectancy and excitement which empowers us to make it past any obstacle along life's way.

I remember making my way to the front row of the church and sitting down for my son's memorial service. When someone from behind patted me on the back and handed me a box of tissues, I quickly responded, "No more tears today!" In that moment I gave myself a personal challenge to find a way to control my sadness. If I must cry I will only shed happy tears for all the many blessings I have received and not what was taken away. I made a commitment to myself and to God, when my tears overflow and overwhelm my heart I would take refuge in the Shelter of the Almighty in Whom I place all my confidence. I made a promise to myself and God that I would no longer sob selfish tears in pity or regret, casting blame or feeling guilt, over things that were never in my control. I vowed to never think that I knew what was best for my life. That day I surrendered to God every emotion that was not pleasing to Him and trusted Him with my life to do as He saw fit. As the choir began to sing, "Jesus Loves Me," such peace and love flooded my soul. I closed my eyes and lifted my hands to the heavens, as I yielded my flesh, will, and way to my Jesus. He gently picked me up and lovingly held me as He exchanged my pain for His peace. He traded His innocent, undiluted joy and took in return all my sadness, bitterness and grief. I had nothing of any worth or value and it concerned Him not, He freely gave me a reward that is eternal and priceless. *"Peace I leave with you, my peace I give unto you: not as the world giveth unto you, give I unto you. Let not your heart be troubled, neither let it be afraid (John 14:27 KJV)* Moments later I stood up, not even knowing what I was doing or what was about to happen. Without the ability to stop myself, I was moving from my seat and somehow made it up eight small, narrow steps in three-inch heels without falling, a feat I'm sure I could *not* have gracefully accomplished in the natural. When I stopped, I was standing at the pulpit looking out over a sea of broken people, saddened faces with tears filling every eye. God needed *me* to tell the crowd of people that my son did not die because Jesus didn't love me and that it was not a punishment to our family or Justin's friends that he was no longer with us on earth. God used me to encourage them that He, and He alone, could give them hope, love, joy, and, yes, peace through the death of a dearly loved one. In my heart, I know without a doubt that God does not cause atrocious things to happen to destroy us. Instead, He brings us, as His sons and daughters, peace in the incomprehensible situations to realize a supernatural understanding of *Who* He is and the magnitude of His great power and abundant ability. I know now more than ever before that we need to cling to Him for the will to carry on. My earnest plea that day was to share the same hope that God had given me so that the tragedy we experienced could somehow help others. Perhaps *if* our family and friends gathered there could see that we still had peace and joy even though we had just lost a most precious, priceless gift, then they could realize that in *their* greatest grief and pain, He would deliver them, also, from anything and everything that held them captive—past, present, or future.

Later, as I made my way back to my seat, my husband began to share a message of hope. The Scripture God chose for him to use is found in *Isaiah 61:3 KJV: "To appoint unto them that mourn in Zion, to give them beauty for ashes, the oil of joy for mourning, the garment of praise for the spirit of heaviness; that they might be called trees of righteousness, the planting of the Lord, that He might be glorified."* His message was that only God could take something which has been depleted of any useful substance and create something exquisite. The service atmosphere immediately went from a somber, hopeless time to one of rejoicing, a perfect depiction of how God takes the nothingness of our lives and turns it into a refined treasure. Family and friends who had entered the church doors distraught and in despair left filled with God's love, tranquility, and forgiveness.

We're all called to be ministers of God's Word, and amazingly, my son's death played a huge part in others' having their lives saved and set free. As the altar filled with people of all ages during the closing prayer, it was comforting to know that many lives were forever changed that day, mine maybe the most. For you see, what if *I* were the one in whom God caused the biggest change? What if it were *I* who would have missed Heaven were it not for the departure of my son? Did the thought of never seeing him again increase my motivation to strive for Heaven? Could it not have been enough reward to know that I'd go to heaven to be with Jesus Who died for me and through Whom I have my salvation? Is it possible? It's hard to think that *I* may have been one of the ones left behind at Christ's return. I'm grateful that through *that* revelation, I've put all doubt to rest and will continue to trust my salvation which assures Heaven as my reward, the bonus of which will be seeing Justin again. For now, I know that every day I have, I try my best to live a life pleasing to God. He is my Jesus, the Lover of my soul and the Healer of my hurting heart. He is my Savior and my salvation, He is the One and Only King of Kings and Lord of Lords. Holding onto the knowledge of Who He is and knowing that when I cross over to the other side, I *will* see Jesus makes my life sweeter amidst all the bitterness this life tries to inject. I will enter the gates of that great city where there's no more pain, no tears, no sadness, and no more grief, to share with my son the joy he has come to know. It's longing for that day that sparks me along the path God has chosen for me and not to become worn out, tried, and lazy. So, from now on, I do my best to cry only tears of joy for the happiness I have been privileged to experience instead of sour sobs for the afflictions I've been chosen to endure. May I have the persistence and discipline to continue to run, walk, or crawl until I'm able to complete my course and finally be able to breathe a huge sigh of relief, resting assured that every tear, sleepless night, anguish, and heartache were worth it in the end. *"Commit thy works unto the Lord, and thy thoughts shall be established." (Proverbs 16:3 KJV)*

What a joy and blessing to know that even though he was only twenty years, five months, and two days young, our son was able to reach more lives for Christ during his heavenly home-going than many of us would ever be able to achieve on this earth if we lived to be one hundred. To God be all the glory and honor for remarkable things He has done. Justin was always giving and helpful to those in need. I wonder *if* he had known that by losing his life, other people might be saved, would he have done it without hesitation. I can venture a thought that would not be a choice we could make in the natural realm. There would not be many, myself included, who would be willing to give their lives up for a friend, much less a stranger. If given a choice I would gladly lay down my own life so my sons could live, but this time it wasn't part of God's plan. I continue to trust God's ways are higher and greater than anything I can plan on my own. *"Your kingdom come, Your will be done, on earth as it is in Heaven." (Matthew 6:10 NIV)*

Chapter Sixteen
The Struggle Is Real

The sorrow from the loss of a child makes even the simple tasks more difficult than they ever seemed to be in the past. What once seemed hard before heartache, afterward becomes excruciating. With Justin gone from my life the daily grind of getting out of bed each morning seemed to be a monumental struggle. By the time I thought I had conquered one battle, there was always another waiting not far behind. The things we used to enjoy doing together as a family became bittersweet; the memory of what "used to be" brought sadness and anguish. It was entirely evident that our whole family desired things to be like they "were," but also that it was one battle we would never win. If we were going to continue with some quality of life, and enjoy some degree of happiness again we needed to find a new plan of action. We would have to push past our disappointment and intense emptiness and find a new way of being a family. I knew if things were ever to be better, I'd have to learn to fight through the overwhelming grief that tried to convince me it was easier to give up than to keep going. That's when the struggle is the hardest, since you must fight at the point of complete and utter despair when you're not even able to *stand* on your own. Even though you are a wounded soldier left for dead--beaten, battered, and bruised beyond recognition, somehow you must continue to fight no matter the pain, knowing that if you give up and quit, the enemy will leave nothing untouched in its path. You have to keep going no matter what; otherwise, you'll never have any quality of life. You have other family members and friends who still need you, now more than ever. I'm speaking only from what I've learned through my grief process. I pray that as I continue to share my journey and thoughts, somehow, in some way, it can also help you if you've ever been through a similar experience.

One of the main ways our family has been able to make it through is to do things differently from before the loss. The first

Christmas after our son's death, we opened our gifts in a different room. The previous year we had put up a second tree in our dining room, and I strongly felt that I shouldn't remove it after the season ended so I wouldn't have to go through the trouble of putting it up again. I'm thankful I listened to my inner voice which said the year before, "Just leave the tree up." My laziness afforded the luxury of not having to go through the hardship of dragging out the ornaments and I was spared the ordeal of putting the tree back together. Somehow the traditional routines were just too painful; the only natural solution seemed to just do the normal things abnormally. Since our lives had been altered radically, nothing would ever be the same again, so everything had to change for life to become balanced again; how long that would take would be determined on our willingness to give our cares and concerns over to God.

Everyone always says to me, "I bet the holidays are hard!" In fact, *all* routine celebrations, such as birthdays and anniversaries, are remarkably difficult, but the truth is, *every* day is hard. Each one is about trying to figure out how I'm going to survive the unexplainable affliction caused by the loss of a vital part of my life.

Attempting to ease the pain and suffering caused by Justin's absence, I think of happier times. That last Christmas we had with Justin we woke up to a snow-filled wonderland. Everyone couldn't wait to run outside and observe the marvelous sights and encounter the crisp winter air. I was finally able to coax the boys back inside so we could open presents, which was always *my* favorite part. Justin had spent a lot of time preparing his gift for Courtney. He had bought her a pair of shoes she had asked for, and instead of wrapping the box they came in, he proceeded to look for the biggest box he could find; he dropped the shoes inside adding a few bricks for weight and lots of newspapers for filler. He then started the decorating process which began much like all his other projects, with "spray paint." He covered the box with bright colors and then proceeded to secure the seams with duct-tape, another favorite tool he never liked to be without. I used to say, "If Justin had zip ties, duct-tape, and spray paint, he could completely restore any Honda back to *almost* new condition." Those of you who knew him well can testify to that fact. His enthusiastic excitement was contagious so we all joined in the fun. I gathered up as much gift wrap as I could find, but it still wasn't enough to cover the huge present. Caleb added stickers, and Jacob found as many magic markers as he could carry; he also wanted to show off his artistic abilities. To be brutally honest, by the time we all finished putting our two cents into the present, it looked like a package the Grinch would have rejected; but if Courtney could only see the love that went into that package she would know how truly blessed she is to have those adorable Fowler boys on her team. Needless to say, when Justin presented her with the strangely wrapped gift her face was priceless and that made it all worthwhile to each of us.

Afterward, we bundled up and walked the short distance to Nana and Buck-A's to eat lunch. This was a tradition we all looked forward to every holiday. Mom would always say "I'm only cooking the same ole stuff, I'm not doing anything special," but with my mother she has never failed at making the usual extraordinary. With our bellies full, we spent the entire rest of the day sledding down the driveway, riding four-wheelers, and building snowmen. We even had a friendly snowball fight. That was probably the most perfect holiday I can ever remember. Although each Christmas is filled with wonder and excitement, that *one* will always stand out vividly in my heart. Everyone always hopes for snow for Christmas, and when it finally happens, you never stop reliving those precious moments over and over in your mind.

It hasn't been easy to be positive and hopeful throughout my grief encounter. There have been times I was angry, and I now know that's okay. I learned that God understands any and every emotion we have. After all, He created us, and when Jesus came to earth in bodily form, He experienced all that we as humans go through. Then His Father Who, adored Him, but loved us more, delivered Him up, unable even to watch as he died a cruel, horrible death for

149

our sake. Thus, He understands all too well well our human conflicts, disappointments, and heartbreak.

I love my sons with everything in me; they've been my reason for living and, for the most part, my most fulfilling career. As a "creative domestic engineer" throughout most of their lives, I became addicted to their needing me. As they grew up, they learned to do things on their own and weren't as dependent on me, but that didn't ever quench my need to be there just in case. I now am no longer necessary to my oldest son. His needs were conclusively and abundantly met forever when he entered through those golden gates and was greeted by his heavenly Father. Between Justin's passing and my two younger sons' growing up, I learned that I could no longer count on them to be the sole purpose for living. I now find God as my source to give my life meaning. He's the reason I'm able to stand on the days my grief is crippling, and my heart is too heavy to beat efficiently. He's the One Who breathes life into my weary soul and causes these dry bones to live again. Had it not been for Him carrying me on the days when I didn't have the substance, stamina and self-control not to quit I hesitate to think where I would be. *"Thus, saith God the Lord, He that created the heavens, and stretched them out; He that spread forth the earth, and that which cometh out of it; He that giveth breath unto the people upon it, and Spirit to them that walk therein." (Isaiah 42:5 KJV)*

Most ladies consider shopping as great remedy to cure the hum-drums of any kind. This antidote is called known as "retail therapy," and for many years I thoroughly enjoyed it. This ritual did wonders to transport my mind's current concerns to another location but did nothing to help heal the one thing my life desperately needed. What I now know that I didn't know then, shopping was only a temporary fix for fleshly problem. What my real issue was is that I needed a healing on the inside to be completely satisfied. The curse of living in the flesh is that you are always left empty and unsatisfied. Once we are truly made complete through Christ we then gain the ability to be content in all things in every location.

After such a loss, however, the very idea of going into a store where I may have run into someone and not had the courage to speak to them was hard to bear. There was a shadow looming over my conversations, as they were afraid that they would say something wrong or upset me and cause me to cry. Truth is that I love the fact people can feel free to share a story with me about Justin. It lets me know they haven't forgotten him and that in some way, he impacted their lives for good. It's important to me that people not focus on his death but on the fact that he lived. I love having the chance to share my own stories more now than in the beginning. At first, I had to struggle, with the stories about him being told, fighting through my emotions and tears at the very mention of his name. Now I take great delight in sharing about our son and do so every chance I get with anyone who will listen. Friends and family are so kind to sit and pay attention when I feel the need to share a fond memory from time to time. It's nothing short of amazing that most of them have the unique special ability to pretend it's the first time they've ever heard the story. You, too, may also have to grant me the same liberty to share things again and again, as I'm quite certain I've shared a few favorite thoughts in this book more than once. Watching the expressions on the faces of the ones closest to me continues to bring me joy. I often wonder if their endearing declarations of enthusiasm may be of shock instead. Are they genuinely interested, or do they look that way because they are trying to understand how a mother could live through the loss of a child and still be able to speak his name out loud or share a memory without losing her composure? Either way, I'll be forever thankful for those who are continuing this journey with me until the end. As more time passes, I often apologize for repeating the same stories over and over since I no longer have new ones to tell. I'm appreciative that I still have the old ones and that there are so many. He was only twenty years young when he left, but there are many happy, unforgettable memories we have of him from that brief time.

I'm so thankful I was able to watch him progress from a baby I held in my arms to a young man fully grown. I was able to see him graduate high school and was on the front row when he got married. I saw him be a loving and compassionate husband to Courtney and an exceptional "Daddy Justin" to her little girl, Skylar. I shared his excitement when he got his dream job at the Honda dealership working in the service department, and cried as he drove off with his little family when they moved from our house into a home of their own. I know so many people who have lost children and never had the opportunities we had the privilege to encounter. Eventually, after much soul-searching, sleepless nights, and many long conversations with God, I learned not to be bitter and ungrateful for the time I *didn't* have with our son. I've since come to a conclusion over the years that I must be thankful for the beautiful memories and amount of time I *was* given. Many times, daily I must regain the victory of gratitude and not permit greed to make me angry and bitter. I treasure the gift of having my son and praise God for lending him to us even though it wasn't long enough, even if given we had a hundred to hold him; at least I was given a chance to love him as long as I was permitted. God could have easily let us never experience the gift of children, but He *did,* and I will be forever grateful that I've had the honor of experiencing the love of my three sons.

Rest assured, and take confidence knowing that if your heart has been destroyed beyond repair, God will give you a brand-new heart, stronger than you ever had before, and with it you will be able to love even deeper. *"Wait on the Lord: be of good courage, and He shall strengthen thine heart: wait, I say on the Lord." (Psalm 27:14 KJV)* Our timing in no way resembles God's. So often He calls us to be patient and wait according to His divine timeline for answers. May your moments of intermission to be used for a brief pause of reflection. Please use *this* time to reminisce about *all* the blessings God has brought to your life, instead of complaining about how long it's taking. Think back on all the battles won that in the beginning felt insurmountable, overwhelming, and impossible. That in return will fuel the anticipation and excitement of what is to come when

God transforms you through your current circumstance.

Don't think God enjoys it when the things you must go through cause tormenting pain and intense sorrow God's love for us goes beyond what we could ever calculate. As earthly parents, we never enjoy it when our children must walk through difficult times, but we know that sometimes it's necessary for them to learn and grow. When Justin first began to walk, we'd remove every obstacle from the room, so there would be no way possible for him to fall and be injured. Later, we realized we couldn't rearrange the furniture everywhere we went and learned that rather than move the obstructions, we must teach him how to avoid the ones that might cause him pain. By learning to walk around the barriers, Justin was able to maneuver anywhere his feet would carry him. He sometimes fell and thereby learned how to get back up again. We must realize that, God won't always remove stumbling blocks from our lives, but He will be there to lead and guide us through the process. We, too, must all learn to get back up when we stumble in our daily walk. There will be days we're knocked down by things we're forced to face, but God will help us if we ever fall too hard to recover on our own. The love we have for our children, grand as it may be, would never even be able to come anywhere close to God's love for us.

Things won't always be perfectly understood by us, especially when they don't go the way we plan, but they do make perfect sense to God. In those adverse times, trust Him as much or more than you do when life is going in complete harmony. There's a Scripture I read often, which says the clay doesn't ask the potter what he's making it to be, but the potter makes it into what he decides: *"Will what is formed say to him that formed it, why have you made me thus?" (Romans 9:20 KJV)* Must we ask God "why" so much? We should realize that God, Who in all His sovereign, omnipotent greatness, spoke the entire world and every living thing into existence, knows exactly how things need to line up for His perfect will to be accomplished, and the only help He needs from *us* is our complete obedience and cooperation. There's another question I often ask

153

God, "When, God, when?" I remember just like it was yesterday, we'd be headed out of town on vacation when the boys were little and it took maybe thirty minutes before one of them would bring up the most asked question ever by kids in a car. Say it with me; "Are we there yet? How much longer?" Gritting our teeth, squinting both eyes tightly, taking a deep breath and trying desperately not to yell harshly, we'd respond calmly and sweetly; "No honey, not yet." Before every trip we always told them way ahead of time that it would take a long time to get where we were going but it would be worth the wait. Unfortunately, they had the same struggles we do when God tell us the very same thing. You see, we all have a debilitating condition called *impatience* that has an adverse side effect of never being able to wait for something very long. The truth is that sometimes good things take time, and lots of it. There has never been an instance after a long ride to the beautiful beaches we often visit that I once said, "Wow wish I'd never made that trip." There has also never been a time when I fully trusted God in circumstances that He didn't come through for me just at the exact moment I needed Him most that I didn't respond saying, "You *were* right God! It *was* well worth the wait!" We all would benefit from being less impatient and more expectant of what lies ahead; it will be worth the difficulties, strife, and turmoil it took to get there if we wait upon God. *"You will make known to me the path of life; In Your presence is fullness of joy; In your right hand there are pleasures forevermore." (Psalm 16:11 ESV)*

One day while talking to God, me doing most of the talking because I always feel like I should explain things as if He doesn't already know, I kept asking over and over, "When, God, when are things ever going to get better?" Almost immediately in my Spirit I heard God respond, "What are you doing to help matters?" Wow! When God does speak, it's always powerful and has the compelling ability to silence my moaning and murmuring instantly. I *am* trying to listen more and speak less during my prayer time as He does have the ability to move mountains and it may require the same fortitude

154

to get me to be quiet, so I can hear Him speak. The fact is God can do anything when we ask in prayer believing, but He needs His children to step aside and not hinder the process. God doesn't need our help to accomplish things; what He does need is our willingness not to complicate His progress and to comply with His plan. We need not spend time complaining that *it's* taking *too* long, but instead be willing to wait because in the end it will be worth it. Stop asking "When, God, when?" and have faith to trust that although we may not know precisely when things will get better or change, He knows exactly how long it's going to take.

When we make a determined effort to follow God after our lives have been tragically impaired, we're finally able to see His light shine through our brokenness, and others can get a glimpse of Him through us. When horrible things happen to bad people, the world says they deserve it, but when tragic things happen to God's people and it doesn't destroy them, the world will be able to know that God is real, because without Him the heartaches and tragedy would overtake us. *"I would have lost heart unless I had believed that I would see the goodness of the Lord in the land of the living!" (Psalm 27:13 NKJV)*

Sometimes I think that God can reach the lost only through their personal catastrophes or by seeing the destruction of others. I've often heard it said that if there were never any problems, some would not find it necessary to breathe a prayer. It would be very disheartening to think *my* children would communicate with me only when they had problems, or wanted something never taking the time to share precious moments at every opportunity. I desire for God to be the most significant part of my everyday life. In my heart, I know He cares about every detail, so I intend to place Him in the very center of my world. Since He is all around us at all times, why not make Him feel welcome in all things? I believe it's through watching others triumph over tragedy that we finally see that, truly, there must be a God! How else could we explain or understand how others could be abundantly restored and be able to stand in the midst of significant loss and devastation. It's only by God's grace and mercy that we could ever withstand the trials of this life. *"It is of the Lords mercies that we are not consumed because His compassions fail not." (Lamentations 3:21-22 KJV)* I believe that by watching other people conquer impossible situations through Christ and seeing them arrive at the other side of defeat, our faith and courage will then increase by our realizing that just as others have overcome, we to will cross over and be carefree conquerors. Remember it was when the disciples were going across to the other side that they faced mighty storms with forces strong enough to destroy them; they trusted God and He delivered them safely to the other side. God will do the same for us. He is the same God now as He was then. *"Jesus Christ is the same yesterday and today and forever. (Hebrews 13:8 NIV)*

After a tragedy, you must do your best to find enjoyment in even the smallest of things, such as a taking a long walk or a drive on a sunny day, with the windows down and the radio turned up way too loud, blasting out some encouraging worship music would be my suggestion. Don't do only the things you *have* to do, but do the things you *want* to do. Yes, we all have everyday, mundane duties, but you have earned the right to savor life. I now feel an immense pleasure in getting chores done, for there was a time after we lost Justin I never cared whether or not I accomplished a thing. Now I feel a deep sense of enthusiasm when I conquer a large mound of laundry and get the dishes, done all in one day. That may not seem like such a great feat to most, but from the pit I've lived in for days, weeks, and months, which turned into years, it's a tremendous personal victory. Always set attainable goals for yourself, which will motivate you to continue when you have lost your determination to move ahead. Perpetually fight past the emotions that would cause you to lie in your bed all day and suffer through tears. I'm not saying that you can never be sad and hopeless; just know you don't have to remain there forevermore. You mustn't let a tragedy leave you paralyzed and despondent permanently; know that there's hope and healing in Jesus. I still have days of great sorrow, and *if* I follow those feelings and become submerged in sadness and marinated in grief, pretty soon, I discover I've lost valuable, precious time that I'll never get back. I've learned to recognize immediately when those feelings of complete despair try to consume my thoughts, and know I must come against it with God's Word. Then I can gain inner strength to resist the feelings to which my mind tries to hold me captive. *"For God has not given us a spirit of fear, but of power and love, and a sound mind." (2Timothy 1:7 KJV)* We need to acknowledge that those feelings of loss and sadness are going to be forever there; once we make it over the hurt hurtle there's always something to take its place, *if* we accept the invitation; but we have the power through our Lord and Savior to move past those disruptions. Difficult as it may be, the choice is ours to make.

I've learned many tricks for keeping despair at a distance. When I find myself missing my son so much that I can't hold on for one more day, I force my mind to go back to a time when he was here with us and try to remember every aspect about that occasion as well as his face and his unique expressions. I strain to hear his voice and remember the words he spoke. I focus on what we did and what he was wearing. I concentrate intensely not to let one fraction of that memory slip through unnoticed. Eventually, a smile comes across my face and overwhelming happiness enters my heart and, I forget for a moment how much I desperately miss him. Another thing I do is try to picture myself the way I used to be before I changed along with everything around me. I focus on the things I liked to do and the fun I had and think back to how I was before my heart shattered. When I regard myself in that light, it gives me the motivation to strive for a place of excitement and contentment. I realize that there was a time I had endless "sunny days" and that gives me the fortitude that one day I will have unending sunshine again! I tell myself to "Soak up the sunny honey!" I don't want only what used to be; I want to be better, stronger, and more hopeful than I ever was before. Realizing I will never be completely the same as before tragedy came knocking, I know that in God there is a healing and a restoration that He is more than able to accomplish when I surrender my will to His ways.

I want to encourage you to take advantage of every second of the good days. Take the long way home sometimes; don't waste one moment hurrying through life. Sit and watch the sunsets, chase the beautiful butterflies, race after the rainbows, relishing the moments wherever possible, and let them propel you out of sadness, remorse, and despair. Your days will not always be happy ones, nor will they all be miserable. However, when you choose to take every opportunity to find at least one positive thing, as you press on and move forward what you will soon realize is that the loss you have suffered will make other difficulties pale in comparison. A difficult day takes on a whole new meaning after tragedy strikes, and what you once thought was unbearable becomes not so detrimental after all.

It would be great to think that because you've been through a debilitating loss, you'd never have to be devastated again and that your heart would never again have to break, but unfortunately, that's not the case. As I've said over and over, I think that actual resistance in a struggle builds your strength. So, when you conquer something that seems unachievable, take pleasure in the fact that you gained courage, which will enable you to defeat the opposition in the next battle. We can never completely recover from the things that hold us prisoner until whatever they are is uncovered. You must let your pain rise to the surface for the sake of being healed. Until we give up the fight of trying to pack down deep inside everything we refuse to deal with for whatever reason, we'll remain captive to that which keeps us chained. This process reminds me of how gold is refined. When melted, the impurities in the metal rise to the surface so they can be skimmed off, and all that remains is pure. As we give permission for the pain to surface, its ugliness will be revealed, so we can be made stronger within ourselves and be a blessing to others. What we've had to go through isn't fair, nor is it beneficial to continue to sink into our sadness when there are others around who depend on us so very much, some of whom we haven't yet met. God can take all our brokenness and pain and make something beautiful when we choose to permit Him to do so.

Without a doubt, I know Justin wouldn't want us to be sad, broken and devastated any longer than necessary to work through the grief process. He received everything he could ever imagine when he crossed from this world into his heavenly home. I know in my heart that if our son felt we were suffering in sadness over his absence, he would be heartbroken. I would be devastated even more than I am, to know that my misery could cause his heavenly reward to be any less than the best; and so, on days that seem intolerable, I remember the look on my son's face when he saw me unhappy and tearful. He would be just so distraught and try anything he could to bring a smile back to my face. He was special in so many ways, but that remains to be one my favorite illustration of his kindness and love toward me. He was always the peacemaker in our family and did his best to make sure everyone was happy, and conflict stayed at a bare minimum.

I have since come to know the ultimate peacemaker in God, Who has been my rock and my fortress when the cares of this life are overwhelming. I now run to the rock which is higher. *"From the end of the earth will I cry to You, when my heart is overwhelmed and fainting; lead me to the rock that is higher than I." (Psalm 61:2 KJV)* If only we'll surrender our struggles to Him and rest in the promise that He'll work all things out for our good. *"And we know that all things work together for good to them that love God, to them who are called according to His purpose." (Romans 8:28 KJV)*

Chapter Seventeen
Shining Through Darkness

If I wholeheartedly and honestly meant what I said in my beginning, that I want to try and help my readers, especially those who have experienced the loss of a child or other loved one, then I cannot neglect to relate the hardest and darkest part of the despairing, grieving process. Please note that this chapter, as well as the entire book, expresses *my* views and personal opinions. With the hope of helping others, I've decided to permit myself to be extremely vulnerable. I acknowledge that every one of us has beliefs and unique ways of dealing with grief so that you can take my thoughts and ideas to heart, or you can choose to disagree with part or all of everything I say.

I've never spoken with a psychologist or sought out other counseling for help navigating through my feelings or emotions of this experience. I've merely tried to face my grief, fears, hardships, and brokenness head on as they come unsolicited to bombard my heart, mind, and soul. I've given only those closest to me an opportunity to give their opinions to advise and help direct me. That's not to say I'm against going to doctors or professional analysts for help; I'm just saying I didn't choose that plan of action. I believe that *each person* needs to pray and seek out wisdom for the right method of leading them through their own grieving process. *I* am daily depending and leaning on my Savior. *"Out of my distress I called on the Lord; the Lord answered me and set me free. The Lord is on my side; I will not fear. What can man do to me?" (Psalm 118:5-6 ESV)* I trust and believe that when I remain patient and wait for His direction, the God I serve is more than able to carry me through every conflict and every bit of strife I face, now or ever. I know with all certainty *if* He has appointed me to go through this unimaginable grief, I have faith that, with His help, I can and will make it somehow. I'm committed to believing that God will not permit me to fall past where His arms cannot catch me, or let me wander so far

160

away from Him that His love and mercy can't maneuver me back to His loving embrace.

There were days in the beginning when I didn't want to live. In fact, because of the constant torment I feared would never end, I prayed each night not to wake up the next morning or begged God to take my life another way. When my prayers went unanswered the way I intended, I tirelessly contemplated ways I could end my own life because I was convinced that with the amount of sadness I was harboring, my quality of existence wasn't worthwhile. I can remember feeling immensely embarrassed even to think about admitting these feelings of hopelessness to anyone. To this day, unless my family members are reading this now, they have no knowledge of that fact. I tried to deny even to myself that I could sink that far below the surface, drowning in a tempestuous sea of despair. The guilt I felt from the constant draw of death kept me in a deep state of depression. I felt I was a heavy burden to my sons and other close family members, but mostly to my husband. I shamefully felt I had no value to God; why would He ever want me when I had nothing left to offer Him? All I had inside was brokenness, anger, and bitterness. I had no self-worth; in fact, I felt insignificant as a human being. I had no dread of dying; my fear was in living. Dying seemed like a way to end what was suffocating me and distorting my vision as to what God had planned for my life. My desire to die was overwhelming my will to live. I know my statements are dark and dismal, but I'm being as honest as possible and bluntly truthful in the hope of shedding some light to others who may be feeling the exact same way. I felt so insecure with many uncertainties and fears; I wanted my old life back! Knowing that was not an option, I felt I needed to find a way to make what had happened to disappear from memory. Please understand, all of you who are unstable, mourning hurting parents, all the gloom and despair you're feeling is part of the process. There *is* help and healing available to you; please don't lose hope.

After many days of soul searching, I can see now that all I was worried about was myself and how *I* was feeling. I had completely lost my compassion for the people around me who were also hurting. I was being selfish and unkind, not even thinking of or even considering them. I despised feeling this way and finally concluded that I had to strive to find a way somehow to turn my sadness into gladness and get my derailed life back on the right track. I decided to turn the evil apathy I had into a pure affinity for others. I realized I needed to have genuine affection for and rapport with others in order to come out of all the madness and strife the enemy was heaping upon my life.

When I miraculously survived the first few months, it encouraged me to know that God had more confidence in me than I had in myself and obviously had a better design for my recovery than I did. I finally come to the conclusion that God had a distinct work especially designed for me that only I and no one else would be able to accomplish. I realized that finding out the nature of His purpose and fulfilling it would take a lot of determination on my part and an ample amount of patience on God's part. If I were going to be who God had called me to be, He would also have an intense job to do on my inside, as I was an complex work in progress. I would be the clay and consent to God's molding me and making me into a vessel for His glory to flow through. *"For God, Who said, 'Let light shine out of darkness.'" (2 Corinthians 4:6 ESV)* I had to act, *not* on how I felt, or fixate on the scared, disquieted face I saw in the mirror, but use what little faith remained and multiply it by putting it into action. I learned to stop focusing on my current condition and look at my life from God's perspective. I realized that if I were going to arrive on the other side of devastation, I'd have to set my eyes on Heaven and the victory I would one day achieve if I would not give up in defeat. By setting my sights on the finish and not on my fear, I felt a sense of power in knowing that God defended me in the biggest assault through the most horrific conflict that I had ever known. In Him, I found the tenacity and the stamina never to settle, but to push on and break free from the chains of fear and death.

Knowing and trusting Him helped me to see that although I felt like I was dying a slow, painful death, He was transforming and restoring me piece by piece, moment by moment. *"For which cause, we faint not; but though our outward man perish, yet the inward man is renewed day by day." (2 Corinthians 4:16 KJV)*

During my loneliest, darkest, deepest pits of sadness, I continued to read my Bible, even when it seemed impossible for me to grasp its content. I would repeat the same verse over and over just trying to discern its meaning. The more I studied, the more confused I became. I knew it was important that I keep God's Word hidden in my heart, so I continued to delve into the Scriptures. I believed that if I were diligent, the Word would become deeply rooted in my spirit and at the precise moment I needed it most, it would assuredly come to the surface to give me spiritual encouragement and keep me going in the right direction. *"Your Word I hid in my heart that I might not sin against thee." (Psalm 119:11 KJV)* There are millions of people in this world who, if honest, will admit that the reason they don't read their Bible is because they don't understand its meaning. I discovered the way to overcome that is just keep reading it; the more you read, the better you will understand its content as your Spirt reveals it to you. Now I know that to be a *fact* in my life. I have the assurance that every time my mind starts to venture off track, my spirit gently speaks a promise from God's book to direct me back to where I need to be.

In many of my most desolate times of depression, I didn't listen to God, maybe because I couldn't hear His voice above the distracting chaotic clamor. All I could hear were voices inside my head that created a ridiculous racket and perpetual strife. While God was trying to whisper to my heart, the enemy was busy filling my head with deceitful lies. He was determined to convince me of my weakness while God was speaking to my strength through Him. What we must recognize is that satan is always attempting to come against our knowledge of God. When he called me feeble, I rebuked him by saying, "If I were weak I would have already given up!" It takes more

163

strength and determination to keep going than it does to surrender to the enemy, who constantly tries all he can to manipulate and deceive us. *"Casting down imaginations and every high thing that exalted itself against the knowledge of God, and bringing every thought captive to the obedience of Christ." (2 Corinthians 10:5 KJV)* If our adversary can make us doubt God's love and devotion, God's power to overcome in our lives will be ineffective. We must take to heart in the very last part of that Scripture and take every thought in our mind captive. To this day I confess out loud that I have the divine intellect of my heavenly Father, as *1 Corinthians 2:16 ESV* promises: *"For who has understood the mind of the Lord so as to instruct him? But we have the mind of Christ."* If our thinking doesn't line up with what God's Word tells us, then we need to kick the untruths out of our thoughts immediately. Never permit the deception to linger long enough to take root in your life but cast it out immediately before the damage begins to fester and decay your thought process. During the moments of doubt and fear, it was challenging not to give in to the evil propositions placed in my mind. In those times it felt less bothersome to quit than it did to strive for victory. I knew with God's divine help I would survive the satan's plot to destroy me. I now realize that I must seek out God's voice at *all* times through everything and resist *every* idea that is contrary to His Word. Most days are a constant crusade between the two extremes, but I know that in the end if I surrender to God and listen enthusiastically to *His* voice, the enemy will no longer have a hold on me. *"My sheep hear my voice, and I know them, and they follow me." (John 10:27 KJV)*

The devil is relentless in his efforts to bamboozle God's children. There has never been a day when my faith hasn't been tested in one way or another. I gage the level of my closeness to God by the degree of the devil's attack. When the adversary is at my heels, I know my witness must be upsetting his intentions; when he's absent, I assume I'm no threat to him. I focus my thoughts on God, knowing the closer I draw to Him the more ability I gain to ward off the invasion of the assailant. If ever I feel hopeless and unsteady, I press into God, praying and studying His Word to encourage my heart to continue, knowing the battle belongs to the Lord. With each passing day, I take joy in knowing that over time my confidence has increased and been reinforced by the difficulties I've conquered with God's help.

Depression gives no warning of the onset of its attack, often taking its victims by complete surprise with no logical reason for its invasion. I never really understood this before I experienced it for myself. I knew people with severe depression and had prayed for them and quoted the Scripture that compels us to *"Submit to God {to the authority of} God. Resist the devil {stand firm against him} and he will flee from you." (James 4:7 AMP)* Some may read that Scripture and not realize it has two parts. First, we must surrender our will and our ways to God and then we can have the ability to resist the enemy. Submitting means to relinquish our control and give it over to God. We must lay aside all of our self-imposed authority and let God have the drivers-seat. I used to think that you could choose not to be depressed. However, from the impact of great depression myself, I learned that it *could* be resisted but requires God's deliverance to be overcome. I don't have an answer for the reason some people are healed of depression or other various illnesses while others must rely on medication for relief. It's something I just don't know. I can speak only about personal circumstances. No way am I saying God plays favorites and won't do for all what He does for some. It was only after undergoing this debilitating disease of the mind that I was able to understand the fact it comes on much like a virus or other sickness, and I myself chose to trust the healing power of God to stand against it. I confessed out loud daily, I know my God would not call me to this trial if He didn't intend on seeing me through to the end. Just as Jesus heals the lame and the sick in body, He can also heal the mind and remove the curse of depression: *"I said Lord, be merciful and gracious to me;*

heal my inner self for I have sinned against you." (Psalm 41:4 KJV) It was apparent *my* inner self was making my outer self sick and tired. The voice I was hearing, which wasn't God's, caused me to feel powerless and weary, contrary to the Word which says our spirit man will quicken our mortal bodies. Instead, my emotions and thoughts were destroying my health from the inside out. Depression made me feel as though I'd sinned against God, that somehow, I'd let Him down when I fell victim to it and gave it an opportunity to steal the joy, hope, and peace He'd so freely imparted. That, in turn, made me feel even more hopeless. Many times, it was as if I were on a never-ending merry-go-round that was far from merry, a ride I did not choose to get on, and didn't possess the ability to get off by myself. I felt like I was constantly going in circles and getting no-where, forever losing any ground I had gained the previous day. For me, the key to victory over this state of mind was learning not to go by how I felt, but on what I knew by faith. I had to put those healing Scriptures to work in my life if I was ever going to recuperate and have my shattered heart rehabilitated.

I am by far not expert on depression and as I said, I can only speak from my own dreary disturbances with utter darkness. I've found it to be void of any light, a dismal, horrifying place, a dreadful destination no one would ever choose to visit on their own. I have learned that many people don't respect this disease as a *real* illness. Most respond by saying, "Snap out of it," thinking you chose to be despondent and unhappy. The truth is depression is a real disease just like cancer and diabetes or any other health-altering sickness. Please don't ever regard people with depression as weak. Unless you have been affected by it for yourself, *you* can never comprehend how strong someone really is that's fighting this perpetual anguish.

God has now given me a brand-new compassion for people un-der the attack of depression. I believe having come to grips with it in my own life, I can more effectively minister to dejected, downcast individuals, just as I once was with new and better understanding of its brutal effects on the mind, soul, and spirit. *Galatians 6:2 KJV:*

"Bear you one another's burdens, and so fulfill the law of Christ."
My prayer is that I will do my part by communicating the truth He
tells me, thereby shining forth His brilliant light to dispel the darkness. My desire is to be confident in all He has called me to do for
His name's sake. I no longer look to my ability and qualifications
but instead put all my faith in Him through Whom my power and
assurance are manifested. I did not come to the knowledge of God's
plan and purpose for my life overnight. In fact, it's a daily discovery;
I declare victory over myself and my family every single day. I
achieve renewed courage from past battles, and yet gloom and
doom continue to invade my mind. My spirit knows I have authority
over every circumstance, but the ongoing fight rages from time to
time in my human, selfish thoughts. I must warn you that we'll *all*
deal with this mental war occasionally, so fix your mind on God's
promise in *2 Timothy 1:7 KJV: "He has not given us a spirit of fear,
but of power, and of love, and of a sound mind."* As I've mentioned
many times throughout this book, every morning I'm faced with the
ultimatum of going forward or backing up. I must resist the temptation to stay in bed and pray for the day to end quickly while I hide
from the challenges this life often brings. I must remain resolute
and make a conscious choice to get up and fight to maintain sound
judgment. My spirit knows better than to retreat, but my fleshly
thoughts remain relentless and continue seeking to imprison me,
trying to convince me that I will never be satisfied resting in the assurance that God is my Comforter, my Shield, and my Defender. I
confess daily that I have the mind of Christ that this war belongs to
God, and Jesus is *for* me. I know His promises, every one of them
are eternal and irrevocable, which gives me the guarantee that
there's nothing He will not do for me, if it is what He deems best. I
let go of the guilt I was holding on to from the thoughts, feelings,
and emotions that nearly cost me my life. I no longer believe my
family would be better off without me, neither do I feel unworthy of
God's love.

Early in my Christian walk, I learned that *"Without faith, it is impossible for us to please God." (Hebrews 11:6 KJV)* and it goes on to say that *"He is a rewarder of them that diligently seek Him."* Knowing that our faith activates God's divine power in our lives, I began to pray for the substance I would need to overpower the obstacles.

I learned a valuable lesson in trust from my earthly father when he taught my sister and me to swim by showing us to believe that so long as he was with us, he would never take his eyes off us, so we would *not* drown. My dad promised he would always be there to save us if we ever got into trouble. Although at times he used to tease us that *if* he threw us in the water, we'd either learn to swim or we would surely sink. Thankfully, he never put *that* plan into action. His first lesson on swimming was teaching us to float. We got into the water and lay on our backs as he held his hand beneath our shoulders. If we ever started to go under, he would steady us, and we'd *magically* levitate on top of the water. When we were finally able to trust that he wouldn't let go, we rested peacefully as we learned to bobble around in our favorite swimming hole, "Pinkard's Pond." We were amazed at how easily we could hover on top of the water with no help at all. God, also, requires us to have faith that *He* won't ever let go. Never will He abandon us, no matter what sea of torment, sickness, or grief tries to defeat us. However, there may be times He may permit us to go through some sort of of "sink or swim" period that is not so He can sit by and watch us perish, but so that He can develop our faith and see it in action. He's a loving, merciful Father Who would never place us in harm's way. Should we ever be in a fiery trial, He'll be right there with us in the middle of the flames. Just as my earthly father would never take his eyes off his daughters or steer us into grave danger, God's protection is even greater. Never once has He not heard my cry for help in times of great distress. He runs to me when I am weary, wavering, and worried. As the psalmist says, *"Your mercy and loving-kindness O Lord extends to the skies, and your faithfulness reaches to the clouds." (Psalm 36:5 KJV)* It is for these very reasons that I can get up each

168

day and proceed on this journey He has called me to travel.

I'm reminded of a day my faith in God was tested especially severely. As my husband and I were driving to the funeral home for Justin's viewing, we had to stop several times because I was under the attack of tormenting fear and extreme panic. I was so riddled with stress and anxiety I could barely breathe and felt as if my shattered, broken heart would implode inside my chest. When we finally arrived and the funeral director met us at the door, my symptoms had worsened; and I was now sick to my stomach and shaking uncontrollably with cold chills even though the temperature outside was well into the nineties. My husband and the director lead me into a waiting area where we were joined by Jacob, our middle son, and Caleb, our youngest, along with other immediate family members. Not wanting my boys, including Justin, to sense I was so upset, I tried to control my sickness and emotions as best I could. We walked into the viewing room, and as I looked into the casket where my firstborn child lay, I was overwhelmed. He looked so peaceful and angelic as if he were asleep, and I felt that if I called out his name, he would wake up and ask, "Where am I, and how did I get here?" My eyes were stationary on his face, convinced that I would see a twitch of his grin or a flutter of his long, dark lashes. I inwardly pleaded for God to open his sparkling blue eyes. Oh, how I yearned with unshakable anticipation to see his chest begin to rise and fall and we could all rejoice that indeed he'd only been sleeping. In that moment of great expectancy, my faith began to overpower my flesh and my sickness subsided as my hope gave way to healing and I began to breathe freely without panic overcoming me.

When people began to form a receiving line, signaling that, in fact, this was a funeral, and not the homecoming I'd anticipated, my symptoms of sickness returned. I felt the room close in and begin to spin out of control. I looked for the nearest exit and bolted out the door; I ran down the hall into a small restroom where I collapsed on the floor. Moments later a couple of my friends joined me. Shaking and scared, I asked each of them how in the world I was ever going to be able to do this grievous task. As each of them tried to console me as best she knew how, another familiar face entered the room. It was Robie's mother, Gina. Shocked to see her, and not even sure my swollen, blurry, eyes could be trusted, I gazed at her as she leaned down and said softly, "One day at a time." "How do you know that?" I asked. Her answer was, "That's what you told me when I lost my 'Robie.'" My mind went immediately back to that very day when I stood with her as she said her final goodbyes to *her* son. She must have noticed by the look on my face that my thoughts had lost all focus on what she was saying, and so she beckoned me back with the question, "Did you lie to me?" I carefully contemplated my answer, knowing that if I could not trust what I had told her to be true, she could lose all her hope and desire to carry on, and it would be all my fault. I quickly responded, "NO! I would never lie to you!" So, she said, "Then that's exactly how you will make it, just as I have, one day at a time." Wow! At that very moment it was as if God were speaking directly to my heart using my friend as a willing vessel for His Word to come forth. I had to once again "practice what I preached." *"Then Jesus said, 'Whosoever has ears to hear, let him hear.'" (Mark 4:9 NIV)* It is one thing to listen to God's Word but entirely different when we *hear* and put it into action. When we discern His voice, and apply it to our lives, it empowers us to do mighty and wonderful things. I've always tried to encourage our church members to rely on God no matter what; now it was my turn to put faith into action. In my heart I knew that if I made it through Justin's entire life, being present at every baseball game, field trip, school play, awards ceremony, and graduation, that somehow, I'd be able to continue to support him in his last and most distinguished promotion ever. With help from my friends, I made my way off the floor with greater strength from God than I thought I could've ever dreamed. We all walked back into the viewing room and made it through the evening, with the peace that passes all natural understanding. I had never felt God's power as alive inside me as it was that day. When I look back on His unending grace and mercy during this time, it encourages me to press in and move ahead, having been privileged to have this example of how He never gave up on me even when I had lost all hope in myself. Just as Jesus gave all He had on the cross for me my prayer is that I'll live each day of my life giving all the glory and honor to Him which He so richly deserves.

I want to take this moment to make one fact crystal clear: I have not for one minute ever *blamed* God for the loss of my son, and I'm convinced that Justin's time here on earth was complete; thus, he was chosen to receive his well-deserved reward in Heaven. I've learned in the most punishing way possible that the plan I had envisioned for my life was far different from God's plan. He has thoughts and ideas for me, for everyone, which I am unable to understand without revelation. That's why I know when things seem unsettled, tossed and shaken or as Barry says, "When our waters have escaped past the water banks, God alone can calm the seas." I must focus on His Word and accept it to encourage, empower, and sustain me every day I'm given. He is God, and I am not; how could I ever understand His ways? God knows what the future has in store, and, I, on the other hand, can see only what is right in front of me. I must walk ahead, using God as my guide. He does, at times, however, reveal His plans to us in part. *"Call to me, and I will answer you and show you great and mighty things {fenced in and hidden} which you do not know." (Jeremiah 33:3 AMP)* If God Himself had chosen to show me a moment-by-moment depiction from day one of my life until now, every single detail of every season, all the breathtaking highs and the gut-wrenching lows, if I had to visualize every time I'd be devastated, depressed or broken throughout my life, I'm convinced I'd have been so overwhelmed I would've quit my journey before it ever began.

Knowing deep in my heart that God had a plan and knew what was best for me far better than I knew myself, did not stop the hurt or make it disappear but did give me a renewed hope that one day life *would* be bearable. I believe pain is a repulsive symptom of grief,

171

much like the daunting darkness that entered my mind at times was another hurdle I had to jump over to get closer to my victory. I don't say this lightly, nor do I believe anyone ever truly makes it out of sorrow entirely without a divine miracle from God, but, in time, it loosens its hold on the heart, mind, and soul. Occasionally the heartache from losing my son feels deeper and harder to bear than in the beginning; other times the ache is lessened each time I direct my thoughts to God and not dwell on my current catatonic condition.

Some days are easier than others, and after some time had passed I was able to feel little better as each phase of the sorrow season came to an end. Unfortunately, so far, however, at the six-year six-month mark, I still have not gone one minute of any day without missing Justin, longing to hear his voice, or see his beautiful smile, desperately wanting to look into his beautiful, shiny, blue eyes. Knowing that day will come eventually and having the love and support of my husband, sons, and extended family, I keep moving forward. *"I press toward the mark for the prize of the high calling of God in Christ Jesus." (Philippians 3:14 KJV)*

When we live in darkness unable to see the dawn, it sets the stage for a dreary, dreadful, dejected, existence. The blackness causes us to encounter obstacles that we could've avoided in the light. One late night, due to the doorbell *magically* going off over and over, Barry stumbled around in the dark to see why this kept happening. Moments later when he didn't return in a timely manner, I got up to see why. Seconds later I was nursing a bruised head. While I was walking out of the bedroom door towards the light, he was walking towards the darkness of the bedroom and we clashed hard, both yelling, "Didn't you see me!" Truth was, I did see him as I was walking toward the light, but he never saw me because he was walking into total darkness. This was a substantial multilayered lesson for us both, the main thing being, never get up without first turning the light on. Much like he ran over me while walking blindly ahead we sometimes get into messes we need not be in while trying to walk in darkness of this earth. Jesus said He is the Light of the world and in Him there is no darkness. When we walk with Him, darkness dispels, and we can clearly see what lies ahead. *"Again, Jesus spoke to them, saying, 'I am the light of the world. Whosoever follows Me will not walk in darkness, but will have the light of life.'" (John 8:12 ESV)*

Chapter Eighteen
What Would It Be Like?

1 Corinthians 2:9 KJV declares this great promise: "*But as it is written, Eye hath not seen, nor ear heard, neither have entered into the heart of man, the things which God hath prepared for them that love Him.*" Have you ever sat and thought about what it would be like in Heaven? Have you wondered if it's for a fact perfect as you've always heard, with streets of gold and walls of precious jewels, a place where there is no sadness, no tears, no sickness or infirmities of any kind? I've often heard it said that Heaven would be precicely what you thought it would be, a place where, when you get there, you'll never want to leave. Have you ever wondered what your heavenly mansion would look like? Would it be big or small? Would it be made of wood, brick, or stone? I am persuaded it's a place that is nothing short of breathtaking, flawless, without one blemish of imperfection to be found. Even though it's depicted to be a matchless place, I'm certain each person has an entirely different definition of what "perfect" means to them, because everyone has their own distinct version of paradise. Of course, being in the presence of Jesus is the most important part of the ideal location. After all, isn't that our main purpose for carrying on through all life's experiences, good or bad, happy and sad, to complete the course and at last arrive at our ultimate destination to be with our Lord and Savior. If you could even begin to imagine it, what would you deem to be the very best of the best? My idea of perfection as you probably already guessed is a long stretch of beach with the whitest sands along the edge of the purest, sparkling, turquoise seas. It could also manifest by displaying visible peace without a ripple of discord as the relaxing waves carry me to complete calmness, where I could sit for hours by the shore and watch the waves perpetually ascend and descend. Another bonus would be to look at the sunrise and, with just a pivot of my head, see it setting and marvel at the saturation of the glorious colors of the sky on both occasions. As glorious as the sun setting and rising looks from earth's perspective I can only imagine how spectacular it must look from Heaven's viewpoint. Aside from all the obvious expected beauty, I especially anticipate this place of knowing how it feels never to have the trials, hurt, and sorrows of this life and no longer feel my endless tears falling from my sleep-deprived eyes. To be able at last to lay my head down at night without fighting even one attack of worry or fear would be my everlasting Promised Land. Until that day I will continue to seek out the contentment here on earth that I have come to know through my relationship with Jesus.

Other people's depictions of Heaven may be filled with beautiful mountains and flowing waterfalls, or perhaps tropical jungles brimming with beautiful, succulent flowers and plants of every kind. I've often wondered if when God created the Garden of Eden, He fashioned it exactly like Heaven. Could we, in fact, get a bird's eye view of Paradise on earth when we read about the lovely courtyards in which Adam and Eve resided before the fall of man? As I haven't personally known anyone who has seen the Pearly Gates and come back to report vivid details, I can merely make my own assumptions about its beauty. Again, I can wait patiently with expectation until the day I'm called to my heavenly home when my eyes will finally behold all the wonders so great and glorious.

I can imagine that on Justin's arrival in Heaven, he would be eagerly greeted by the loved ones who had gone on before him, his great-grandmothers and great-grandfathers who especially loved him since he was their firstborn great-grandson. There is no doubt in my mind that they were the first ones in line to grab him up and shower him with love and affection. I wonder if Justin would recognize the child I lost through miscarriage and be there to take on the role of big brother so they could enjoy eternity together. My heart can hope in what my mind cannot fathom.

Many times, I've wondered what thoughts I'd have as we gather around God's throne. Would I continue to have dreams and see visions of goals I'd like to obtain, or would all previous passions vanish in the light of God's glory? As my son has gone there before me, I often speculate whether or not his thoughts of the life he had before having been erased so that he doesn't know what used to be? Will he never know the heartache of the ones who loved him so much and the sorrow we feel each day when we wake and realize he's no longer with us? Do the heavenly residents lack the ability to miss *us*? How could Heaven be Paradise if we must wonder where our earthly loved ones are and why they aren't surrounding us? If truly there is no heartbreak, sadness, or tears in that land, it's evident that our loved ones may not have the capacity to miss us and their former lives. *"He will wipe away every tear from their eyes, and death shall be no more, neither shall there be mourning, nor crying, nor pain anymore, for the former things have passed away." (Revelation 21:4 ESV)* The best answer my heart can find is to assume that memory of previous life is somehow blocked from consciousness, and all they are aware of is what's ahead of them, having no recollection of what was left behind. What a priceless gift to be present with the Lord and have no concern or regret.

The one conclusion I've hidden inside my heart that gives me peace in my wondering is found in *2 Peter 3:8 KJV*: *"Beloved, be not ignorant of this one thing, that one day is with the Lord as a thousand years and a thousand years as one day."* God's Word tells us that on earth a thousand years may pass that would be equal to only one day in Heaven. What we count here on earth as a number of years will equal seconds in Heaven. We'll have many days to miss our son, but we're thankful because he possibly won't ever know what it's like to be without us. Just as we continue to sense his presence with us, I hope that is the exact feeling he has about us! When he has taken in all the wonders of Heaven, walked on the streets of purest gold to stand before the throne of the One Who died so he could experience life everlasting, Justin will look up and there we'll all be together again just as if time had stood still. *"For as the new heavens and new earth that I make shall remain*

176

before me, say the Lord, so shall your offspring and your name remain." (Isaiah 66:22 ESV)

Whatever your concept of your heavenly home may be, the best part for every believer would have to be finally inhabiting the kingdom of our King Jesus! For, most assuredly, God's Heaven is a perfect place whether the surroundings are mountains, sea, gold, silver, or precious stone. It's guaranteed to be a spectacular paradise and a sight to behold, no matter what, and the most important decision you'll ever make in this life is to choose Heaven as your final destination. *"For we know if the tent which is our earthly home is destroyed, we have from God a building, a house not made with hands, eternal in the heavens." (2 Corinthians 5:1 AMP)* I think a lot more about my eternal life since my son left. I often wake up and ask the Lord to tarry not a moment longer, as I feel my heart heavy inside me from a longing for my heavenly home. I sometimes want to ask God to "Send Jesus back soon to get *Your* sons and daughters." I picture it in my mind as His coming on a cloud when the trumpet sounds to call us home. Before I plead selfishly, I remember it is His heart's desire that not one of His children perishes. Just as I would never be able to leave one of my sons and loved ones behind I know God's affections and longing for His children is greater still. So, I quickly ask forgiveness and for the courage to carry on until His return. *"The Lord not slow to fulfill His promise, as some people count slowness, but is patient toward you, not wishing that any should perish, but that all should reach repentance." (2 Peter 3:9 ESV)* May God continue to use me to help spread His Word so that His purpose shall be fulfilled, and every man, woman, and child will have the opportunity to come to know a right relationship with Him. Realizing God's love and compassion for His children cannot be measured, I know that I could never pray God's return without knowing every person had been given the freedom to accept Christ as their personal Lord and Savior. I am so very blessed and thankful Jesus didn't return before my family and I had a chance to receive that salvation. *"And this gospel of the kingdom shall be preached in the world for a witness unto all nations; and then shall the end come." (Matthew 24:21 KJV)*

Chapter Nineteen
Purpose in the Pain

Even though I despise exercise with all that's inside me, I eventually realized that I could improve greatly physically and mentally by being in better shape, so I became determined to participate in some physical activity every day. *Knowing* isn't much help, however, in getting something accomplished, and sometimes I steadfastly refuse to do so. Have you ever contemplated how much harder a task seems if you don't enjoy it? Still, I tried to convince myself that, in the end, it would all be worthwhile. I've since found it to be a great stress reliever, helps to clear you mind and positively keeps depression at a bearable distance. When I feel the onset of desolation hovering all around I load up the dogs and we find a good place to take a hike. The fresh air and the outdoor atmosphere does us all good.

On days I felt motivated, I enjoyed exercising and tried to eat healthy foods. If I saw results from my efforts, I continued the process because I was pleased with myself for the strides I'd made. More often than not, times would come when I felt as though I had achieved nothing and that my efforts were in vain. I perceived myself as a complete failure, exactly the feeling I experienced a lot throughout the grieving transition. When my emotions were all over the place, I learned I must walk by faith and not believe what they're trying to make me accept or feel. Then there were days that no matter how hard I fought, I knew I lost miserably. I felt dejected and defeated, unable to find even the smallest amount of courage to continue.

When I got started and made exercise a daily habit, it wasn't so hard; but once I got out of the routine, the idea of going back through the soreness and pain was a condition to which I didn't look forward to. With each failed attempt I grew less and less interested in the perks and more interested in doing *what* I wanted to do *when* I wanted to do it.

When you're able to look past all the discomfort in any endeavor and trust that there's a purpose, you know that by going through it, you will one day receive the payoff of excellent benefits. Would the knowledge that, for all the agony, one day you'll get a valuable reward for not giving up cause you to keep going? *"My brethren, count it all joy when you fall into diver's temptations; knowing this, that the trying of your faith worketh patience. But let patience have her perfect work, that you may be perfect and entire, wanting nothing." (James 1:2-4 KJV)*

For most of us, if we can work out in our minds that there's a *reason* for doing what we do, even if we don't *want* to do it, we'll eventually realize we *can* do all things. For example, you go to work every day knowing you'll receive a paycheck at the end of the week and will be able to pay your bills, buy food, and have a home and car. It's not necessarily that you love to work, but by doing so, you can reap the advantages. The key is to keep the prize in sight and know that even if it isn't easy, you can do it if you don't give yourself permission to grow tired and give up. *"Let us not be weary in well doing: for in due season we will reap if we faint not." (Galatians 6:9 KJV)* That is a promise from God's Word to encourage us to look for the ultimate reward we'll receive if we stay the course.

Once we realize there's a purpose for the pain, we'll be able to take it all in stride, knowing that one day the prize we receive will far outweigh our tribulation. That is unequivocally what I had to do so that I was finally able to realize I could get to the other side. To heal, eventually I had to go through this uninvited wretchedness and feel every hurt and the afflictions that go along with the loss of a child. I couldn't pick and choose what I wanted to do, or what I thought I *could* do, but had to realize I must walk this pathway one step at a time, knowing some days I could take a *few* steps, and other times *one* step could take weeks. The main goal is to advance forward doing the very best you can to make steady progress. If I ever had to ability to make it an entire day without crying, I felt as though I were gaining massive amounts of good ground. Then those desperate days would come when I could barely get out of bed, and I thought all hope had been lost. Grief resembles a marathon in which it's long, tiresome, and strenuous. In a real race you are allowed to continue even if you slow down, get behind, or fall. However, during the mourning process, if you falter you *feel* like you must go all the way back to the beginning and start over, which deceives you into thinking you're fighting an unwinnable battle. How many of us feel like we're always taking two steps forward and three steps back when we go through strenuous seasons? As mentioned before, the main thing to remember during the hardest times is that *all* days will not be detrimental and that on those you do win, you'll grow stronger and more able to endure the next difficult day with a new level of confidence. Please understand when you feel as though you are always getting knocked down and falling short of the desired victory it's because you are trusting in your own ability and not in God's. We will never lose if we refuse to quit. We will absolutely not ever be defeated no matter what the struggles may be when we trust in God are realize that with Him we have been made to be overcomers in this life. My husband often reminds me that God's ways bear no resemblance to man's ways. With God, if we slow down or even fall, He never makes us start all over, but lovingly and tenderly picks us up and permits us to get up from the place we stumbled and carry on. God permits us to throw up the white flag of surrender at any time we can't continue, and in return, He'll carry us when we no longer have any strength left, another reason to be grateful for His much higher and greater ways. It should encourage us to think of those in Heaven enthusiastically cheering us on. *"Wherefore seeing we also are compassed about with a great cloud of witnesses, let us lay aside every weight and sin which doth so easily beset us, and let us run with patience the race that is set before us." (Hebrews 12:1 KJV)*

I've always been well aware that *our* timing is not the same as *God's,* the Bible assures me that His plans are far greater than we could ever ask or imagine. No matter how long an individual journey ensnares us, we must walk each step at our own pace, faithfully doing as much as we can, so that when we arrive at completion, we'll have accomplished one of the hardest races ever to present itself. Yes, there'll be others in this life we'll have to face, but with each one, as I have said many, times over, the confrontation becomes a little easier due to the courage we acquired in the previous victories. Remember that even the longest, most laborious encounters begin with that one first step. *2 Thessalonians 3:3 KJV* declares: *"Yet the Lord is faithful; He will strengthen you and set you on a firm foundation and guard you against the evil one."* The struggles we face on this earth are growing our faith stronger, enabling us to withstand anything the adversary tries to throw our way to knock us off our promised path. Just as our physical bodies must have stamina, we must also have the power to resist spiritual attacks such as depression, anxiety, and grief: *"So you, my son, be strong (inwardly) in the grace (unmerited favor) that is in Christ Jesus." (2 Timothy 2:1 AMP)*

My son finished his race here on earth and moved on to his heavenly reward far sooner than I was ever ready for him to go. Not realizing what God had in store, I hadn't yet found the courage to rejoice. I didn't understand that if I pushed through the pain and found its purpose, I'd be able to have the peace and joy that I so desperately desired. *"Rejoice and be exceeding glad for great is your reward in heaven." (Matthew 5:12 KJV)*

A lot of times we create our own pain through wrong choices or failure to seek God first, but even then, God's mercy sustains us. *"The Lord is gracious and full of compassion, slow to anger and abounding in mercy and loving kindness." (Psalm 145:8 KJV)* Regardless, there will be tribulation along the way, but when it's over the joy will far outweigh the agony. Have you ever met a mother who has gone through childbirth, enduring hours and sometimes days of intense, extreme labor, would ever say, "Whoa, I wish I'd never done that"? No, not one would admit that even the hardest, most excruciating, painful deliveries didn't fade from memory the moment she held that priceless, brand-new, God-given gift in her arms

I pray that my Father will continually forgive me when I get so overwhelmed by my afflictions and despair that I forget there truly *is* a purpose in them. I don't completely understand the entire purpose for my heartbreak, but I know God does *not* permit unnecessary suffering, and I trust He does have a divine intention for everything we go through. *"Rest assured that the affliction which is now for a moment worketh for us a far more exceeding and eternal weight of glory." (2 Corinthians 4:17 KJV)*

My hope to encourage you to stay focused on the finish line and not to let the pain and sadness blind you so that you miss out on enthustacially living your life to its fullest potential possible. If we remain sad and defeated, we'll miss some of the greatest blessings God has in store for us. Circumstances that caused tremendous suffering may never make sense to us here and now, but I believe that one day it will be entirely evident why we've been chosen to face specific hardships on this earth. The difficulties we encounter along our walk will make Heaven that much sweeter, the same as we appreciate the radiant, glowing sun placed in a brilliant blue sky after the darkness of a raging, storm-filled night. I know that our God will never leave us no matter what. He is emphatically for us and will never be against us. He would not, could not, ever forsake us, even though debilitating depression and overwhelming despair may try to swallow us up in its vengeance. God is our strong tower, our hiding place, and our shelter from the storm, yes even when life is tumultuous and falling apart. *"God is our refuge and strength, a very present help in trouble." (Psalm 46:1 KJV)*

I draw great strength and boldness from the Bible when I read about Paul and how he was able to say, *"I count all things but loss for the excellency of the knowledge of Christ Jesus my Lord: for Whom I have suffered the loss of all things, and do count them but dung, that I may win Christ." (Philippians 3:8 KJV)* Though Paul suffered much, as he surrendered to his calling, he knew there was a far greater reward to gain than the affliction he had to undergo for a season. What a great encouragement to know he took all his sufferings on earth and counted them all joy for the reward of knowing Jesus as his Personal Lord and Savior. He realized that we are in fact God's hands and feet on this earth and that although he'd have days of great trials, he was able to spread God's Word which enticed many to be saved. Jesus Christ Who bore our sins and hung on the cross as the ultimate sacrifice. On that day, Jesus looked ahead in time and realized that for all He would have to withstand, it fit perfectly into His Father's purpose--which was that the world might be saved from eternal damnation. *"For even here unto were ye called: because Christ also suffered for us, leaving us an example, that we should follow His steps."* (1 Peter 2:21 KJV)

I pray that you will be encouraged to know it doesn't matter how horrid the pain or how long the journey, if you will pace yourself and hold onto God, you will one day enjoy the beautiful bounty He has in store for you. As my husband says, "It's not how you start, but how you finish." Also, it's not important *when* you finish, but that you never give up! *"But the God of all grace, Who hath called us unto his eternal glory by Christ Jesus, after that ye have suffered a while, make you perfect, stablish, strengthen, settle you."* (1 Peter 5:10 KJV)

Chapter Twenty
Seashells

The fall of 2011 our family packed up our suitcases and loaded the car. We decided to follow through with the vacation we had been planning before Justin left on his heavenly departure. We did the best we could to prepare for an annual beach trip, which was usually a time of excitement and anticipation of some much-needed rest, and, of course, lots of Fowler fun-time. This one, however, was filled with emotions that we had never experienced before. The thought of going on vacation without our oldest son Justin seemed inconceivable. In the past we had traveled some without him since he'd recently married, but those times had been *his* choice not *ours*. On this trip neither of us chose for him not to go, *this* was one of those situations enforced upon our family. We had fully intended to bring the *whole* family on this particular trip, and, if you remember, I had purposely discussed it with Justin the day before he left this earth. God had another trip for Justin planned, we were left to travel without him for the rest of our natural lives.

As I've mentioned further back, *forced* change isn't something that's easy to accept. I once heard a wise old saying which went something like this-- "You can't pick the cards you want; you must play the hand you're given." We can live our lives thinking it's always going to be a "bed of roses," but inevitably we'll face difficulties. However, when God is on our side, rest assured we can survive these challenges whether they choose us, or we choose them. Time goes by so quickly; let's not waste one moment here on earth. Instead, may we search out the positive in all things and learn of God's goodness in every season of our lives.

The first thing I've always looked forward to when we got to the beach was a leisurely walk along the shoreline as a family. It was the perfect way to stretch our weary bodies after hundreds of miles of highway and finally see the ocean waves and endless miles of sand. This time our arrival was plagued with distressing memories and emotions. I can speak only for myself but can venture a thought that each of us probably felt the same amount of sadness, grief, and, guilt. *I* felt guilty because I was thinking, "Part of 'us' is missing, so how can I enjoy anything that we all used to enjoy together?" I remember an overwhelming sadness at the realization that on this side of Heaven we would never be complete as a family again. We would always be lacking a vital branch of our family tree. My eyes filled with tears as we walked along the water's edge, and I assumed the people we passed along the way might have questioned our sad, weary faces. This being a happy, magical place for most, I'm sure not many tears were shed while at this beautiful, breathtaking destination. As I bowed my head to hide my uncontrollable emotions, I looked down at the sand and saw one of the most extraordinary "signs from above" I had seen thus far on my journey of grief. There before me was an astonishing pathway of the most beautiful, shiny, bright orange seashells I'd ever seen. I quickly picked up some of them to make sure what I was seeing wasn't a mirage. As I scooped up a handful, I felt someone staring at me as if I were intruding on private property. When I looked up, a lady standing on the beach caught my attention. As she walked closer, she said she lived in a nearby condo and had never seen so many orange seashells at one time, so she came down from the porch to see the unusual sight. At that moment, an unbridled smile came across my tear-stained face. I *knew* that only God Himself could have organized such a beautiful pathway of shells, strategically placed so that there was no denying our Justin was still with us. Although we couldn't reach out and touch him, he was there and forever would be, albeit in a new and different form. We look for him in places we need him to be, and there he is, whether in the orangeness of a seashell or the brilliant fiery, orange colors of the sunrise and sunset, which fills me with an overwhelming feeling of hope and peacefulness each time I discover those fabulous creations of nature and cherish the "signs from above." There are times I presume it was no accident that our son's color of choice was orange from an early age. *Could it be* that he was led to pick it because God knew that one day we'd be able to look at the brightness of the orange hues on His earth and have peace knowing that not only was He with us but that our son, also, was always there, too? That once again confirms that God has ordained each and every step we've taken or will ever take on this earth. I know that *if* I follow the footsteps He has ordered for me, I'll be led to that certain path He Himself has specifically designed especially for me. *"The heart of a man plans his way, but the Lord establishes his steps." (Proverbs 1:9 ESV)*

Chapter Twenty-One
Choices

My years in ministry have proven to me how quickly some people are to blame God when they are confronted with dreadful things. What we need to realize is that it's not *God* who causes disastrous things to happen, but they're often times the result of poor choices *we* make. There are many times we open the door to the enemy and permit him to come in and do as he pleases and run rampant "willy-nilly," then blame God for adversities caused by inadvertently or even unintentionally inviting evil into our lives. Many times, I've heard people declare that they are not responsible for the things they do. Some go as far to blame others or even the devil and all of his deceiving demons for the wrong choices they make. I have come to know that very few people can make me do something I didn't want to do. Furthermore, there is no one can make me participate in things that are harmful, bad, or dangerous if, I wasn't an able and willing subject. For example, I know very well it's best to choose water over soda but, after I finish a buttery bowl of salty popcorn my cravings then go to wanting a huge glass of cola. In my mind I know water is the right choice but the battle rages in many areas of my life between the right option and the wrong. I realize that is a mild example, but the same principle works if you are choosing between drugs or alcohol, promiscuity over abstinence or engaging in criminal behavior and dishonoring your parents. The list could go on forever, but I know you get the point. Everything we decide to do matters and has its own set of consequences. I want to encourage you that we all can opt for the correct choices, if we condition our hearts and minds to abide in agreement with one another. We all have a spirit and a flesh man warring on the inside of us. The flesh is always hungry, constantly wanting for anything and everything to satisfy. The spirit yearns to be Christ-like at all time in all things and is easily content to trust God in all things. The one you feed the most is the one that will grow the strongest. Learn to pray and seek God's leading on which way to turn and your life will be not only bearable but more enjoyable.

I don't shove the blame on the driver that caused the accident that took Justin's life, although there *were* times in my deepest pit of lamentation I did try to do just that. After all, he had children of his own and would never drive impaired with them; why would he drive drunk with my son in the car? Furthermore, I don't hold God responsible for my son's losing his life. Some question, "Why, in fact?" I woefully realize that it was Justin's catastrophic decision to get in that car with a drunk driver, which ultimately caused his death. That is not to say it took God by surprise. Even with the poor choice Justin made had it not been his time he would still be with us. What we all must recognize is that the choices we make affect not merely ourselves, but everyone around us. Justin's choice that night ended his own life and also forever changed *our* lives and every aspect of the way we now live. Life as we knew it has been completely obliterated and we no longer resemble the family unit we once knew. Although permanently scarred, from now on all we can do is live as best we can with a vital part of our family missing, with the hope and faith that one day we'll be together again, which provides motivation for staying steadfast in my efforts to continue seeking restoration throughout this life. I feel it honoring to our son to live as *he* did, enjoying life, taking chances, and experiencing new and exciting things. The most remarkable decision he ever made was to accept Jesus Christ as his Lord and Savior, thereby granting him entrance into God's presence when he took his last breath in this world.

We must realize we do maintain the power and have the authority to hasten the end as well as extend our time on earth. *"And if you will walk in my ways, keeping My statutes and my commandments, as your father David walked, then I will lengthen your days." (1Kings 3:14 ESV)* We can have confidence that God will protect us from harm, but at the same time that doesn't mean we can jump off a cliff or the roof of a house, or go speeding down the road, without consequences. We should always pray for wisdom in our choices and never tempt God because the decisions we make most assuredly have long-term effects, which is something I've tried to drill into my sons at every opportunity. We live in a society that promotes, "If it feels good, just do it." We are deceived into thinking our actions won't impact anyone but ourselves when, in fact, nothing could be further from the truth. We have to be competent enough to take responsibly for our choices and not be selfish, wanting only what we want when we want it. Determine to live your life purposefully, with the ambition to make sound, conscientious decisions, thereby making a positive impact on yourself as well as all those around you.

I think back to a priceless memory my heart often recalls. A few months before the accident, Justin had been at our house having dinner as he often did. When he was ready to leave, I walked him to the driveway, and as he made his way to his motorcycle, I shouted out, "JUSTIN!!" As he turned to face me, our eyes met, and I said, "I *love* you, Son!!!" He flashed me the biggest grin and said, "I know, Mom; I love you too." I've always told each of the boys how much I love them at every opportunity. This time it was a feeling that ran throughout my entire being as if my love for him was pouring out of me and being absorbed into him. At that moment, time stood still, and I no longer doubted that he felt or understood my love. That was the exact moment I was absolutely convinced that he sincerely believed how much I loved him unconditionally. One days when I'm missing him the most, I return to those moments that make my heart smile. His face that day is the picture I hold close each time I close my eyes, and his voice at that time is the one I strain to hear daily. It brings me the most joy on my loneliest, wearisome days.

I thank God daily for granting me these rare, treasured moments. I also had the chance a few days later to let him know how proud I was of him for the great young man he was becoming. He was providing a good living for his family and trying to make wise decisions, as his choices affected not only him but also Courtney and

Skylar. He was kind and always giving more than he received from others, a good Christ-like trait to possess. He was looking at life more seriously and not wasting precious time on frivolous things, which made me feel an unselfish pride to think that, maybe, I *was* a good mother, as I often felt inadequate in so many areas. I had peace in knowing I didn't leave any words unspoken, that everything I wanted to tell him I'd been able to say. I give God all the glory and praise for those memorable occasions. *"Surely goodness and mercy shall follow me all the days of my life." (Psalm 23:6 KJV)* I'm very thankful and so blessed that God granted me the time with my son to tie up all the loose ends before He called him home. May you please permit me to prompt you never let a day slip by without letting your loved ones know how uniquely special they are to you. Spend more time loving than fighting and cherish every moment you are given with those closest to you. Let the dishes go and let the yard grow. Those remarkable children are yours only for a little while before they go off into the world and make their own way. It's then that you can breathe a little less labored, knowing you did the best you could do during the time you were given. Make the most of what you have remembering, "It's not what you have, but what you *do* with what you have." My Mamaw Conley which was my grandmother on my dad's side, was a wonderful example of this phrase; she knew it well because she lived it. When Barry and I were first married, we lived in a small country farmhouse provided to us by my dad's twin brother and his wife. We were rich in love but poor didn't begin to describe how much money we didn't have. When my Mamaw came to visit with me, she must have noticed the windows could use a good cleaning. She asked if I had old newspapers and some water with baking soda. I asked, "what for" and she said, "I'm going to show you how to make these windows shine like new pennies!" I grabbed up what she asked for and we went to work; and what do you know, she was right. The view out those old worn panes was crystal clear, shimmering like expensive diamonds. It's advantageous that we take the time to spend with those we hold precious and priceless. Do your best to make as many memories as you possibly can with those you cherish most in your life. When they are gone from this earth it only takes a brief second of remembrance and you're right back to those special times, and it's as if they never left your side. Through the treasured times you can visit them anywhere at any time you choose. I was able to spend a lot of time with her as we lived very close. We often walked together while I was pregnant with Justin. We always ended up afterward at her house enjoying a nice lunch, usually a turkey sandwich with farmer's cheese and her famous homemade dill pickles. When my sister and I were little, my dad brought us to visit we were never allowed to leave empty handed. She would always full up a bag full of chips, cookies or candy. As a matter of fact, no one ever left her house without something good to eat. I suppose that is why she never went without. Whenever she gave, God always blessed her back with more. We spent every holiday and most Saturday's eating with the Conley side of the family until Mamaw was no longer around to cook. She didn't have a lot but what she did with what she possessed was incredible. We all crowded in a basement apartment her sons had fixed up for her when she had surgery and was unable to maneuver the stairs easily. Everyone gathered to eat wherever we could find an empty spot. To her it didn't matter how fancy the place she lived or what she had in it; what she cherished most were the people in her home. She was the one that helped me see soon after Justin was gone that a messy house didn't matter; it meant you had lots of love growing there. When people came to visit our family the day after the accident I sat on the couch completely distraught by agony and remorse; crowds of people were in and out of our home. My friend's daughter wrestled Willow until it looked as if it were snowing in my living room, fur flying in every direction as the ceiling fan blew, depositing fluff on every surface, and throughout the entire house. It was then and there in that surreal moment I finally grasped the meaning behind the lesson my priceless Mamaw preached by her actions.

There were many days in those first few months I was faced with fear and doubt that tried consuming me. Although these thoughts may come, it's our choice to accept or decline their invitation. Most of the ideas that tempted me were along the lines of, "How do I know my son is in Heaven?" The enemy tried to come against me with that one so many times in the beginning. I quickly choose to believe by faith and not agree to let doubt enter into my thought pattern. Many books I've read speak of life-after-death experiences. I know of only one Man Who has ever returned from the dead; being placed in a borrowed tomb after three days, He arose. He came back with the promise of life and an eternal home in Heaven for all believers. I made a choice a long time ago to believe in God no matter what, and although I've faced many unfathomable situations throughout my life, He has always been there with signs to encourage me to continue on the journey created just for me. I cannot walk anyone else's path but my own and He's given me the confidence, mercy, and grace to make it if I trust in Him every step of the way.

It was a blessing to have not one but two grandmothers throughout most of my adult life. There were vast differences between my two of them, but the one similarity was they each brought a great amount of happiness, wisdom, and love to my life. Several years ago, I was forced to deal with the unexpected death of my maternal grandmother. I was her firstborn grand-daughter, and we had an extraordinary relationship. My Mamaw lovingly spoiled me every chance she could. She always talked about how she bought me a brand-new Sunday dress every week, and then added, "Until your sister came along; by that time, it became too expensive." Even then she *continued* to provide us with new ones for Easter each year. There were times when my sister and I were younger; she even *made* our dresses. When the grandsons came along, she continued to do as much as she could and provided them with new shoes as needed. I've never felt loved by someone on this earth as much as I did her, not because she overindulged me with material things, but because she made me feel important, as if there were nothing I could not do. In my heart, I felt she was my number one fan. She cheered me on to do many things in life that I'd never had the confidence to tackle otherwise. She loved to sing in the choir at our church, so I stood right beside her believing I could sing as well. I'll never forget the time she offered me five whole dollars to do solo at our church. Wow! I thought I had hit the jackpot! She supported my cosmetology career and was even my model for the state board test. She had to let her hair and nails grow long for the exam and said, "I look just like an '80's rock star with this hair-do." To this day I can still see the look on her face and hear her voice as she insisted I had better hurry and get my required state board hours in so she could finally get a much-needed haircut. I believe that woman would have done anything in this world for me, and I felt so blessed to have her by my side almost all of my life. I often said she loved me as Jesus does. In her eyes, I could do nothing that would ever cause her to love me less. It's a rare treasure on this earth to have experienced a love so genuine and unconditional.

When Justin was born, she was over-the-moon excited and could hardly wait for his arrival. She ran out and bought him his first pair of Air Jordan tennis shoes and always had him a brand-new pair waiting before he could outgrow the previous one. My Mamaw spent two days at the hospital waiting for him to arrive and never complained about how long it was taking. She promised whoever tried to make her leave that it would not be without them dragging her out forcefully. When the time had finally come and Justin was born, she was the first one at the nursery room window letting everyone know he was her first great-grandson. My husband's uncle overheard her bragging about how beautiful Justin was and determined to get a rise out of her; he responded, "Why, that's the ugliest baby I've ever seen." She turned around as a lioness would attack its prey and let him know in a few choice words that he obviously must be blind not to know that her great-grandson was adorable and perfect in every way. When I was permitted to have visitors, you know

194

she was the first one to inform me of the event that had just happened. She was still quite angry, even though she eventually realized it was all a joke; I was surprised that Uncle Jim didn't have a black eye when he made his way into my hospital room. They shook hands, and both decided to call a truce, and Uncle Jim quickly learned not to mess with *my* Mamaw Hannah when it came to her children or grands and great-grands.

Mamaw and Justin also had an exceptional, unbreakable bond, much like the one she and I shared. Justin and I were with her as much as we could be, taking every opportunity to spend precious time. She always sat with him on her lap as I continued to do her hair each week. As the time passed, I failed to notice that she was aging quickly. Although the years were marching on, in my eyes, she remained a timeless beauty, never showing the lines or wrinkles of her actual age.

As long as I live I'll never forget the day my mother called and said that I needed to hurry to the hospital because my precious Mamaw had taken a turn for the worse. She had fallen and broken her hip a few weeks before, and due to complications had been placed in the intensive care unit. The sound of my mother's voice let me know it was serious and that I needed to get there as fast as possible. Justin was old enough, so I left him in charge of his brothers, as I knew they would not be allowed in ICU. I flew out the door and jumped into the car. As I sped down the road, I pleaded with God not to take my Mamaw away. She had been developing signs of Alzheimer's, and her memory was getting foggy at times. I had prayed every day since that dreaded diagnosis, begging God never to let my Mamaw forget me. She always said she loved me *most*, and for her to forget me would be impossible for me to bear. Even though I knew she loved us all the same, she must have sensed I was the one who needed to *feel* a special unconditional love from her until I was able to find acceptance in God. My eyes kept filling with tears and made the road difficult to drive. I'm thankful God was by my side and got me to the hospital just at the exact moment I needed to be there. I quickly ran back to my Mamaw's room where most of my family members had gathered. As I walked in, she slowly turned her head to notice me at the door. As I made my way to the bed, she asked if I'd come to sing with her. When I responded that I was much too sad to sing, she said, "That's okay; we can sing in a little while." I took her by the hand and agreed that we would harmonize together again very soon. She began to say that she felt so warm, which was unusual because she'd been having a tough time keeping warm as a result of her lack of movement due to the recently repaired broken hip. She then began to speak about the crowds of people in the room. I said, "Yes Mamaw, all of your family members are right here with you," and then she asked, "Who are those people behind me?" We all looked at each other with confused expressions because we didn't see anyone in that space; her bed was against the wall so that no one could possibly have been there physically. She began to speak about the light in the room, saying it was so bright she could hardly open her eyes. We all looked at each other, puzzled because the room was entirely dark; with the curtains tightly closed, there wasn't even a sliver of sunlight streaming in. The only glimmer was in a far corner of the room from the small flicker of a night light above the sink. She couldn't have been speaking of that tiny light, as it wasn't even in her line of sight from where her bed was positioned. She was completely mesmerized by the glow she saw to the point she appeared to be having difficulty holding her eyes open. As moments passed, she continued with a soft, whispered voice to speak of the sights she saw through squinted eyes. Baffled, we chatted among ourselves and tried to figure what was actually happening in that hospital room.

As we stood bewildered at the realistic description of events my grandmother was explaining, we continued to question her about what she was "seeing," and soon a nurse quickly rushed in and made us all leave the room immediately. As we gathered in the hallway, my grandfather sat down in a chair and began to cry softly. I bent down and tried to console him, telling him that everything was going to be okay. He was convinced that *if* he had done something differently, his beloved wife would have been all right. At that moment, it finally became apparent what was taking place. My heart began to pound fast and hard inside my chest, and my hands were trembling as I knew God was speaking to my soul, I began to explain to my Papaw, just what God was revealing to my heart through His Holy Spirit. My Mamaw was preparing for a joyous journey to her eternal home. The people that only she could see were Heaven's angels coming to carry her to her final resting place. The bright, blinding light she spoke of was God's glory coming down as Heaven's doors opened wide for Mary Imogene Hannah to enter. That was the warmth she was describing which she had so long been denied. My grandfather's eyes were now overflowing with tears; at that moment he realized that no longer would he enjoy my grandmother's companionship here on earth but must surrender her to God's compassionate care. Moments later, the nurse confirmed our conclusions. None of us expected Mamaw's departure to come only a few days after entering that hospital, but the signs were all around us when we stopped to pay close attention to her vivid descriptions. She had received her long-awaited reward of heavenly blessings, and we were left without a single doubt as to her destination.

My hard-working, strong Papaw recently joined my Mamaw at the ripe old age of 94. He was an honorable, dedicated man who served in World War II. The stamina and tenacity he had exhibited rendered him the endurance to continue for a long time after losing his beloved sweetheart of 64 years. I'm fortunate God blessed me with the benefit of spending his last few hours on earth with him. He was slowly fading when the nursing home called and told us that we needed to come quickly. I was able to hear him speak only one thing over and over as he walked his last mile. He kept repeating the name, "Paul." I imagined he was speaking of the apostle Paul, because no one had an idea of anyone he knew named Paul, so I quickly asked, "Can you also see Jesus, James, and John?" I leaned

197

over and whispered "Papaw, will you please give a hug and kiss to Mamaw and Justin from me and tell them how much I dearly love and miss them both?" I had read that even though he may have seemed incoherent, he could still hear but perhaps not be able to respond. I watched as my Papaw's legs made walking motions almost continuously. Was he running over to deliver my love and hugs? Knowing his strong-willed personality, I also wondered if he was resisting being carried through Heaven's portals, insisting he wanted to proceed under his own capability to his mansion in the sky. Sometime later he stopped the struggle, accepted his escort willingly, and entered Glory Land in perfect peace.

I have no reservations the events that transpired enabled me to catch a peek of Heaven coming down and touching earth on those sacred days of my grandparents' home goings. In that manner, God sustained me after the loss of our son, with the knowledge that indeed Heaven is an absolute, irrefutable place, and precisely where we who have committed our lives to Jesus will spend eternity. From that day until now, when unbelief tries to consume my thoughts to the point it is impossible to breathe, I go over in my heart every single detail of those precious moments spent my beautiful grandmother and remembered the moment she and my Papaw went to Heaven, and here on earth, we caught a glimpse of its beauty and wonder. *"And if I go and prepare a place for you I will come again and receive you unto myself; that where I am, there you will also be." (John 14:3 KJV)*

Chapter Twenty-Two
Peace

A peaceful life doesn't just automatically happen, and it seems most days there is always something constantly trying to rob you of all the serenity you've achieved. To neutralize the conflicts that confront us, we need to hunger and thirst after a place of refuge, never settling for a fake fortress. *Isaiah 44:3 KJV* declares: *"I will pour upon Him who is thirsty and floods upon the dry ground. I will pour my Spirit upon your offspring and my blessing upon your descendants."*

The enjoyment the world tries to offer can never be compared to that which God brings. The world provides satisfaction only for a moment but what God freely gives lasts a lifetime when you choose to partake of its benefits. To be able to take advantage in this highly sought luxury, you must first believe it's available to you and then search diligently after God who freely gives perfect peacefulness. *The Lord gives strength to His people; the Lord blesses His people with peace." (Psalm 29:11 KJV)* I've decided that I'll walk in complete self-control throughout the rest of my life no matter what my current conditions reflect. That is a possibility available to all who are willing to walk in knowledge of Who Christ is and believing and trusting His Word. Remember what I talked about earlier; we can't always control what happens, but we can decide how we will react. Position all your hope and trust in Him, and don't look at the situations which instantly devour the delight and relaxation right out of you. Don't try to make sense of everything, but rest in the assurance of knowing that God will work all things out for the very best outcome possible. He knows the beginning and the ending of your life, and every detail in between. *Isaiah 46:1 KJV says, "Declaring the end and the result from the beginning, and from ancient times the things that are not yet done saying, My counsel shall stand, and I will do all my pleasure and purpose."* The ability to remain in complete contentment, no matter what situation may be, is total freedom. When I look past the circumstances and trust that everything will be all right, it is then and only then I am able to triumph through tragedy.

Once we obtain order and rest in our lives, we have to declare that nothing or no one will ever steal these gifts away. There's an ongoing conflict each day not to give in to how I feel but to walk in what I know. My mind has thoughts contrary to what God's Word tells me, and when I listen to those comments in my head, I'm discontent and discouraged, but when I listen to God's voice, my spirit can rest. *"Finally, brethren, whatsoever things are true, whatsoever things are honest, whatsoever things are pure, whatsoever things are lovely, whatsoever things are of good report; if there be any virtue, and if there be any praise, think on these things." (Philippians 4:8 KJV)*

After a devastating loss, many fall into sorrow and deep, dark despair. We somehow conclude it's our *right* and that we deserve it because of the pain we've endured. There are times I felt peace was unattainable due to the overwhelming sadness that had been heaped upon my life. I've learned that you can settle into suffering and make your home there, or you can *choose* to desire, seek out, and claim the peace that passes all natural comprehension. Make a conscious decision that the hopeless and discouraged state you find yourself in at times and is not your final destination but only an unplanned stop along the way to a glorious place with no more heartache. With determination not to quit and God's unrelenting support you'll eventually discover your way out of darkness if you continue to search for the light at the end of your tragic tunnel.

The Bible tells us to ask whatever we need from Him. *"Ask, and it shall be given you; seek, and ye shall find; knock, and it shall be opened unto you." (Matthew 7:7 KJV)* If we knock once and that door doesn't open, we should keep right on tapping until it does. The walls of Jericho didn't fall the first time God's people marched around the city. The faithful continued to walk, never giving up in defeat, and one day the walls came tumbling down. If you ask God for something and don't get an immediate answer, you can do as my boys always did with me and keep asking; or you can wait in faith knowing that God is moving and working at all times in every situation in your life. There have been times when I thought God was too busy to answer my endless cries for help, when my whining turned to begging, pleading, and demanding. I eventually gave up, thinking He was deaf to my prayers. I've since realized it's in those times He's teaching me to wait patiently while He's working out the details. If you take only one piece of advice I've offered, please make a note of this part and stick it on your refrigerator door, when you've asked over and over, knocked on Heaven's door until you are weak, weary, and worn, have faith and know God hasn't abandoned you and He never will! I've learned through the years when I need God, He's always with me, even when I refuse to acknowledge Him. When I can't feel his constant presence, it's not because *He* is absent; it's because *I* have turned away from *Him*. Wherever I go, God is already there. The Bible says in *Psalm 139:8 KJV: "If I ascend into Heaven, thou art there: if I make my bed in hell, behold, thou art there."* When I choose God's path for my life, He has already prepared my steps and the way I'm to go. Should I decide not to follow after His plans, He will still be with me. *"A man's heart plans his way, But the Lord directs His steps." (Proverbs 16:9 NKJV)*

It's God's intense pleasure to bless His children with exceptional gifts. Peace is one of those, that like the others, is free to all those who will ask and receive. *"And let the peace of Christ rule in your hearts to which as one body you were called to live and be thankful."* (*Colossians 3:15 KJV*) We can have the hope that we need not worry and stress over what may come our way and can rest assured that He holds the universe in the palm of His unchanging hand. *That* is the tranquility we should all seek, for without it our lives can be filled with a lot of chaos and turmoil. I always say, "Yes, life is tough, but can you imagine how hard it would be without God' assistance?" I try to encourage people to pray through adversities of every kind. Even though it may still be difficult, I'm convinced it would be impossible without God. Complete peace is not worrying about what happened in the past and not stressing over what may or may not happen tomorrow; it's resting in the assurance that God is your source and He will provide what is needed to bring you refreshing restoration. There's not one trial or hardship we face that He can't manipulate and make a beautiful masterpiece of perfection. When we accept the truth of that, we can begin to walk in the freedom His life operating within us brings.

There's an ongoing battle with your adversary when you decide to walk with the Lord. The enemy would like nothing more than to keep you oppressed, overwhelmed, depressed and discouraged, without hope of *ever* having serenity in your life. You must not fall prey to his evil plot and easily give up what Jesus so brutally died to give you. You must take a stand and not enable His blood-bought peace, a rare, precious treasure, to be carelessly stolen from you. When you have something so valuable, there's always a chance it can be lost or taken away, but it's your choice whether you'll let go quickly or hold onto it with all of your might. I've heard time and time again; a thief never breaks into an empty house. Keep in mind that if it seems like the enemy is continually trying to intimidate and aggravate, realize it's because you are a threat to him or he wouldn't bother you. Make sure your temple is filled to overflowing with God's blessings of joy and peace physically and spiritually in a bountiful supply. You must tirelessly seek to possess tranquility and let nothing to rob you of its matchless worth. To control what restricts our contentment, we must make up our minds that nothing or no one is going to take from us what is rightfully ours. The same principle works whether it be happiness over sadness, victory over defeat, or speaking life over death in our situations. We must speak life over the dead things in our lives. Because Jesus conquered death, hell, and the grave, do not let death win. *Revelation 1:18 NKJV* assures us that *"I am He Who lives, and was dead, and behold, I am alive forevermore. Amen. And I have the keys of Hades and of Death."* Things that were once lifeless can be revived by God's power actively working through us. We can have joy knowing that happiness is caused by a reaction to an event or an encounter, but joy is *remaining* in a state of contentment that cannot be taken away without our letting go of it. If we do not permit people or circumstances to dictate what we have to accept, we'll conquer every obstacle in our way. As fifty is quickly approaching, many women have warned me of the heath issues in my future. I've decided not to accept their offers of unpleasantness and have chosen to play the trump card of Jesus is my Healer. I may have to muddle through some undesirable side effects of middle age, but I will do it with God's help making it bearable. Don't be so quick to take other people's word for what will invariably happen to you; trust the Word and believe God; in doing so, your future years will be greater than the past ones! *"The glory of this latter house shall be greater shall be greater than the former, saith the Lord of hosts; and in this place, I will give peace, saith the Lord of hosts." (Haggai 2:9 KJV)*

Has anyone ever physically tried to take one of your belongings away from your grasp? Did you willingly give it up or did you put up a struggle? I don't know about you, but unless God specifically asks me to do so, I don't often freely give up something that's rightfully mine. So why is it we carelessly let go of our peace and joy when we discover ourselves staring at difficulties? To all the nay-sayers, I'm not declaring that I'm selfish, or in any way a lover of material things, because anyone who's ever lost a child places no value on such stuff that can easily be replaced. I'm merely trying to make a valid point as to how we excessively protect possessions that are valuable to us. Shouldn't we have that same determination over our own physical well-being?

The word "peace" is mentioned in the King James Bible 420 times. Knowing that there are 365 days in a year, that is once for every day and then some, as God always blesses us above and beyond what we can ask, think, or imagine. He knew ahead of time there would be days we'd need an extra dose of peacefulness in our hectic lives. We often introduce chaos by adding more to our schedules than we can do in one twenty-four-hour period. That, in turn, creates discord which robs us of our patience and composure causing an axexity-fueled stressful day. For God to bring His comfort into our lives, all we have to do is ask for, believe in, and accept it; *then* we can begin to walk in it. *"But let him ask in faith without wavering. For he that wavereth is like a wave of the sea driven with the wind and tossed." (James 1:6 KJV)* That means we should not talk ourselves out of our God-given blessing but be steadfast and determined to have the calmness that reaches beyond all human perception. *"And the peace of God that passeth all understanding shall keep your hearts and minds through Christ Jesus." (Philippians 4:7 KJV)* That Scripture means that with God you can have tranquility in every circumstance no matter what the situation may be. When you know the Peacemaker, you can be at ease when nothing in this world lines up according to your expectations. Be determined not to dread, stress, and worry over every hindrance in your life. Before we ever face a trial, we need the determination to stand firm and faithful, rather than walk around beaten down, depressed, and disgusted by everyone and everything. Knowing we have a heavenly Father who loves us, we'll be able to walk victoriously. You have to come to this realization on your own; no one can make you believe. When you get a real realization of Who God is and what He can do you will be completely transformed. I've always told my sons their mother would be their number one fan. That means no one on this earth will ever be prouder of them, whether they do everything right or fail every time they try. I refuse to let my unrealistic expectations of what *I* think they should do disappoint me when they chose a different road to success than the one I had in mind. When they played sports, or participated in other competitions, I never cared if they won or lost; it was way more important to me that they had a fantastic time. I celebrated with the boys when they achieved the win; and cheered them up when they faced great loss. Their father would always remind me that, "It's no fun losing;" and yet it was always more important to *me* that they never stressed over their performance but learned to enjoy the activities. God desires both for us to enjoy life and excel in all that we do. I'm sure it grieves His heart when His children walk around dejected and disappointed, trying to make it on *their* efforts when He's waiting for us to ask *Him* for help. It's one thing to read the Word and know what it says, but until we actively walk in it, there's no power. When we're aware of Who God is inside of us, we'll be able to stare defeat square in the face and cause it to run back to where it came from in such fear it will be hesitant to return.

My favorite message preached by my husband is titled, "Your Attitude Determines Your Altitude," meaning that your thoughts, which eventually become words and actions, will determine how far you go in this life. The Bible refers to our tongue being like a rudder on a ship. *James 3:4-5: "Look at the ships also: though they are so large, and they are driven by strong winds, they are guided by a very small rudder whatever the will of the pilot directs. So also, the tongue is a small member, yet it boasts of great things."* That Scripture speaks of how powerful our words are; they determine how far you will go in this life. If we approach life with negativity through all the situations we encounter, how can we ever expect to enjoy our days? Have you ever met people that no matter what the circumstances, they always find a way to complain? It's as if they never have anything to say unless it's a negative comment. These people are the ones who rain on everyone else's parade; they are the ones upset when it's cold and also when it's hot. For fear it might be contagious, it's not surprising that no one would ever want to be within one hundred miles of them and their griping and complaining ways! I'm pretty sure it's a proven fact we mimic those we associate with; at least it's that way in the Fowler household. If ever my boys leave the house without telling me who they are going to meet, within thirty seconds of them returning home, I can tell you exactly who they were with. It has to do with their actions, demeanor, and vocabulary. Good or bad, we often resemble in our words and actions who we spend time. When we run around with the wrong crowd we quickly take on their character traits, and when we spend time with Jesus, thankfully we resemble His glorious countenance. A friend once told me that she acted one way when she associated with her non-Christian friends and took on another persona when she was with her Christian friends. In order to live a peaceful life, we must choose to "get on one side of the fence or the other; you can't ride the middle," as my dad says. The Bible tells us we need to be hot or cold because warm just doesn't cut the mustard so to speak. *"I know thy works, that thou art neither cold nor hot: I would thou wert cold or hot." (Revelation 3:15 KJV)* Both hot and cold water serve a purpose, while warm water is unsatisfying and is what you get if you mix the hot in with the cold. To the coffee lovers out there, no one drinks their favorite mocha latte or frappuccino lukewarm; you like your hot specialty java heated and the ice coffees chilly. God goes on to say in verse 16 that, *"So then because thou art lukewarm, and neither hot nor cold I will spue thee out of My mouth."* No one that drinks coffee settles for sipping barely hot coffee; some would follow God's example in the above verse above and spit it out.

To walk in perfect peace, we always must try to get out of bed with a positive attitude every single day, speak life and power into the atmosphere, and claim it in Jesus' name over your life as well as the lives of family and friends. Never communicate statements contrary to what God's Word says. Remember the enemy seeking to devour us cannot read out thoughts, but when we announce them out loud, he knows our secrets, plans, and desires. The Bible uses references about planting, reaping, and sowing. When our evil antagonist is throwing out seeds of bitterness, hurt, and anger do not let them take root. Just as natural grains won't thrive on stony, hard soil, the enemy's seeds of discouragement won't grow in you mind if you are strong in the Lord and steady in the Word. When you read your Bible, you increase in wisdom and knowledge of who you are in Him, which gives you the ammo to destroy your enemy's plans;

in return you will reap a bountiful harvest of God's amazing blessings. You should never make it easy for your opponent to get the best of you. Remember he comes against our minds and into our thoughts; if we give attention to the ideas that rotten, low down, dirty villain is using to discourage our walk and he gains a cordial invitation into our lives. The enemy has no power over you unless we open the door and welcome him in. We need to put on the whole armor of God each day so that we'll be able to withstand all his attacks. *"Stand firm then, with the belt of truth buckled around your waist, with the breastplate of righteousness in place, and with your feet fitted with the readiness that comes from the gospel of peace. In addition to all of this take up the shield of faith which you have to extinguish the flaming arrows of the evil one. Take the helmet of salvation and the sword of the spirit which is the Word of God."* (*Ephesians 6:14-18 NIV*) It is Christ Who gives us the ability and endurance for whatever we're called to do, but we, too, have a responsibility to do our part and be ready when trouble knocks at the door. Aside from Him, I can do nothing, but with Him, I can and will do *all* things. As I've said over and over throughout this book, in every way, fashion, and form possible no matter what the circumstances may dictate, we have to maintain God-confidence so that we can avoid a devastating, downward spiral when things do not go our way. We must set our minds on things above rather than below, and fixate our focus on all God's promises so we'll not get caught up in the negativity of life and miss the moments of generous joy and vast happiness. Hard, desperate times make us who we are; we can live life dejected, discouraged, pitiful, and powerless or we can choose to walk in victory. *If* we determine early in the day that we'll have freedom from disturbance no matter what may happen, then we set ourselves up for great blessings. The enemy would like nothing better than to continue robbing, destroying and killing. *John 10:10 ESV* warns: *"The thief comes only to steal and kill and destroy. I come that they may have life and have it abundantly."* Do not ever doubt that God is for you, and when we are His children, His power

207

is in us; therefore, whatever force may come against you, God is greater! *"Ye are of God, little children, and have overcome them because greater is He that is in you than he that is in the world." (1 John 4:5 KJV)*

I understand all too well devastating pain, horrible heartache, and sorrow of all kinds, specifically with the loss of our son. I've chosen to let the pain push me onto a road of tranquility that is hard to discover, but with persistence is achievable. I refuse to sit back or lay down and let my constant disappointment and discouragement take me out of the race for serenity. That's not what my son would want for me and not part of God's plan for our family. When my life begins to disintegrate before my eyes, I bend my knees, bow my head, take a deep breath, and ask God for the fortitude to continue. He's my source of comfort like never before, and *nothing else* in this life can bring the peacefulness, contentment and joy He can.

What God has done for many other grieving parents and me, He will also do for you. The decision is yours to make. No, we didn't sign up for this journey of heartbreak, but God permitted it because He knew He'd be available to bolster us up every step of the way when we would welcome His assistance. May your attitude soar with the eagles throughout your journey so that you will know the reality of *Isaiah 40:31 KJV: "They that wait upon the Lord shall renew their strength: they shall mount up with wings as eagles; they shall run and not get weary; they shall walk and not faint."* Learn to wait upon God; be patient, and He will give you incredible might to soar above the storms of life. The eagle is admired all over the world as a symbol of power, freedom, and transcendence. A commonly known fact, however, is that eagles aren't known to have a vast amount of stamina, but they recognize the power of the wind. Once these magnificent birds have captured the mighty gusts of air under their wings, they use the currents to lift and carry them effortlessly far above the turbulence, so they can reserve their energy and fly longer and stronger. While other birds refuse to fly with such damaging winds, the eagle is unafraid of the storm and soars majestically in spite of the danger. If we could all learn this ability not being tossed back and forth by life's storms but use their force to our advantage, it would cause us to rise above and remain consistently stable. When we get confused, frustrated, and bent out of shape in an "impossible situation," we are likely to destroy all our hope and will to keep going. Much as it is very unlikely that you will be able to save a drowning man until he stops fighting, surrenders to assistance, and permits you to pull him to safety, we must recognize that Almighty God *is* an ever-present help in troubled times. He stands ready and willing for us to lean on Him. If we chose not to do so, we would almost certainly drown while trying to be rescued, as the man in the illustration above would. May we always submit to God and find silence in every storm as we consent to His being our power when we are weak.

The real victory will come when you learn to *rest* in Him. Stop trying to lift the heavy load of grief with your limited power. I'm reminded of a biblical illustration in which Jesus had just performed the miracle of feeding five thousand people with five small loaves and two fishes. When the meal concluded Jesus insisted his followers climb into the ship and cross over to the other side. He then dismissed the others and stayed there praying well into the night. In the meantime, a storm developed and the disciples were in complete distress because it appeared as though the storm would consume the boat and drown all passengers. The Bible describes Jesus walking on the storm-tossed sea, without worry or concern. Because He knows the Master of the winds, He knows no fear. The Scripture describes that Jesus was moving toward the vessel and quickly responded when they cried out to for help. (This verse was paraphrased from *Matthew 14:27 KJV.*)

Much like the turmoil of that day, many times we are faced with rough waters when going from one place to another. When we're being battered by the waves of life's assults we must remain steadfast and call out to God knowing He will answer. Most times we reduce God's ability when we refuse to step aside and let Him move in our lives. When we relinquish all pain, stress, and heartache and consent for Him to remove the burden, we can begin to have more successful lives. After all, He created the entire world and all its contents with His spoken Word. Is there anything at all too difficult for Him? *"Behold I am God of all flesh: is there anything too hard for Me?" (Jeremiah 32:27 KJV)* All you have to do is entirely surrender your load of cares, trusting and believing that everything that happens to us has to pass through His hands. God has not called us to walk through this life alone. Should you choose to do so, you need to realize that is not God's plan for you. He desires for us to be wholeheartedly, confidently, and solely relying on Him. We must develop a divine dependence, believing that we will make it in this life no matter what detours we may encounter along the way. *"And Jesus looking upon them said, with men it is impossible, but with God all things are possible." (Mark 10:27 KJV)* His grace and mercy will continue to encourage me all my days through whatever may come my way until my time on this earth is completed. All we have to do is admit we need help, allow Him to move in our situation, and He will bring reconciliation to calm every storm we're facing. Then and only then can breakthrough come, and with it, the most incredible victorious peace. There is an overwhelming freedom in knowing that when we walk according to His will, permitting Him to direct our steps, we can live a life of absolute contentment!

"Thus, saith the Lord, which maketh a way in the sea and a path through mighty waters." (Isaiah 43:16 KJV) My hope and constant plea each day are that I may rest in the comfort I have in my relationship with Christ. I'm convinced that when my struggles take me out past my ability to hold myself above the angry waves, having God's Word living inside me, and believing He will be my support, He lovingly rescues me so that I will never be consumed by conflict. I have heard that having peace on the outside comes from knowing God on the inside. Complete, unrelenting peace comes

from *knowing* Him and that there will never be a storm we have to go through that He won't be there to hold and keep us from all harm. *"For thou hast been a shelter for me, and a strong tower from the enemy." (Psalm 61:3 KJV)* Our God desires to make every mountain level or give us the ability to walk over them with His unyielding, endless assistance. He will also make every crooked way straight if we'll submit. *"And I will bring the blind by a way that they knew not; I will lead them in paths that they have not known: I will make darkness light before them, and crooked things straight. These things will I do unto them, and not forsake them." (Isaiah 42:16 KJV)*

While on vacation one year when the boys were small, we all were enjoying a relaxing, cloudless day on the beach. Justin and Jacob wanted to go to the pool and Caleb wanted to stay near the ocean. I left Caleb with Barry and the other two went with me. When we returned a brief time later, I saw Barry talking with another couple and Caleb was nowhere in sight. I hurried to him and asked where Caleb was, to which he responded, "I thought he was with you." Within moments we each went in opposite directions frantically searching for our son. Barry was grabbing up random children thinking each one was Caleb; he was completely blinded by his fear. A lady approached me and said, "Are you looking for a little boy with blue swim trunks?" "YES!" I exclaimed. She then replied, "He's right over there, I've been watching him chase sea gulls down by the water's edge." We all quickly ran over to Caleb, grabbing him up holding him tightly. I looked for the woman to thank her, but she had vanished into thin air; we looked all around but never saw her again. I feel strongly that dear lady must have been sent as an angel from Heaven to watch over our son. Fear may come and leave our vision grossly distorted much like my husband was that day. We may be in total darkness, unable to see what lies ahead, but God will be the light to show us His way and restore our sight. Was it not until Saul was struck down with blindness that he was then able to truly see God? *"And he trembling and astonished said, Lord, what wilt Thou* have me to do?" *(Acts 9:6 KJV)* What a glorious promise to know that although grief may blind us awhile, God will lead us to a brand-new way we would never have known on our own. What pure contentment we can have in Him, trusting, believing He can lead us through the utter darkness when tragedy has taken our sight. To know that He will deliver us from unbearable places in our lives gives me calming consolation.

God never guaranteed this life would be easy and trouble free, but He does provide tranquility during the troubled times. *"Though the mountains be shaken, and the hills be removed, yet My unfailing love for you will not be shaken, nor my covenant of peace be removed, says the Lord, Who has compassion on you." (Isaiah 54:10 NIV)* That's a blessed affirmation from God to all who seek after and have an honest and humble hunger for contentment. Just as He has given me incredible solace through my journey that often takes me places I have no desire to go, He will do the same for you because God has no favorite children. What He has done for one, He'll do for all. Won't you accept *His* peace unlike this world can ever offer? *"You will keep in perfect peace those whose minds are steadfast because they trust in You." (Isaiah 26:3 KJV)*

Chapter Twenty-Three
Trusting in Him

I've not always had the relationship with God that I now have; it has grown deeper and stronger over time, particularly since the loss of our son. The bond I had with God in the past was average and very vanilla. So, if you detect even one ounce of might or boldness in these rambling, wandering chapters, know that it is not of my own effort or ability that I can stand; but by His unmerited mercy and undeserved favor! I believed in Him for my salvation, and I kept up with all my Christian responsibilities. I prayed, read my Bible, and loved others, and did all of the self-imposed duties we feel obligated to do as believers. Even knowing that God requires none of those things to receive salvation, I still felt like I needed to do them so I could somehow feel as though I'd done my part to let God know I loved and appreciated Him. I now rest in the divine assurance that His grace covers all my inconsistencies and lackluster attempts at trying to be worthy of His love, which I now accept as a free gift. I realize His affections can never be earned or deserved. I no longer worry so much about "messing up," but try my very best to do what is pleasing to God. When I miss the mark, His Holy Spirit quickly pricks my heart to remind me I'm still a work in progress. *"And I am sure of this, that He Who began a good work in you will bring it to completion at the day of Jesus Christ." (Philippians 1:6 ESV)*

Through the events of the last six and a half years, I have learned to lean on Him even for the courage to get out of bed, and there were times I was grateful simply that God had commanded my heart to beat, and the act of breathing had happened naturally without any thought on my part. Had this not been the case, I know without a doubt that at the beginning of my extreme heartbreak, most days would have been too overwhelming to do that much. I am so thankful that God in all His wonder keeps this grief-stricken body functioning properly that I may be used for His glory, a testimony to others of His power and grace. Now, more than ever, I have to rely on God's Holy Spirit in me to direct my life. I can no longer make it by my own efforts but must depend wholly on Him and His life in me, which gives me the power to exist. *"For in Him we live, and move, and have our being; as certain also of your own poets have said, 'For we are also His offspring.'" (Acts 17:28 KJV)* I have discovered that when I focus on what I see in the natural, it causes me to lose sight of what God is trying to show me supernaturally. I have learned that when I trust God in every area of life, He causes my faith to be strengthened and the things that used to get me sidetracked and sideways no longer hinder my course. To explain it more clearly, when I focus on God and not on my problems, all my troubles seem to disappear. One of my many favorite verses in the Bible has always been *Proverbs 3:5-6 AMP: "Trust in and rely confidently on the Lord with all your heart. And do not rely on your own insight or understanding. In all your ways know and acknowledge and recognize Him, and He will make your paths straight and smooth {removing obstacles that block your way}."* I dare not trust the thoughts that race through my mind but confidently believe in God's wisdom to give me understanding and guide me the way I should go.

God has the unique ability to speak words of encouragement directly to my heart. I'm convinced that without His help, I would have never been able to function under the constant strain of the grief I've felt through my trials. In times of trouble before, all I had to do was read my Bible and glean instruction of how to make it in my daily walk. *"Behold the Lord will help me. Let him rely on, trust in and be confident in the name of the Lord, and let him lean upon and be supported by His God." (Isaiah 50:9-10 KJV).* After tragedy struck, however, it was nearly impossible for me to concentrate on one thing for any given period. During those days of complete darkness and heartache, my mind was in such a paralyzing stupor, I couldn't even understand God's Word. As I read the lines on a page, they all seem to run together in a muddy mess. My mind would not

214

retain what I had read long enough to get through even one sentence. As I continued to read the Scriptures daily, as I'd always tried to do, my mind seemed to grow more and more confused even by the simple ones. It was as if my thoughts were filled with such chaos that I feared my head might explode. All through my Christian walk, I've believed that when you plant a seed, God will bring the harvest, so I continued to study. I trusted that even when I lacked the natural ability to comprehend on my own, that, in time, He would reveal to me the fullness of His Word. I knew that it would become planted deep in my soul, and in His perfect timing, it would spring forth when I needed it.

With my desire to hear from God so important, and my inability to understand even greater, God chose to get my attention through Christian songs during the first few months after the accident. I was able to hear Him speak through them when I was exhausted both physically and mentally. The way verses of the Bible were incorporated into the lyrics saturated my spirit and soothed my sorrow. He chose to reach me through music, so I didn't have to think or try to study the meaning of the Scriptures. All I had to do was relax and listen to the words of the songs and let them minister to my heart. I made it a habit of playing music all through the day so that just at the moment I needed to be lifted up; I could hear God's voice of encouragement as if He were speaking directly to me. There were so many times while driving a song on my car radio would confirm something I had just talked to God about moments before. Every time this happened, it was as if God Himself reached down from Heaven and held me in His arms. I'm firmly convinced that God knows positively what we need before we are aware of it ourselves. He even knows our thoughts before we think them.

I'm convinced He takes much pleasure in seeing His children prosper, just as we do ours. *Psalm 37:4-5 AMP* says, *"Delight yourself in the Lord, and He will give you the desires and petitions of your heart. Commit your way to the Lord; Trust in Him also He will do it."* Some may argue that God doesn't give His children their

215

hearts' desires, but as I've lived this life, I have found that the closer I draw to Him, and the more I rely on Him, *my* desires become *His* desires. It was through time spent at His feet that passion for the things I once thought relevant began to fade away. Through my days of unrelenting trials, I yearned for the ability to survive moment by moment, day in, day out. Being directionless in efforts to find my way, I finally focused more intently on God and grew dependent on Him for guidance. I felt His arms around me the tightest when I kept my eyes on Him rather than circumstances. He strengthened, motivated, and cheered me on and proved that with His ability actively working, there was nothing I couldn't accomplish. When I needed comfort, He would be my peace. Every time I desired joy, He was my delight. When I needed love and compassion, He provided an abundant supply.

It is in those times, of being fully immersed in His goodness that we learn His strength is made perfect in our weakness. *Jeremiah 17:7-8 KJV: "Blessed is the man that trusteth in the Lord, and whose hope the Lord is. For he shall be like a tree planted by the waters, and that spreadeth out her roots by the river, and shall not see when heat cometh, but her leaf shall be green; and shall not be careful in the year of drought neither shall cease from yielding fruit."* Wow! What a promise, that when we place all our hope and trust in Him, we will be successful and multiply. That particular Scripture proclaims that even during the hard, dry, thirsty times, we'll never be without the things we need; even when things are bad God is still a good Father. He delights in being our heavenly Father Who helps in difficulties and rejoices with us joyful times. Do not be conditioned to pray simply when things go wrong. Make it a priority to go to Him at all times in every area of your life. *"Show me Your Ways O Lord; teach me your paths. Guide me in Your truth and faithfulness and teach me, You are the God of my salvation; for You do I wait all day long." (Psalm 25:4-5 AMP)*

I once listened to an old-timey, hellfire, and brimstone preacher say, "Lord, save 'em no matter what it takes!" For so many years I was too afraid to pray this prayer for my loved ones, the fear of what might happen scared me to death. What if having their souls saved meant enduring great calamity or even losing their lives? After a very long struggle of back and forth with God, I finally came to a sobering thought. *Why* was I too paralyzed to ask, "Save 'em no matter what"? Rather than relinquish their "fate" to the Lord, did I think I could assume the challenge of winning them on my own? Was I deceived into thinking *I* loved them more than God does, in that He might allow a great misfortune for them to be saved? Was my trust in God not genuine? All these questions continued to flood my mind until one day the Holy Spirit revealed that I was all wrong in my thinking. I learned that because God loves us more in a moment that we can love anyone in a lifetime, I didn't need to worry and fret about praying this prayer for my family I could freely and easily speak undaunted prayers of this nature and be completely trusting in God to "save 'em no matter what it takes." I realized that if they were ever to discover salvation, I'd have to surrender them for Him to work in their lives. My job would then be to make my petitions known to God and get out of His way, rather than trying to convict others by "preaching" my "sermonettes."

It's so challenging to trust someone or something you cannot see, to rely on and have confidence in what you cannot physically embrace. That, however, is why God says we must have *faith* in Him which seems impossible, but in reality, if you could see or touch Him, would it be faith? People often say that "Seeing is believing," but faith believes in what you cannot see. It's like walking in the dark, not knowing what's ahead but trusting you can make it to the other side. The confidence you must learn through tragedy is possibly one of the hardest lessons of all, but if you *stretch* your faith to reach past your normal way of reasoning, you'll be amazed at how God will move on your behalf.

How many of us are willing to walk by faith? *2 Corinthians 5:7 KJV: "For we walk by faith, not by sight."* It's not easy to trust in what isn't apparent to the human eye. Many may call us fools for believing in an invisible God. Although I can feel His presence moving in my heart, my mortal eyes cannot detect Him; however, there's evidence of His existence every moment of each day. We cannot *see* the wind, but we can't deny its presence. We watch its force as it causes trees to sway gently side to side or brings the pandemonium and extensive damage of a hurricane. Although we may not be able to *touch* it, we feel its effects when it gently blows across our faces on a breezy spring day or during storms that try to knock us off our feet. You also cannot visualize the air you breathe, but without its life-sustaining power you would definitely not continue to live. That's how I believe it is with God. I cannot see Him physically, but I can feel Him in my heart as He enables me to conquer each day's obstacles. The power He gives me through His Holy Spirit is the same that raised Jesus from the dead. *"And what is the exceeding greatness of His power toward us who believe, according to the working of His mighty power, which He wrought in Christ when He raised Him from the dead and set Him at His right hand in heavenly places." (Ephesians 1:19-20 KJV)* Knowing that exact power is living in me gives me hope that He will also rejuvenate and restore my life after tragedy has caused me to feel like death has invaded and devoured my body, heart, and mind.

So much of the time it seems I'm reluctantly going through the motions and not truly experiencing life, unable to enjoy what once brought me great elation and delight. When I don't analyze and contemplate the past, going over every detail of what used to be, and simply rely on what I have learned through the Scriptures, my determination increases and my enthusiam rises to the sky. *Isaiah 40:28-29 ESV* says *"Have you not known? Have you not heard? The Lord is the everlasting God, the creator of the ends of the earth. He does not faint or grow weary, and His understanding is unsearchable. He gives power to the weak and to him who has no might He increases strength."* When I read this passage, I get a renewed sense of power, and hope begins to rise in my spirit as I gain motivation and stamina. I trust that when I call upon His name, He'll hear me; He's never so busy He doesn't take time to listen. God is no respecter of persons. He hears the faintest whisper of a sinner's prayer as quickly as the prayers and praises of a life-long, seasoned Christian. Hear my heart and know that God will meet you wherever you are, whether you're a Christian or not, have just begun your walk with God, or have been traveling to your promised destination for many years. I know this for a fact, as He has proven to be trustworthy time and time again in my walk with Him. Never has He relented in His pursuit of me, even when I refused to acknowledge His presence. He has never failed me even though I've failed Him many times. *"Though he fall he shall not be utterly cast down; for the Lord upholdeth him with His right hand." (Psalm 37:24 KJV)*

God is the only one Who has the unparalleled ability to see into the future. He knows precisely how everything in our lives will work out from the day we are born until the day He calls us home. *"Before I formed you in the womb I knew you, And before you were born I concecrated you; I appointed you a prophet to the nations." (Jeremiah 1:5 ESV)* Just as God prepared me to accept His will for Justin and for our family, He has also trained me to trust in and completely depend on Him. All my life, up to the very night of the accident, I tried to plan in detail, according to my desires. I always knew what I wanted to do and did whatever I could to make it happen. I tried to live my life by a set schedule and often said that if it wasn't written in my daily planner, then it didn't happen. I liked to be in control, and what I could and could not do was evident by the kitchen calendar I made for myself. After losing my son, I was rudely awakened to the realization that I was not the one in control, but that I did have a close relationship with the One Who *is*. That night, I learned that I could no longer try and plan my life according to how I wanted it to go, but instead had to trust in the One Who set this world in orbit. He's the One I confide in and pray to each morning and night for help to accept and understand the things I cannot control. I haven't always been accepting of God's design, but have learned to trust that He has remarkable things in store for my family and me. I now realize that even though I may have some great ideas, God, Himself has extraordinary plans to which even my finest, most outstanding dreams cannot come close to comparing.

Many times, I've wondered, as most people do, "Why me, Lord?" My dad, a long-time pastor, would always answer that question with a question: "Why *not* me, Lord?" I also heard of another preacher who took that statement one step further posing the question, "Who would you suggest?" *Romans 5:3-4 NKJV* gives us an idea of one reason we suffer afflictions and adversities. *"We also glory in tribulations, knowing that tribulation produces perseverance; and perseverance, character, and character, hope."* However, would any of us *volunteer* to go through torment so that our confidence in God can become more developed? To take trust one step further, who do you know that would agree to go through extreme ordeals in order to use them as a solution for others' troubles? Would we ever be willing to go through pain, tragedy, or misery to help someone else prosper from our experiences? I will answer that very few, if any, would agree to that task. However, God calls us to endure certain circumstances so that we can grow and gain a more compassionate understanding of others who have gone through similar testing and learned a trust that extends beyond the limits of our human capacity to comprehend. That is precisely what Jesus did for us when He died on the cross for our sins. He came into this world and walked as a man on the earth and died so that we could have life and live it through Him to its fullest potential. He, too, had to have an incredible faith in His Father to trust beyond what He could understand. *"O my Father, if it be possible, let this cup pass from me: nevertheless, not as I will, but as Thou wilt." (Matthew 26:39 KJV)* As Christians, we are called to be Christ-like, doing things as He does. It's not easy, but when we make each decision based on that benchmark, we quickly learn when we are walking after *His* way or straying from the road having our own agendas often leading to undesirable destinations.

Going through difficulties will also help build our trust in God. You see, I don't believe there's another mother on this earth who would be willing to do what Jesus' mother did. In the first place, she was a young virgin woman, at risk for being stoned when people knew she was pregnant without being married. She also risked losing Joseph, to whom she was engaged. How would he understand, and would he accept her anyway? She knew this baby was the Messiah, come to save His people from their sins. Did she in fact also know that in order for Him to do this, she would have to give him over to death? That had to be the most painful insight *if* she knew the child she carried in her womb would be called back to Heaven after only 33 short years on this earth. Were these part of the things Mary thought about? *"But Mary kept all these things, and pondered them in her heart." (Luke 2:19 KJV)* I believe God chose Mary because He trusted her. He knew that what was required of her wouldn't be easy, but I'm persuaded God knew she could do it, even if she, herself weren't sure. Because Mary loved God and was willing to fulfill His call on her life, He knew she would be more than able to walk it out to accomplish God's plan for the world.

I cannot begin to count the times people have come up to me since the loss of our son and said, "I don't know how you make it. I could never do that." The truth is that many days, I don't know either. Through much prayer and seeking of the Lord's will and His way, I've sought for the answer as to how I *can* continue. I say to myself that if God had given me a choice, I'd have said, "NO WAY, ABSOLUTELY NOT, NOT ME EVER, NO NEVER!" *He* chose me, however, knowing, just as He did with Mary, that by myself I would crumble, but with His help, I could survive. *"But thanks be to God, which giveth us the victory through our Lord Jesus Christ." (1 Corinthians 15:57 KJV)* In every impossible situation we face, we need to look not to man but place all our confidence in God. Man will often let us down, but God will always provide relief. He is the *only* way when there is *no* way. If you get this fact rooted deep in your spirit, when tragedy strikes, your recovery can begin.

My family is blessed with more happiness than hardships. I cannot let one tragic night, no matter how horrendous, distort all the wonderful times we had with our son. One catastrophic interruption wasn't going to derail God's purpose and plan *if* I didn't submit to its assault. I think of Mary at times and wonder *if* God had made her aware in the beginning that she would have to give Jesus up at His expected time, would this knowledge have hindered her ability to love Him to the fullest. When I say that I trust and believe I'm chosen for this particular journey, I don't take it lightly, nor do I try to insinuate in any way that I'm a modern-day Mary. I merely suggest that God called me to this road because He knew that, like Mary, I would be faithful to His will. I presume that not only did God know I would depend on Him but He was persuaded I would comply with His calling. He supplied supernatural strength for me to make it through encountering my worst fear and still have the ability to praise Him. Learning that He had faith in me and would equip me for my walk was perhaps the hardest part of the learning-to-trust process. However, that has been one of my most valuable life-altering lessons. What I've undergone has also brought a lot of freedom and much-needed victory. I honestly believe that *if* God has called you to do something, He will supply everything you need to bring Him glory and honor. I've often heard it said that "God doesn't call the equipped, He equips those He calls." To think that my son may have been chosen to give up his life so that someone might come to know Jesus, causes me to speculate whether or not he would have been willing to make that decision for himself. As a Christian, Justin knew there would be no sting of death because his salvation was a guarantee, of eternal life in Heaven. Even still with that glorious guarantee would he or I or anyone ever be willing to give our lives for the life of another? *"We are confident, I say and willing rather to be absent from the body, and to be present with the Lord." (2 Corinthians 5:8 KJV)*

In this very moment, I'm brought to a fond memory of my son

when he had come home from school one day in his sock-feet, asking me not to be mad. When I inquired as to where his shoes were, he explained that a boy at school had no shoes for P.E. class, so he gave him *his* shoes because he knew he had another pair at home. I believe God placed that situation in my mind to help me better understand my son's sweet-spirited nature. Justin had so much love and compassion for others, the depths of which I will never fully understand. He was always willing to share what he had so that other lives could be enriched. I share that memory not to brag on my son, but to invite you to capture a brief glance inside his heart. He was the most unselfish, caring, compassionate person, always willing to help and give to others. That brings an incredible sense of peace to my heart, knowing the character of my son and the numerous qualities he undeniably portrayed. God not only knew they were in him, but He had placed them there to begin with. *"Every good gift and every perfect gift is from above and cometh down from the Father of lights, with Whom is no variableness, neither shadow of turning." (James 1:17 KJV)*

It was once recommended to us, that the best way to honor our son was to do as he did. Realizing his most outstanding traits were being kind and helping others, if we too performed prominent and generous acts of kindness, his memory would continue to live. We all can profit by showing a heart of compassion to the ones God places in our paths. That's also a wonderful way we can bestow honor unto God, too, when we decide to serve Him not only with our words but also with our actions. *"Wherefore, I beseech you, be ye followers of Me." (1 Corinthians 4:16 KJV)*

Chapter Twenty-Four
Thankful

The question I disliked most of all after my son was gone was, "How are you?" How could anyone ask a mother who had recently lost her child *that* question and not already predict the answer? I realize those who asked were just trying to make conversation. Obviously, they couldn't think of anything else to say so relied on what was probably the most used appropriate generic greeting, except for a grieving mother. Therefore, I've come to the conclusion that it's never an innovative idea to pose this question. I don't believe many would have been patient enough to sit still and listen to the long, drawn out details of how I actually felt. I wasn't angry with them or upset; it was just so frustrating never to be able to come up with a condensed version of my condition at that time. After all, there had to be a way to relate exactly how I felt without denying God's power to speak life into my situation. Day after day, I would think about the perfect response to that constant, dreaded question. I didn't want to reply with the all-too-common, "I'm fine" or, "I'm alright." Truthfully, I was *not* alright by any definition of the word. In those early months "fine" wasn't even registering on my radar.

I often thought that some people were just waiting for me to slip up, testing me to see if I really believed God would faithfully see me through. There will always be people praying for it to rain on your sunshine when *they* have trouble believing in God's power or feel as though you are blessed more than they think you "deserve." The truth is, none of us are *deserving* of God's blessings; it's only by His amazing grace that we can stand. I'm so very relieved that God doesn't ever give us what we are justly entitled to receive, but instead chooses to love us and cast all of our wrongs into the sea of forgetfulness. *"He will again have compassion on us; He will tread our iniquities underfoot. You will cast all our sins into the depths of the sea." (Micah 7:19 ESV)* My belief that God desires to see His children walking in the truth of His forgiveness helped me realize that a fulfilled life is available even though at times it seems out of reach. When we trust in God's truth and apply it to our lives, it will not only bring us joy but also greatly pleases our Father. *"I have no greater joy than to hear that my children walk in truth." (3 John 1:4 KJV)* Once again I fully relate with God on this fact. I can think of no greater pleasure than watching my sons walk in wisdom and knowledge, serving Him with their whole hearts and lives.

After a lot of soul-searching and longing to discover a way to describe my feelings, I decided to steal what a great friend of mine always said even though she had suffered numerous hardships throughout her life. So many of her struggles taught me that if God had helped her through, He would do the same for me; so, I believed and received God's blessings just as she had always done. As long as I've been acquainted with her, she always answers the same. She told me that whenever anyone asked her how she was, she responded, "I am blessed." That was it! I *was* blessed. That said it all! She is blessed, I am blessed, we are all blessed! "Blessed" was a phrase that worked no matter how I was feeling or what I was going through that day. With God, we are favored when everything turns out perfectly and comforted by Him when things fall apart. *"Though I walk in the midst of trouble, You preserve my life; You stretch out Your hand against the wrath of my enemies, and Your right hand delivers me." (Psalm 138:7 ESV)* My attitude about the dreaded question began to improve immensely, and when I saw my friend again, I confessed that I'd stolen her answer. She smiled and said, "Well you know it's true!" When we take our minds off of our prolems and start to count all the good things God has given us, it doesn't take long to see, we are all greatly blessed by God in one way or another. That is a fact! God has blessed us in so many ways we don't even know or could ever begin to understand.

For a very long time my mind wouldn't let me comprehend what my spirit already recognized. I remembered the Bible story of Paul and Silas. They were destitute, beaten, battered, and left for dead, chained and locked in a dungeon. Instead of feeling pain and pity they began to let praise flow through the penitentiary and when the foundation began to shake, the jailhouse doors broke open. *"About midnight Paul and Silas were praying and singing hymns to God, and the other prisoners were listening to them. Suddenly there was such a violent earthquake that the foundations of the prison were shaken. At once the prison doors flew open and everyone's chains came loose." (Acts 16:25-26 NIV)* Through reading this Scripture my heart was enlightened to know that *if* I was willing to praise God in my own barricade and bands of bondage, my chains of grief, pain, and torment would be broken off and I would finally be free! I then decided that *if* I were ever going to be able to trust in God again and have the ability to partake of His goodness, I'd have to find a way to give Him thanks even when I couldn't make sense of circumstances I faced. I had to give Him unlimited praise even when I was upset, angry, hurt, devastated, and falling apart, unsteady, and undone. *"All this is for your benefit, so that the grace that is reaching more and more people may cause thanksgiving to overflow to the glory of God." (2 Corinthians 4:15 NIV)*

After some time of replying to, "How are *you*?" with, "I am blessed," God began to show me that I wasn't just blessed but that I should also be very grateful with a thankful heart. I knew from early teaching that the Bible says we are to give thanks whether things are good or bad, happy or sad, easy or hard, if we are in want or have plenty. *"Giving thanks for all things unto God and the Father in the name of Jesus Christ." (Ephesians 5:20 KJV)* I believe I received a huge breakthrough when I finally decided that I could be content in all things. *Philippians 4:12 KJV* tells us that, *"I know both how to be abased, and I know how to abound: everywhere and in all things. I am instructed both to both to be full and to be hungry, both to abound and to suffer need."* Simply explained, it means to be appreciative in *all* things, not that I would necessarily be happy or understand or even approve of everything, but know that it's not always left up to me to decide the outcome. It is, however, *my* choice as to how I will react to situations. *1 Thessalonians 5:17-18 KJV* says, *"Pray without ceasing. In everything give thanks: for this is the will of God in Christ Jesus concerning you."* Deciding to be appreciative makes it possible for me to go through the challenging situations with the right attitude. I've had to place my all my confidence in God when things didn't go the way I wanted. The truth is, you *can* be mad at God for what happens unexpectedly, and can yell, scream, and be angry and bitter, but in the end, you'll have to come to the knowledge that without Him you have no hope of making it through this life with your joy and sanity intact. My constant prayer even still was for this horrible tragedy to all be a nightmare that I would wake from and have my son safe and sound here on this earth. Knowing *that* is not our reality and is an unattainable dream, in order to continue on my way, I have to dig deep and locate a force greater than myself, which I discover daily in God. He graciously has been with me every step of the journey and never grows tired of my unending need of His miraculous mercy. Just as the children of Israel had only enough manna for one day, which could never be stored up, due to mold and decay, we can never hoard more than one day's amount of God's mercy and must be satisfied with His provision. He gives us a new bountiful supply of grace and strength to accomplish each day what we must do, and also the faith not to worry over tomorrow, for that day may never come.

Many months after the accident, I was finally able to discover the positive and begin to give God thanks for His many blessings. I did still have my husband and two amazing sons with me, for which I give Him my best enthusiastic praise. I began to identify many areas of my life when things could have turned out way differently had God not stepped in and intervened. You see it only takes a minimal amount of time of counting your blessings, and you'll begin to realize how truly thankful you should be. The truth is, when I gravitate toward praise instead of self-pity, it brings my heart boundless joy to be able to say, "Lord, I'm certain that I've now learned to give you thanks and praise in all things. Even when I can't understand why I will still trust you." *"I will say to the Lord, He is my Refuge and my*

Fortress: my God; in Him will I trust." (Psalm 91:2 KJV)

Most of you are probably asking how I could conclude to be content in all things, especially since we had lost our firstborn son not that long ago. I'll have to be honest, as I've tried to do during this whole book; I've learned along my way that thankfulness is based on my faith in God and His ability to take me from a place of total devastation to one of gratefulness. Since it's a daily walk, I can sometimes fully surrender my emotions to God and appreciate the time we *had* with Justin, but there are also times when it's terribly difficult to give thanks for the things I cannot conceive. When my suffering seems to run deeper than my faith, that, I trust not in what I'm feeling but fix my spiritual eyes on God because He knows me by name. His Word tells me that: *"Even the very hairs of your head are numbered." (Matthew 10:30 ESV)* God has that special ability to make me feel as though I am the most loved person in the world, which comes when I realize how unworthy I am but that He pursues me anyway. You see, it's not who *I* am, but the One alive in me that bolsters my self-esteem so that I can get through even the hardest days. *If* I fully trust Him, He will see me through each one, every step, until the time comes I will no longer suffer the pain of heartache and despair. Through the devastation I've suffered from the loss of our son, I'm indebted to God for choosing *me* to be his mother. God saw fit to bless me above and beyond what I could have ever dreamed. Each of my sons has contributed a vast amount of adventure and extreme pleasure to my life, which brings undeniable satisfaction. On the most difficult days, I try my best to remain thankful for all things, and it takes only a few minutes of gratitude to bring me to a place of contentment in Him. When I set my mind on my Creator and not on my problems, my heart is at peace, and I'm overflowing with praise to my God. He puts a song in my heart and a smile on my face.

I'm glad that God still loves me and never gives up trying to send me signs and wonders to encourage my spirit every day. As I wait upon and seek after Him with my whole heart, He is easily located.

When I surrender all of me to His power and rest in His grace, and wholly submitted to His will and His way, I discover peace and endurance like I've never had before. Teach me, Lord, to learn to wait upon you and to be patient and steadfast so my strength may be renewed, restored, refreshed, and revived in you. *"He gives strength to the weary and increases the power of the weak." (Isaiah 40:29 NIV)*

Chapter Twenty-Five
Songs Just-in Time

I will never forget my very first visit alone to my son's grave only a few days after the funeral. That would be my new normal, and I couldn't always depend on someone to go with me. I felt the need to go as often as possible so he would somehow realize I still treasured my time with him. I knew he couldn't really sense that I was there, but it seemed the only thing I could do to continue showing the love and devotion I still carried for him. Even though he was no longer physically here with me, his grave was the one place I felt closest to him, and I knew I was never completely alone, as *God* is always with me. I remember thinking that this was not the way things should be, not my plan. My son's life was just beginning. He had been able to experience just a tiny part of life and had been able to finish only a few chapters of his story. He had been married less than a year, and he and his wife Courtney had just moved into their own home. He was privileged to learn how to be a father to Courtney's little girl, Skylar. He had so many new and exciting adventures ahead and numerous worlds to be explored. His life was just beginning and not supposed to be over so fast. Parents should never outlive their children. It's just not the way life should be. My mind was running rampant with all the thoughts and plans I'd made in my heart. I hadn't yet surrendered to the idea that God knew best, thus, the reason I still walked around broken, defeated, and discouraged most all the time. However, my spirit once again wouldn't give up the battle for victory that my flesh tried desperately to destroy.

In time I was finally able to let go of *my* ideas about how things *should* have gone. Although, today was not that day! My eyes began to overflow with tears of sorrow and grief. My heart was quickly reminded of a time I had talked with a friend on the phone late one night, and she asked me, "Alisa, will there ever be a time you'll no longer be sad and cry unending tears?" I couldn't answer. At that time in life, I felt I may have been forgotten by God, left alone and unloved. That night I, too, questioned Him as to whether or not my tears would ever totally stop. Would there ever be a time I wouldn't be sad? Would there be come a day eventually when I could experience uninterrupted happiness? As I lay down to rest, that night seemed to last an eternity, my mind being bombarded all night with worry and doubt flooding my thoughts. I finally saw the morning light coming through the window and got up and turned on the radio, only to hear a song that answered every question. Its title is "There Will Be a Day." There IS a day coming when there will be no more sorrow, no sickness, and no pain. It will be the day we see Jesus face to face. Until then we'll all face difficulties of every kind, but rest assured that with Jesus as our Savior, we can experience joy unspeakable and full of life. *"He will swallow up death forever. The Sovereign Lord will wipe away the tears from all faces; He will remove His people's disgrace from all the earth. The Lord has spoken. In that day they will say, "Surely this is our God; we trusted in Him; let us rejoice and be glad in His salvation." (Isaiah 25:8-9 NIV)*

With this truth, I was able to encourage my heart in the Lord and began to talk myself out of crying as I wiped the tears away. At the very moment I lifted my weary eyes, I was able to see more clearly, and the amazing God I serve had caused the most beautiful surprise to appear directly across from where I was. I didn't have to look to the left or the right, but straight ahead to see the brilliance of the bright orange colors of the sun as it rose above the mountaintops--a picture so perfect no one but the Creator of the world could have painted it. Seeing this sunrise at that very moment of utter despair and complete hopelessness gave me the fortitude to make it another day. My heart grew new substance; I realized if I would look past the tears, God had a message of help. He gave me renewed hope that everything would work out somehow if I placed all my concerns, stress, and anxiety on Him. I learned that day that if I was ever feeling down and out, all I had to do was look to the heavens, and my courage and determination would be renewed.

After a spending a few moments to give God praise for the care and compassion He had shown to me that day, I made my way back to the car, climbed in, placed my foot on the brake, and pushed the start button. The timeliness of the song on the radio amazed me: "This world is not my home; this world is not where I belong. Take this world and give me Jesus. This world is not my home." *"For this world is not our permanent home; we are looking to a home yet to come." (Hebrews 13:14 NLT)* What a glorious day that will be! The words of that song, along with the Scripture, brought my heart great peace and reassurance that although I may be *in* this world, I am not *of* this world. Our Lord Jesus is preparing a magnificent place where we'll reign forever with Him and all of our loved ones who have preceded us in death. We're merely passing through this life on our way to our Heaven. I could see clearly that there was a concrete reason for my feeling out of place many times in this earthly realm. *"But {we are different, because} our citizenship is in Heaven. And from there we eagerly await {the coming of} the savior, the Lord Jesus Christ." (Philippians 3:20 AMP)*

When Justin's headstone was ready to be placed, I received a call requesting that I stop by the cemetery to make sure I was pleased with the way they had completed the job. I didn't want to go alone so asked my mother if she would come along. As we made our way to the graveside, an overwhelming realization came to me. I felt completely broken once again. It was as if all the hurt and pain I thought were carefully buried and the gains I'd made in the healing process quickly dissipated like a flame in the wind. The sight of this huge, shiny, black rock with Justin's name etched in stone caused a large knot to form in the pit of my stomach. My throat began to close, and my aching heart pounded with a force to the point I felt it would explode. My eyes immediately filled with bitter tears. That large boulder would be a constant reminder that Justin is no longer with us on earth, as if I ever needed a memorial stone to remind me what I try constantly to forget every day to no avail. No words can describe how my heart was being ripped apart, shredded beyond recognition. It was as if I was losing my son all over again.

As I wiped my tears and tried to suppress my emotions, I inspected every detail of my son's headstone, making sure his picture was as identical a likeness as possible. I gazed upon the description of who he was: "Son," "Brother," "Grandson," "Husband," and "Father" My heart was full; Justin was loved by so many. He was our firstborn son as well as the first grandson and great-grandson. He was a big brother to Jacob and Caleb. He was a husband to Courtney and will always be "Daddy Justin" to Skylar. Even though he is far away, His memory will be forever in our hearts and minds. I'm eternally grateful we each, in diverse ways, had the privilege of sharing an extraordinary bond with him. I looked at the back of the stone that displayed our last name in bright, white, bold letters and studied the quote God had given me months before to help the aching in the very core of my being: "Never Apart Always in Our Hearts." No matter how far heaven is from earth, it will never weaken Justin's impact on our hearts and in our lives.

The time had come to leave, so mom and I made our way back to the car. My thoughts of what should have and could have been subsided for a moment. As I started my car, immediately the very same exact song began to play that was on the radio the first time I visited the cemetery several months before. Again, the lyrics were confirmation and a constant reminder to me "just-in time" that "this world is not my home;" God once again used those lyrics to sustain me, and I *know* He will continue that support until He calls me home. Although this song is now several years old and isn't heard as often as before, it continues to play at just the moment I need restoration, which reaffirms that God can speak through many avenues for us to be able to hear His voice in a time of need. We must always be looking and ready to receive from His endless supply of blessings. He will never let us down. *"Set your affection on things above, not on things on the earth." (Colossians 3:2 KJV)*

The heaviness of my heart immediately lifted as I realized that, as always, God has everything under His control. At that moment I felt like the most important daughter of the highest King. He chose to bless me with those uplifting words at that particular time, which let me know all my questions will be answered in God's timing, not mine. I decided to wait patiently for God because He is more than able to mend every wound, whether emotional or physical. What a mighty, awesome God we serve! He reminds me daily through His Word to make the following decision: *"And be not conformed to this world: but be ye transformed by the renewing of your mind, that ye may prove what is that good, and acceptable, and perfect, will of God." (Romans 12:2 KJV)*. I have taken this Scripture to heart, particularly during the most difficult parts of my journey, and concentrate on it when this world insists I am "deserving" of my right to be sad, discontented, and mad with God. It's not always easy to stay positive in a negative world, but I trust God's heart, and I desire to fulfill His call and be all He needs me to be. I strive to bring honor to His great name. I cannot for one moment imagine trying to conquer this life without the help of my Savior because I believe with all certainty that had it not been for God, I would've never made it this far. I am so thankful that even when I had given up on myself, convinced I would never make it through, God Himself never once gave up on me. He had faith in me that I could've never had in myself, and I now focus all my confidence in Him. *"And I am sure of this, that He who began a good work in you will bring it to completion at the day of Jesus Christ." (Philippians 1:6 ESV)* There are days when fear and doubt still tries to overshadow me and take control my thoughts, but I do my best to resist at its first suggestion never admitting defeat. I trust by faith that through the heartache, torture, and pain, God will create in us an exquisite work of His creative design that will most assuredly be used for His honor. I hope beyond all expectations that one day *my* story, will in fact bring Him glory.

After every visit to my son's grave, the car radio is without fail playing a song which speaks to my heart, as if those encouraging words were coming directly from the mouth of God. There are still times when I'm feeling down that I pull up to the grave site for a brief moment just to *see* if a song will play to speak to my situation, and God has never failed to lift me up. I call them my Justin songs because they are always just in time and because of him that I started searching more intently for HIM.

Every reminder of Justin is both a blessing and a curse. Reminiscing can bring joy one moment but pain, sorrow, and sadness the next. A decent day can quickly turn dreadful with thoughts of your loved one's absence. The hardest part is the difficulty of controlling which emotion wins. Your thoughts and words dictate your direction. Therefore, concentrate on the goodness of God and the happiness your loved one brought, so that your joy will multiply. Never let yourself dwell on your sadness, or your grief will grow. In *Romans 7:18 NASB,* Paul lets us know that he, also, struggled with this battle. *For I know that nothing good dwells in me, that is, in my flesh; for the willing is present in me, but the doing of the good is not."* Therefore, first *choose* which emotion will take priority. It's pivotal that you not let grief overtake your gladness. I was able to surround myself with people who spoke life into me, and I avoided those who appeared to enjoy misery. I would urge you to do the same. In taking these steps on a consistent basis, you will become the victor rather than the victim. I had to learn reliance on my faith in God to speak peace to my heart and still the questions that tormented me both day and night.

Along the way, I would frequently make a mental note to remind myself of all the questions I wanted to ask God when I finally saw Him face to face. I try not to dwell on all of the questions I so deperately want to ask as I fear it may hinder my faith and cause doubt to grow. My husband often reminds me that answers frequently lead to more questions. I'm convinced that by that time all my concerns and comments I desperately wanted explanations for will all fade away at the very moment, I finally see Jesus. All the issues I thought were so important on this earth will matter no more when I can finally savor the pleasures Heaven has to offer. Nothing else will hold any significance compared to the goodness God has in store when we reside with Him and all our loved ones in our heavenly home. As I've said before, I fully believe our Father doesn't intend for us to suffer a broken heart and endless hardships the entire time we're on this earth, just to discover joy and contentment *only* when we get to Heaven. I rest assured that God desires for us to lead happy, blessed, fulfilled lives while we're awaiting our greater reward one day. With all my being I believe that we are to enjoy our time here, to be blessed and be a blessing to others. Will you choose to walk in the freedom God provides?

God blessed me with numerous other *Justin* songs over the past few years. One, in particular, was voted number one in 2011, the year our son died. I'm sure He meant it to lift me up, but each time I listened it caused a black cloud of despair to hover over my hurting heart. With the first note of the song entitled "Blessings," my eyes immediately began to burn with heavy, hurtful tears. The words speak of all the times we pray for protection, wisdom, and other blessings, and for God to heal our suffering. They proceed to ask the question "what if" when we ask for all these things, God sends us rain, tears, and sleepless nights. Those lyrics have the connotation that we can receive calmness when we discern that perhaps our hardest times were blessings in disguise. What *if* the hardships we've endured were protecting us from a worse fate? Perhaps through the suffering, we're being shaped for Heaven. Through much heartache and pain, I finally concluded that sometimes God must send the storms to cause us to grow. I in no way believe God causes terrible things to happen to us, but I do think *if* we're willing, He will work through the hardest nights and manipulate them into something extraordinary, and in return our faith in Him will increase. The catastrophes we encounter are not meant to destroy us but to cause us to become stable on the firm foundation of Christ. If we never faced an impossible situation, we would never trust and know His great love and mighty power at work in our lives.

I am so very fortunate that I've had my relationship with God during this great trial. This connection has strengthened and grown over the loss I've suffered. He has revealed to me many beautiful and glorious sights that, in fact, may have always been there but went unnoticed. The truth is, God, also, has always been there through all the "busy-ness" of life. It took a great tragedy that made me finally slow down, look for and listen to God, and search for Him in every moment of every day for the boldness to continue. I know that in His mercy He sought after me through music and Scripture, and for that, I will be forever thankful. *"He has put a new song in my mouth, a song of praise to our God. Many shall see and fear and put their trust and confident reliance in the Lord." (Psalm 40:1-3 KJV)*

Chapter Twenty-Six
Signs From Above

As a Christian, I believe with all my faith and might that God alone *is* the Healer of the wounded and brokenhearted. He's the only one Who can raise the dead, cause the blind to see, and give the leper a reason to dance. Healing from God is sometimes instant but *may* take a tremendous amount of prayer and time to manifest. I've witnessed immediate healing in others and have even been privileged to encounter it for myself. You can ask me all day every day why some are healed and others are not, I'll answer you as honest as I know how. It's simply put and easy to understand: "I just don't know why." As I've reiterated throughout this book, if you are going through something physically, mentally, or financially, I know God can move in His timing if you allow Him to do so. Will it go the way you want? Not always but I can assure you if you hold on to God watching for His signs and wonders along the way He will give you whatever you need to conquer your opponent, cross your Red Sea, and climb your biggest mountain.

As I said in a previous chapter, we sometimes pray for something, and when it doesn't happen quickly, we assume God didn't answer. We may think we didn't pray the right prayer or that we asked for something we didn't need. Some would go so far as to say that prayer just doesn't work. The truth is there are times we pray, don't get the response we expect, and so assume that God didn't hear us. I have a dear spiritual friend who says that we pray a microwave prayer when God's way is slow and simmer, meaning that we want things instantly while God sometimes wants us to wait. He cannot be rushed. May we continue to learn to trust in His perfect timing. We must have faith and wait patiently on God and recognize that He is actively working to bring us the best outcome in every area of our lives. *Psalm 62:1-2 KJV: Truly my soul waiteth upon God: from Him cometh my salvation. He is my rock and my* salvation; *He is my defense; I shall not be greatly moved."* The security and blessings I've received from God throughout this journey haven't come without much perseverance. I've had to learn how to stand firm and not be easily swayed by my feelings or by other people's opinions and beliefs. My faith in Him has increased by leaps and bounds. Learning patience was not an instantaneous process but instead happened over time through trial and error on my part. *God* has patiently, lovingly walked beside me every step of the way. Sometimes He carries me, other times it feels as though He's dragging me kicking and screaming when I would rather quit than keep going. Knowing that's not God's best plan for me, I appreciate the fact He never quits on me even when I'm stubborn, un-agreeable, and un-submissive.

One morning in December of 2011 as we stood to have the closing prayer at our church, I was busy putting away items Skylar had dragged out of the diaper bag and make certain I had everything that belonged to her so we'd be ready for Courtney to pick her up. I gave the space one final glance to make sure I hadn't left anything on the floor, then scooped her up in my arms, held her close, and began to pray for the fortitude to make it through the holidays. The thought of our first Christmas without Justin weighed heavily on my heart. My emotions were taking my breath away, Sky looked concerned as her eyes began to puddle. I told her, "We *will* be okay, Justin is still with us, and he lives in our hearts, just like Jesus does." As I turned and reached in my purse for a tissue to wipe the tears, I noticed on the floor a slip of paper which moments before had not been there. I bent down to pick it up and saw that Justin's name was written on it! My mouth fell open, and I immediately began asking the people around me if anyone had dropped the small piece of paper. The look on their faces told me without a word spoken that they were as bewildered as I was to see the name of my son written in what appeared to be a young child's handwriting. I showed the piece of paper to Skylar and told her, "See Justin was here with us and left

239

a note!" I know most of you are thinking that it had to be my grand-daughter's paper used for scribbling during the church service, right? To bring your wondering minds to rest, she was so little then that she couldn't even write *her* name, so there was no way possible she could've written Justin's name on that paper. *My* mind was racing, trying to figure out just how it might have gotten there. After a few moments of overwhelming excitement, I tried to regain my composure. As a calmness covered my soul, my spirit began to speak and reminded me there was nothing too difficult for the God Who created everyone and everything in the entire universe, which were spoken into existence at His sovereign command. Would it be impossible for Him to drop a letter from Heaven just for me? The answer is *no*! Nothing, no nothing, is too hard for God to do. *"Alas, Lord God! Behold, You have made the heavens and the earth by Your great power and by Your outstretched arm! There is nothing too hard for You!" (Jeremiah 32:17 AMP)*

As I took some time soaking up the undeserved love and kindness God had shown that day, my heart began to overflow with excitement. I wanted so much to share my experience with anyone who would listen. My heart was overwhelmed that the God of all creation would take time to bring joy to my shattered heart during that Christmas season. Once again, He wanted to let me know that He was with me and that I could see His signs and wonders all around *if* I were keenly aware of their presence.

To this very day, I do not doubt that God caused that paper to be in the exact place where I would be sure to see it; whether it was directly from Heaven or not is something that can never be explained this side of eternity. I had a profound sense of peace and reassurance that because God has the power to move mountains, most assuredly He can deliver a message on a Sunday morning near Christmas time to let this mother have increased faith that everything would be okay. I now know that indeed He *will* be with me until the end of time.

That would not be the only Christmas God would send me a

sign. Since I like to get each of my sons an ornament yearly, the next Christmas while shopping at a local store, a crystallized candy cane "J" caught my eye. I had searched the year before for one just like it when I had decided on the candy cane initials. I could find only one "J" and one "C," and that would not work because I needed two "J's." I gave up the search and settled for matching ornaments that had each of the boys' names on them. So, this time I ran over and snatched it up, before anyone else decided they wanted it and then searched for another "J" and a "C." Not only was I unable to find either of the others needed, but there were no other candy cane ornaments anywhere in the store! I made up my mind that this had to be the missing "J" from the year before and knew I had to have it. God once again was trying to focus my attention on the fact that He can do the inconceivable and make something beautiful appear out of complete nothingness.

I made my way to the checkout counter and patiently waited in line, bubbling over with excitement, overjoyed at the significance of the small reminder that God never forgets a prayer. The substantial importance encouraged me once again that things work out how they are supposed to. He is never early and never late so we must find treasures in the valleys while we wait. When it was finally my turn to pay, and the lady began to ring up the merchandise, she scanned the ornament but couldn't get it to show on her register. She tried over and over to get a price, but nothing worked, so she asked if I wanted to get another just like it because this one was not in the system. I explained that it was the only one in the entire store and pleaded with her, saying that I had relentlessly searched for another to no avail. She then called someone else to determine what to do in this situation. The second clerk arrived and tried unsuccessfully over and over to run the item through the scanner, but nothing they did revealed the price of the ornament, making the treasure, as I already had discovered, "priceless."

After a while, the clerk informed me that since they could not locate a price for the ornament, they wouldn't be able to let me purchase it. She explained that this particular item might not even belong to that store but had no explanation of how it got there. I knew once again, as in the year before when the small handwritten paper had appeared on the floor, that this ornament had been placed by God for me to discover. Whatever means God used to get it there at the exact time I would uncover it will remain a secret until some future time it may be revealed.

As the lady watched my eyes fill up with tears, I took a deep breath and began to explain why this ornament was so dear to me, and that I knew I was meant to obtain it, whatever the price, so there was no way I could leave without it. A nearby store manager must have overheard the conversation and saw the sadness on my face. She immediately told the cashier that she should locate a similarly sized ornament and let me have it for that price. I was overjoyed that the situation had been resolved and I would be able to have my unforgettable ornament and also a memorable story to share. To this very day, I believe that God has used everything I've encountered, not just to inspire me, but to encourage those around me, because He cares about every detail of our lives, so nothing is too insignificant to Him.

You may be wondering if I continue to get heavenly signs, especially at Christmas, and my answer would be a resounding "yes!" The following Christmas was the third one since we had lost our son. I was watching and waiting each day in December wondering if the year before would be the last one God would choose to reveal a sign letting me know that he was still concerned about my needs. Had He instead decided that I was strong enough not to need those physical signs from above? Had I depended way too much on signs and songs? Was God taking my proverbial "training wheels" off? As the days turned into weeks, I truly began to think that God may have been nudging me to lean on Him and walk by faith and not by sight, as He tells us in His Word. Should that be His will, I would accept it, trusting that He is intently aware of what He's doing and needs to accomplish in my life for His glory.

As December 25th began, I felt God must think I was stronger than I'd been in the past, since I hadn't received that sign I'd been anticipating. Still, from the bottom of my heart and in the depths of my soul, I yearned for that affirmation. *"But if we hope for that we see not, then do we with patience wait for it." (Romans 8:25 KJV)* I'd grown so dependent on "God nods," to the point I searched for them in my daily walk but was particularly expectant of these divine manifestations at Christmas time. It was as if I were a child again, looking for that gift I'd hoped for all year long. I longed to experience the joy of Christmas morning when I'd run over and unwrap the desired present that had brought such excitement the night before that I could hardly sleep. It's as if we all become wide-eyed, exuberant children again during this very special, joyous season. We all get so consumed with the presents we often forget the best ones are the kind that money couldn't buy. The merriment of gift giving becomes lackluster and ordinary when one of the best gifts you've ever had won't ever be seen again this side of Heaven. Reminds me to be thankful that God didn't bless us with only one priceless gift, but three. Having the boys to carry on the holiday celebrations help to bring back the flavor of Christmastime.

As the day marched on, we enjoyed all the family traditions as best we could with the emptiness of Justin's not being there to keep the momentum going as he'd done in the past. He was always full of contagious enthusiasm during the holidays, so full of ideas and plans that would include everyone, young and old, participating in a friendly competition of some kind. He was all about family and being together. This year, we didn't hurry the day but sat around enjoying one another and shared stories of times gone by with smiles and laughs and not so many tears as the previous two years. We spent our time looking through pictures and remembering a time that was, honestly, the best of times, which passed by all too quickly. As minutes turned into hours, I looked around only to discover I was all alone. Everyone had gone their separate ways but would return later for another round of food and fellowship. I sat with my sister's computer, scrolling through pictures and reliving each memory. Wrapped up in the moment, I went back to the time I felt life was at its best, but I hadn't even realized it then. With each passing year I gain momentum that in time things will be good again. I heard a noise, my little "fur baby," Gracie Belle, began to scratch on the door, letting me know she needed to go outside. As I got up and opened the front door, I looked up at the sky and there it was, one of the most glorious scenes I'd ever witnessed in my entire life, by far one of the biggest signs from above I'd ever had. Words would never even begin to describe the wondrous glory my eyes beheld. The sky was lit up with the most beautiful, fiery shades of orange as if the woods were ablaze; it was as if the sun sat perfectly still waiting to set just for me. On the left side of the sunset was a cross placed in the sky so that I would realize it was no ordinary setting of the sun, as if a sunrise or sunset could ever be described as ordinary. The cross was there to signify that God positioned it just for those praying and expecting a sign that day. With tears welling up in my eyes, the extraordinary picture painted by the almighty hand of God was a bit blurry until I could clear my eyes. Within moments, my weeping turned to gladness. An immense joy and peace filled my heart because I realized that God had chosen not to end that day without satisfying my expectations. It was as if I had received a "wink" from God, Who was just waiting for the perfect time to unwrap that present. You may wonder why I should even consider that God would love me so much, to display a gift across the sky like that; truth is, He loves us all that much. The wondrous sight that Christmas day was not just for me but for everyone willing to take the time to notice. Jesus' gifts are available to all who will take the time to receive them. God understands that His blessings cause our spirits to be lifted and motivated so that we may continue in His footsteps. *"Beloved, I wish above all things that thou mayest prosper and be in health, even as thy soul prospereth." (3 John 1:2 KJV)*

244

Within minutes, the sunset had faded away never to be the same again, just as God's mercies are new every morning. All these blessings are near and dear to my heart and have increased my faith because of their meaning. What we see is temporal just like the small piece of paper with my son's name written on it and the candy-cane "J" Christmas ornament. These symbols will pass away, but the unseen things are forever.

That day confirmed to my heart that the God I serve is awesome and amazing, loving, caring, and compassionate, and never gets weary of finding ways to bless His children. He delights in surprising us when we least expect it, just to see our faces light up. The love and excitement I saw on my own children's faces when they opened that especially desired gift are priceless. How much more is the love of our heavenly Father for His children and the joy He receives from blessing us with His gifts? I pray that the surprise He saw on my face still brings a smile to His heart, much in the same way I recall my sons' starry-eyed smiles regarding the presents for which God has provided the money so that we could share with them. We've never let Santa have credit for the blessings God afforded. *Matthew 7:11 KJV* tells us that *"If we then being evil know how to give good gifts unto our children, how much more will your Father which is in Heaven give good things to them that ask?"*

God's commitment is indestructible and irreversible. Whatever He said He would do, He will accomplish. *"For the gifts and calling of God are irrevocable." (Romans 11:29 ESV)* Hold on to that and entrust it to saturate your soul. He never guaranteed this life would be easy, but He did vow that He would walk every step with you and hold you when you cannot walk on your own. Ask God to show you the signs from above to encourage you along the way. *"I would seek unto God, and unto God would I commit my cause: Which doeth great things and unsearchable; marvelous things without number." Job 5:8-9 KJV*

Chapter Twenty-Seven
Don't Leave Weak

"Don't Leave Weak." This phrase radiates through the deepest part of my heart, soul, and mind every minute of every day. All throughout this book many times over I have tried to promote perseverance. My story is summed up by simply saying, "When you get knocked down, get back up over and over, again and again." You may get pushed around time and time again to the point you don't know where to turn, but don't stop, lie down, and never quit. Look up! Upon waking, I greet each day as best I can with a "don't quit" attitude. When I have accomplished the first challenging task of getting out of bed, I can take on the next chore with renewed determination of knowing that I *did* make it out of bed and *didn't* retreat under my covers at the first weak moment. To make extra certain I don't crawl back into bed, I immediately make it up. Although that doesn't always work, it never hurts to try. You too will learn techniques to help you deal with sorrow while you're moving forward.

As I come to the last chapter of this story, God is already writing another story for the next part of my life, just as He will with yours if you are committed to Him. I hope this book has ministered to you as much as it has to me while working on it. It has caused me to dig deep into God's Word and search out the meaning of life, which has given me hope and provided healing. When I first began this book, it was as much of a mess as my life was at the time. Both were full of mistakes and missing parts that didn't fit together; some parts had to be removed while others had to be rearranged. Just as I have had help transforming this book, God has been continually working on me, taking out the unnecessary parts, changing and rearranging piece by piece. Many times, while working on this project I've had to look back and put my own advice to the test. Just as I'm not perfect, I've resolved that this book will have its own flaws and side-tracked story lines. It's quite possible this book and its contents will have no value to people who have never lost something so priceless you lost all hope and passion for living. So, if you must judge, do it gently. For the endless hours of up-all-night writing sessions, and edits from those willing to help, in the end my prayer is that "My story will bring God glory!" He has never asked for our perfection only for our willingness to do as He leads, so I gave it my all. Knowing that God is a parent much in the same way we are, feeling that when our children have done their best, that is what matters most. I am grateful to God for giving me my story and showing me how to walk it out in my every-day life.

The term, "Don't leave weak," has taken on a whole new meaning since my son left this earth. It no longer refers to cars exiting in a cloud of smoke, squalling tires down the road, burning rubber as they leave. It's now a constant reminder to live life giving it all I have, not to do anything halfheartedly but to jump in and give everything my very best. It means never to hold anything back, not to quit, and never to give up. God, also, compels us in His Word to give our very best: *"And whatever you do, whether in word or deed, do it all in the name of the Lord Jesus, giving thanks to God the Father through Him." (Colossians 3:17 HCSB)* To portray the meaning of this phrase, try closing your eyes and think of a time when you've watched the sun rise, paying close attention to its struggle to push with all its might up into the darkened sky to illuminate the morning with its spectacular brightness. It strains beyond itself to make sure it gives the most brilliant light with kaleidoscopic colors. That same extravagant sun has as much splendor when it exits, as it continues to give all it has left to make sure it's as glorious setting as it was rising. If you can get that picture in your mind, then you have an illustration of what the phrase "don't leave weak" means to our family.

I've heard it said that the sun at its appearance promotes hope and at its going brings peace; I agree with that statement one hundred percent. There have been many times I've welcomed a new day with the hope and expectancy that it would be better than the day before. At the end of the same day, I received unexplainable contentment with the stillness and quietness the setting sun brought to my soul. God in His greatness has designed this world to be filled with all of its abundant wonders to motivate us to move continually ahead and never tarry too long in inactivity. He has a work for us to do as He teaches us His unlimited power all through our lives. Rather than just sit and wait for the Lord to come, it's advantageous if you actively wait, by filling your life with praying, spending time in the Word, serving, and planting seeds of faith in others. Wait with expectancy, praising the Lord in your circumstance because the Lord inhabits the praise of His people. *"Yet You are holy, Who inhabit the praises of Israel." (Ps. 22:3 NKJV)*

As I've said before, I thoroughly enjoy our visits to the beach; it's my second favorite place on this earth; the first being wherever my family is found is where I find my paradise. Being away on vacation is a wonderful way to rest and relax and connect with one another in a way we sometimes seem too busy to do at home. I also try to spend extra time with God during our vacations. My husband and I often go down to the beach early to study Scriptures and spend time with our Creator. I've always felt exceptionally close to my Father while at the coast, and it reminds me of how Jesus often ministered along the shores of Galilee. He never needed a fancy tabernacle to proclaim the gospel, but was intent on sharing God's Word wherever He went, which is a great lesson for us all; we should take each opportunity no matter the location and share God's love with the world; if we don't who will? The world is so quick to take every opportunity to reach people; why should the church be any different? If everyone could win one for the God's kingdom, what a mighty army He would have!

Each morning when I wake up while at the beach, I always rush over and look out the window to see if the sun is visible, hoping to run down onto the sand and watch the sunrise. There have been many mornings clouds concealed it, and I was unable to experience its radiance. On one particular day when clouds were not present, I quickly made my way down to the water's edge, camera in hand, to capture the spectacular sight, so I'd have a constant reminder of God's faithfulness and His mercies that are new every morning. Crowds of people began to gather, waiting patiently to see the awakening of a brand-new day. As the sun began to burst its symphony of colors across the sky, I could see the big, bright orange sphere begin to surface, *pushing* up from the farthest part of the sea, revealing its beauty and warmly welcoming another day. It was breathtaking, and my heart filled with hope that *this* day would be great, realizing, *each* day is one the Lord has made, and we are compelled by His Word to be appreciative. As *Psalm 118:24 NJKV* instructs: *"This is the day the Lord has made; We will rejoice and be glad in it."*

Seconds after the sun rose, people began to turn away and go about their day eagerly searching out the next desired attraction. My mind wondered if we are like that as Christians, settling for one moment with the Son, content with just a small amount of time in His glory, then quickly moving on to our own agendas, not perceiving the direction God desires for us.

Recently we were privileged to watch the 2017 total eclipse of the sun. I was somewhat amazed at the interest the community took in trying to catch a glimpse of this phenomenon. We spent time searching for safety glasses to be able to view this event properly; we even spent a lot of time researching and talking about the much anticipated phenomenon with friends and family. My thoughts quickly made the comparison between the sun and the Son of God. Have we conformed to this world and celebrate the creation more than its Creator? God loves nothing more than having us close to His side as he showers us with love and blessings. I hope that we, as His sons and daughters, will all desire more time with Him, savoring all the goodness and love He so freely wants to give through a relationship with us. We should learn that surrendering to God is honestly the only way to be completely strong. *"Finally, be strong in the Lord and in the strength of His might."* (Ephesians 6:10 ESV)

You see, it's not of our own strength that our power flows, but is in Him. If we focused more on the Son, I'm confident it would make an incredible change in our lives. *"The sun shall no more be your light by day nor for brightness shall the moon give light to you but the Lord shall be to you an everlasting light, and your God your glory and your beauty. Your sun shall no more go down nor, shall your moon withdraw itself for the Lord shall be your everlasting light and the days of your mourning shall be ended." (Isaiah 60:19-20 KJV)* When we walk in the fullness of His light, the darkness connected with our grief will disappear in the radiance of God's glory. Although I do enjoy God's creations, the sun fades as the darkness swallows up the day; but His word and the power therein will never die. *"The grass withers and the flowers fade, but the Word of our God stands forever." (Isaiah 40:8 NLT)*

Often when I think of the phrase "don't leave weak," I'm reminded of the time my sister's family took a weekend trip with my family. She is my only sister and, therefore, my favorite, not that I could ever pick another who could ever take her place. She is blessed with three beautiful blonde-haired, blue-eyed children, two girls with a boy in the middle, who have been a joy to all of us since the day they were born. God knows exactly how to bless aunts and uncles with kids they didn't give birth to but were born in their hearts. Since we are not responsible for the way they turn out, we can let them have their way "most" of the time, right? My sister has proven that to be a fact, because my boys always knew that if Mom said, "no," their "Buffy" never understood the meaning of the word.

Justin often went to her whenever he needed help or had a problem he didn't want us to find out about. To my knowledge, it was never anything too serious, or she would have warned us; or I'd at least like to think that would be the case. To this day I question why on some occasions he went to my sister rather than his parents. She always assured me that it wasn't because we were unapproachable, or that he was feared our reactions, but that he never wanted to disappoint us. Being the firstborn, he'd been cursed with the desire to be a parent pleaser, which is something I understood all too well, as I, also, am the firstborn and felt a constant need to please my parents. I am so very thankful my sons have Aunt "Buffy" as a constant in their lives because everybody needs a "go-to" person who understands and will lend a listening ear without judgement or condemnation. My sons believe, without a doubt, that she always has their backs and whatever in this world they need her to do, she will give her last breath to help them.

While on this trip together, we took the opportunity to visit a local water park. As we walked around looking at the different slides, my nephew Evan said, "Look. It's the biggest slide in the park." We were all amazed at its enormity. Immediately he yelled, "Don't leave weak" and jumped in line. We all looked at each other, and I thought to myself, "No way was he going down *that* slide. Even if he *were* going to take the plunge, he positively wouldn't go alone. With his unsubstantial weight being barely sixty pounds saoking wet, and this incline several stories high, his speed would be so intense that he wouldn't even be able to hang on with the force at which his body would be traveling. All I could see in my mind was his being carried away up into the wild blue yonder by the sheer force of acceleration and gravity. After all, "What goes up must come down," as the saying goes. By the time he'd reached the first rise, he would have been catapulted like a cannonball into the great unknown. As we stood there discussing the event about to take place, I remember thinking *surely* my sister wouldn't permit him to do this. Hopefully, this would be the one time she would finally say, "No." After all, he *was* her son, and she could easily tell him "No," and he would have to obey, right? Just as that thought crossed my mind, I heard a voice yell out from across the way. It was my sister, and she shouted his name loudly, "Evan!" I waited for the next words out of her mouth to be, "Get yourself right off of that slide this instant, or you're grounded," but, no; instead, she screamed, "Don't leave weak!!" She was cheering him on as loudly as she could. What? Are you kidding me? Had we not just lost one child? Was she willing to take a chance on injuring one of *hers*? Was she seriously thinking that accidents couldn't happen? Barry and I stood holding our breath as Evan made the long climb up the hill to the entrance; he looked so small and delicate compared to the vastness of the slide. In fact, we could barely see him. As he stepped onto the platform, there was no turning back; there was no exit, the only way out was one step off the mile-high plunge to the wading pool at the bottom. I secretly wished the attendants would inform my nephew that he was too small, too short, or too young to attempt this feat, and carry him safely back to the shelter of his mother's arms. When that didn't happen as I'd hoped, he took one step forward and, like a flash, he shot down that slide at breakneck speed. In seconds, he was in the wading pool at the bottom and on his way back to us, safe and sound. Running as fast as his tiny legs would carry him he exclaimed, "Mom, I didn't leave weak!!" She replied, "No, son, you sure didn't, and I won't either." In the blink of an eye, my sister was gone, making her way up to the top of that gigantic slide to prove she would always practice what she preached. She never looked back, so she missed seeing the dumbfounded expressions on all our faces. She took the plunge and survived, enjoying every minute of the freedom. That day Amy confidently made her mind up she wasn't going to live in fear because of what we had all been through. She refused to be bound by fear or let it influence her children and cause them to be afraid to take chances within reason. How brave she was to win that battle and take a leap of faith, not worrying or letting fear paralyze her into passing up some thrilling opportunities for her and her children.

I took a mental snapshot of that day and still fight with all I have to never live in fear of losing one of my other sons. I strive for the goal of being able to walk by faith and not by feelings. Let me tell you, it isn't easy. To this day, I still struggle sometimes with fear that tries to strangle the life right out of me. I always think that since it happened once, my mind wants to imprison me into believing it could happen again at any minute. My middle son, Jacob reminded me soon after the accident that I had to let him live, that just because Justin was gone didn't mean *he* couldn't live. That was a tough pill to swallow, but he was one hundred percent correct. Jacob helped me to realize that we must live our lives unafraid, not worrying over what may or may not happen, but to live expecting wonderful things that are in store if we aren't afraid to live. I am so very grateful that I can learn from each of my sons' many very valuable lessons. In my eyes they will always be my little boys although I do realize they are in fact truly wonderful, young men.

I'm thrilled Justin was confident in knowing that life was meant to be enjoyed to his utmost ability. There were several times he certainly could have left this earth way before he did. Living the life, he enjoyed placed him in harm's way more than once, but each time God spared him until that final moment when it was his time to leave. I believe without a single doubt that *He* was not taken by surprise when my son climbed into his friend's car that fateful night. From the day Justin's life began, God knew his every future decision along with its outcome. He knew the number of breaths he would take, and the precise moment he would breathe his last. Ever since I realized that Heaven is not the finale but only an introduction to a grander life, I rest assured that it *was* indeed all part of God's plan for Justin. He left him here until his mission was completed and then called him home to live a life worthy of a King's son.

My dear friend that I spoke of earlier in the book often talks about the day she met my son. She told me a little while after the funeral that the first time she laid eyes on him, she knew he was different. She explained that she didn't understand why she felt that way, only that she knew he was special and created to do remarkable things. It was a brief time later God called Justin to his home in Glory, I speculate that his abilities, talents, and determination are now being put to even greater and more profound use. He and Robie spoke often of how they would love to build houses. I have to believe now that is exactly what they're doing. Justin and Robie went on ahead of us to help prepare our heavenly mansions. We will remain waiting patiently until the work is finished and we're all called home. I'm grateful God's plan for my son was confirmed by my friend. It helps me on the most difficult days when my entire soul and body aches to see him again. Some days my severe need to hear his voice and hold him close is intolerable. The hope I have in Christ encourages me to continue. When we rest in Him, surrendering for His Holy Spirit to live in us and govern our lives, we can fully enjoy a life free of confusion, fear, discouragement, depression, oppression, torment, sickness, pain, and grief. The key is that "yes," we will still be confronted with these things at times, for He knows what's best for us even if it causes intense agony for a season. Through Him, however, we have the ability to overcome. *"We are afflicted in every way, but not crushed; perplexed, but not despairing; persecuted, but not forsaken; struck down, but not destroyed; always carrying about in the body the dying of Jesus so that the life of Jesus also may be manifested in our body. For we who live are constantly being delivered over to death for Jesus' sake, so the life of Jesus also may be manifested in our mortal flesh." (2 Corinthians 4:8-11 NASB)* Reflecting on that Scripture brings me to the conclusion that suffering is necessary, and although I don't fully understand, it's all for our good and God's glory. I've said many times and prayed that if our loss brings God glory, then I must be thankful and confident because of the realization that it will be totally worth it in the end. It's not for me to try and calculate all of God's ways, and figure of how or why, but to believe that everything will go according to His perfect plan when we trade *our* lives for *His. "For this is good and acceptable in the sight of God our Savior; Who will have all men to be saved, and come unto the knowledge of the truth." (1Timothy 2:3-4)*

If you are reading "my story" and have no life in your living, are tired of a mundane existence having no purpose, meaning, or direction, you feel empty, alone, discontented, Jesus told his disciples, *"I am the way, and the truth, and the life. No one comes to the father except through me." (John 14:6 ESV)* To accept Jesus into your life is as easy as A, B, C. **A**sk Him into your heart, **B**elieving that He is Who He said He was (the Son of God Who died on the cross for your sins and rose again the third day), and **C**onfess your sins and ask His forgiveness. *"He is faithful and just to forgive us our sins and to cleanse us from all unrighteousness." (1 John: 1:9 ESV)*

When we ultimately put all our hope and faith in God, He will take the damage in our lives, the shattered, crushed pieces of nothingness, and make something great in return. If and when we submit to Him, He will make a beautiful vessel for His glory to shine through just like the glorious sunrises and sunsets that happen every day. The choice is yours to make. I encourage you to have a "don't-leave-weak" attitude and run this race, giving it all you have and permitting God to have His perfect will in your lives. Be committed to accomplishing all that God has in store for you to do with your allotted time and to be patiently, actively waiting for your heavenly reward. Face all life's trials and tribulations head on, knowing that God is with you. I know I want to make it to the finish line beyond the sky with a "don't-leave-weak" determination. So, until that day comes, I pray that each of us will do our best to live, love, and walk in the freedom and victory that knowing the Lord Jesus Christ can bring. Remember we all have our own story, and *if* we give Him permission to intervene throughout of lives, our story will be used for God's glory.

"Not to us, O Lord, not to us, But to Your name give glory, for the sake of Your steadfast love and Your faithfulness." (Psalm 115:1 ESV)

This is not the end but a new beginning.
Dedicated in honor of my sons Jacob and Caleb Fowler
In loving memory of Justin Robert Fowler
February 15, 1991 --- July 17, 2011

Alisa Fowler has been married to her husband Barry for 28 years. Together the have raised three handsome and incredible young men. Justin, the oldest resides in Heaven after a tragic car accident due to a drunk driver in 2011, he was 20 years young when he unexpectedly left this earth. With great expectation this dedicated mother waits for the time when her family is once again complete when they reunite in Heaven where she is convinced her son is living a happy, whole and fulfilled life. The couple's other two sons live in Cleveland. Jacob is the middle son, he is 22 and works and attends college where he is studying business. Jacob is a talented baseball pitcher and third baseman. Caleb, the youngest is 19, he also works and attends college, he is studying psychology. Caleb enjoys singing and playing the piano and leads worship at the family's church. Alisa has truly savored her life as a stay at home mother since the birth of her youngest. She has chauffeured, cheered, and committed her life to supporting her sons through numerous basketball, football, baseball, karate classes, soccer games and show choir competitions. The family have immensely enjoyed countless hours spending time swimming, camping, and boating all throughout the boy's lives. The couple, are Senior Pastors of Cleveland Cornerstone Church in Cleveland, Tennessee, for the last five years. Together they bring a vivid message of hope and healing to the congregation. Through her ministry Alisa desires to motivate others by instilling a deep desire for an enthusiastic relationship with the Lord Jesus Christ. This mother's journey has been filled with great sorrow and despair, but also with hope and joy. Her heart is to bring help to the hurting by being vulnerable herself. Her prayer for her readers is that you will all learn to be victorious over-comers and triumph through your tragedies as you travel your own particular road to recovery, no matter what the circumstance. Please feel free to contact us with your thoughts and comments about the book on our Facebook page. You can search us online at BarryAlisaFowler. Feel free to join the Don't Leave Weak page online for updates and reviews. This book can only be purchased directly from the author.

Never Apart Always In Our Hearts

Our *Three* Sons

Daddy Justin & Skylar Anne

Slick & Sky

My Pastor/Hubby & Mrs. Pastor

Justin & Courtney's Wedding

Buck-A & Nana Slick, Buffy, Jacob, Caleb, Hannah Grace, Evan,
Isabel & Gracie Belle

ISBN NUMBER- 9781973719717
Scripture references and Bible quotes have been taken from the following:
Amplified Bible (AMP)
English Standard Version (ESV)
Holman Christina Standard Bible (HCSB)
King James Version (KJV)
New American Standard Bible (NASB)
New International Version (NIV)
New King James Version (NKJV)
New Living Translation (NLT)

To my beautiful wife,

It is sometimes hard to see things in the context of a journey, but I want you know how proud I am of yours. Journeys' are often like seeing your kids growing up, it's hard to measure how quickly they're growing when you're part of the process. The Bible tells us *that "The steps of a righteous man are order of the Lord." (Ps. 37:23 KJV)* However, that doesn't mean that they are easy to walk in, pain free, or even obvious at all times. Victory starts before steps, it starts in our thoughts, which lead to our steps.

Watching you day by day, find hope in Christ as your victory has been slow at times, but that's what it's like in the process--like watching your kids grow. It may seem slow in the beginning, but when I see where you are today, it's nothing short of amazing, giving all glory to God for His love and care for you. Day by day, you've allowed your life to be transformed by our Lord to find hope and life through His grace and truth. I made a promise to you when our son went before us, that we serve a God who can and will make beauty out of the ashes, no matter the flame of the trial.

Your steps are now that of a lady who has discovered that nothing is impossible to those who believe. Watching your grief and brokenness give way to faith and trust has led to the restoration of joy and victory in your life. I know this book will help make that possible for others who have, or even will, undergo trials that seem impossible to live through. I love you with all my heart and thank God for all He's done in your life.

Barry

Made in the USA
Monee, IL
11 July 2022

99500596R00163